UNSUNG
ORDINARY MEN

Sally Dingo

UNSUNG ORDINARY MEN

A generation like no other

hachette
AUSTRALIA

Permission to quote from the diaries and notebooks of Dr CEW Bean, Australian Official
Historian, courtesy Mr Edward Le Couteur and Mrs Anne Carroll. Dr Bean's collection can be
accessed via the Australian War Memorial.

hachette
AUSTRALIA

Published in Australia and New Zealand in 2010
by Hachette Australia
(an imprint of Hachette Australia Pty Limited)
Level 17, 207 Kent Street, Sydney NSW 2000
www.hachette.com.au

10 9 8 7 6 5 4 3 2 1

National Library of Australia
Cataloguing-in-Publication data:

Dingo, Sally
Unsung Ordinary Men / Sally Dingo
978 0 7336 2524 4

Includes index.
Bibliography

Butler, Max.
World War, 1939–1945 – Prisoners and prisons, Japanese.
Veterans–Australia–Family relationships.
War–Psychological aspects.

305.906970994

Cover design by Christabella Designs
Front cover photograph courtesy of Sally Dingo
Back cover shelf and picture frame images courtesy Getty Images
Typeset in 12.5/19.5pt Bembo by Shaun Jury
Printed in Australia by Griffin Press, Adelaide, an accredited ISO AS/NZS 14001:2004
Environmental Management Systems printer

MIX
Paper from
responsible sources
FSC
www.fsc.org   FSC® C009448

The paper this book is printed on is certified against the
Forest Stewardship Council® Standards. Griffin Press holds
FSC chain of custody certification SGS-COC-005088. FSC
promotes environmentally responsible, socially beneficial
and economically viable management of the world's forests

A love letter to a generation

It was too late to retract the words, for I had – there could be no doubt – I had indeed uttered them. I heard with horror each momentous word as it emerged: another foolish sentence, another lapse that signalled to all those I now knew, in the city-life I was leading away from my small-town childhood home that in truth I was not of them, or like them. I came from a different world. Many I knew already thought that because, well, I had come from Tasmania, that strange state, with its convict background, its dearth of cities and its isolation. And – after all – Tasmania was at the bottom of the earth. I was aware of the perception and hid my heart. But the world from which I had emerged was not of Tasmania's making. Instead, the life I had known was one tainted by those times when the bottom of the world was not far enough away. And today, oh today, how reckless and unguarded I had been. For today I had spoken of one of those times.

I dreaded what would come and grimaced, or so it felt, but my face remained even, for I was working overtime to keep it so. How could I have made such a mistake, got this moment so wrong? How could I have confessed even a little – even to a friend – confessed at all to those who did not know?

'His photo is in a book,' I heard myself say.

My friend nodded, slowly. He stood by the tall antique cabinet in his living room, both the furniture and he solid, firmly grounded on his city turf. I stood by the door, flimsy, an outsider. And female. He was a man, confident of his knowledge, and war was another subject on which he could rake up enough facts. War was men's business, inherently so, even if his specifics were a little shaky. And my specifics – well, there were none. So he refused, it seemed, to accept my comment.

'Well, how long did he fight?' he asked.

'Oh . . . ah . . . a few days . . . maybe . . . Hm . . . Oh . . . I don't really know.'

My friend stared, his lips curling, eyes laughing. He paused before speaking, perhaps through an attempt to locate some semblance of kindness. But he could not. Out it came.

'He wasn't much of a war hero then, was he?' he said.
And snorted.

Almost a blow to the head. Hero? I had never thought he was. And now I was ashamed that he was not. But I didn't really know. How could I know when he had not told? Heroism, though . . . well, that was another thing. I knew full well – had read – that there had been heroism.

'I . . . I didn't say he was a hero,' I attempted.

Feeble. Should never have been said at all. For in my words I sensed a betrayal: I had almost denied him. I had failed him. My heart withered and shrank. I felt a fool for mentioning it.

PART I

1

The letter

My sister eased open the lid of the writing desk, a desk which had been, always, part of our lives, solid and sturdy and positioned on an angle in a corner looking out, and holding our mother's secrets. Elizabeth took out the used envelopes one by one, the papers now somewhat yellowing and brittle with age, the stamps and addresses and watermarks long ago ignored. The envelopes had been arranged to stand upright and each sleeve contained certain papers and documents my sister and I were clearly meant to find.

Some papers poked out of the top of the envelopes, too irregular were they in size and shape, but all had been categorised, like with like. Our mother's filing system: a method of her own devising which veered, we always thought, towards eccentric; yet it was, no question about it, eminently easy to use and cheap to maintain. A model system, a remnant from another age, with a quaintness and practicality that, over the years, had never failed to make us smile.

It had taken us six months to start this, to go through her things and organise and remove some of the traces of her life. But the house was to be let, and there could be no further delay; the memories of our mother in the last few years in this house to be – finally, and to our sorrow – interrupted. Surely, it now was time.

Our mother had prepared for this moment, refusing, as she had always done, to allow such sentimentality as her daughters were now exhibiting to intrude upon her life. Or death. And the papers were ready and waiting.

We were looking for one envelope in particular. Concerning our father. To be able to search openly, say the word 'Dad' again, loudly into the air – speak it across the room to one another – had a tinge of rebellious freedom to it, of triumph released, which we toned down when we heard it in our voices, speaking from then on with a degree of purposeful restraint. *For our mother mattered to us too.* But how wonderful, after all these years, to be able to say his name, to call upon his memory, to include him. And not just on his birthday. 'It's Dad's birthday today,' our mother would say, softly, and we could hear the many moments of thought and effort and resolve it had taken to bring those words to the surface, for our mother was a woman for whom any overt expressions of tenderness were dismissed – through embarrassment, we always knew. Every year. We would nod, and know what those few words meant. And say nothing, add nothing of our own. This was our mother's grief, deep and still there. We did not want to awaken it. We suppressed our own. Mostly. So many years. But we all knew – understood – why.

The envelope we were looking for contained a letter announcing that our father was coming home; a letter sent from Thailand at the end of World War II. It was a letter both Elizabeth and I wanted to see again, one in my father's own handwriting. It was important to us. His hand had written that, held that pen. The letter would connect us, help us feel him close by, bring him back into our lives again.

But it was not that letter which we found first. It was another, one in small rectangular folds that had been pushed thin and flat. The edges of the folds had begun to tear – from too much handling at one time, it appeared – and it was clear that if more pressure was applied, and the unfoldings became too frequent, the letter would end up in pieces. It was fragile, this letter from long ago.

I stood across the room and listened as my sister read.

The letter was from a woman, someone we didn't know, telling of her baby, and her joy, and how she was trying to carry on. Of her love for the person to whom she had written the letter: her husband, whom she called sometimes by his name, and at other times 'Dearest'. And of her longing – oh, how she longed – to hear something, some news, a word.

The ink kisses, from her, and some from her baby to Daddy, went right across the bottom of the page, an attempt to send as much love as possible, if only she could find the means.

My sister and I were confused, and there was a moment of brief anxiety, of terror: a letter like this, with our father's papers? It surely had not been left here, for us – now – to bring life-shattering news in one of those clichéd times upon someone's death when the certainties in your life are then swept away. But our thoughts settled when we realised that our father's name, or a reference to him, were nowhere to be found.

Sad that letter was, heartbreaking even, but surely – my sister urged – an explanation of it, one of no importance to us, would be found. And we could perhaps deliver the letter, even find the woman who waited, in Katoomba, New South Wales. We did wonder, though, why that hadn't already been done.

But no, I said. This had importance to us here in Tasmania – a connection, otherwise it would not be filed in this unique and careful fashion, ready, in the desk.

The letter was refolded, a light touch only, its delicacy too apparent, and we lingered, our thoughts muddled and moved: the woman waiting, her husband, her dearest – their child.

We seemed unable to fully put the letter and all it said away. Then: 'Oh! Look! Look at this! Here, on the back.'

And we both received a jolt. I did not take a breath for some time.

For there, written directly on the reverse of the letter, fitting within the confines of the folds of the paper, was a list, in my father's writing, divided into several columns. A list of deaths. And rank and name. And dates. And causes of death. And place. All the deaths in the couple of months before the end of the war. So close to coming home: those poor men, those poor families waiting.

Our father's life, hidden; unspoken. And with our mother's things. Written on someone else's letter.

2

Penguin

The pubs were always abuzz in my home town. Ordinary men, from ordinary families, came out to be with other men. They would drink, play practical jokes, laugh and carouse. There was much foolery and noise, and voices shouted across the room to one another, for these were life-filled days. Times of peace, when you have known war, are like that.

On many a Saturday night in the front bar of the top pub – or bottom pub, when men chose to drink there, for neither was favoured over the other (fairness mattering a great deal to the men of the town) – at a time when Hedley Deverell, a World War I veteran of the 26th Battalion, served behind the bar, a sizeable crowd at the bar was about fifteen men. There was nothing but laughter and mayhem when Oscar Mather, one of the notable characters in town and an old World War I veteran himself, would issue his standard challenge if someone was hanging back, that someone in question not offering readily enough when it was their turn to 'shout'. And Oscar's beer glass there, empty and waiting.

'Kick the tin, Alec,' his voice would boom across to his old army cobber, Alec Oliver. 'We'll go over the top!'

The place would erupt with a roar and the glasses would be replenished. And the beer, the liquor of friendship all over Australia, had been — well, just about — blessed.

It was a ritual the men in the pub understood — or else it was soon explained to those who didn't. That World War I directive from the fields of France; from the Somme, that war of attrition. The war a game of slaughter by numbers — for a game was what the planning from the official desks had almost become, played with millions of ordinary men; the game that would end, it seemed, with the country of the last man standing declared the winner. The fields of France blood-filled, the battles back and forth for yards of territory mostly senseless. All of it known, in this pub. And known, too, the kick of the kerosene tin to ring out the signal to throw your body up and over the top of the trench, a bayonet charge into the hail of bullets and the bombs; that surge recalled and relived here in the small-town bar.

All who were there in the pub knew what it meant then, what it meant now: no holding back. You do as you are directed — line up, ready, even if the man beside you is not your close mate, and more so if he is — find the courage to do what each of you must do.

'Every time Oscar kicks the tin,' explained Phil Hales, one of the town's most recent veterans (and there were now many of those, a crowd having just returned from the Second World War and for most of those, after three and a half years, beer, and freedom to be in pubs like this, all of it never tasting so sweet), to Hedley's son, Bill, 'over the top we *gotta* go!'

In this declaration of inclusion, of brotherhood, of bravery and men remembered, was much that told of who these men were. For this was a town, like many places scattered far and wide around Australia, where men knew war.

From this town alone, with its top and bottom pub, with its small groups of men who gathered together, and not just in the pubs — men who knew each man's family, each man's life and past, who called in on one another regularly at each man's home, always walking straight in, no knocking, friendship and trust long ago earned, all that was required just a cheery, raised voice *hello* . . . Here in this tranquil place, a place of peace — a place with a population of just over 1124 people when World War I, that foolish war, swept in — *from this town alone*, 107 men enlisted. And twenty-six died. In this town, like many in this state, many all over Australia — such as the small community of Brighton Point in Tasmania, with its population of fifty-four, where ten of their young men died out of the twenty-eight who enlisted – men, and their families, indeed knew war.

Now, another war had ended, and more men had died.

Those who survived had come home: to this town, to towns and cities all across Australia; home to families; mothers and fathers, wives and children, brothers and sisters. They had returned. And here in my town, in that round of beers, that stirring, rowdy and irreverent call to men together, was the offering of a balm, from older men to young men now home. It was mateship obliquely given – the spirit, if not the act, of an arm around the shoulder. For consolation was needed, these older men knew. There had been an added dimension to this Second World War.

These men, at the end of the evening's merriment, the old and the young, veterans nearly all, would leave the bar's warmth and the glow and move out into the spaciousness of the big sky, dark and often star-filled, breathe the salt air, feel the chill and hear the sea. They'd sing out their goodbyes, which echoed in the late night's largely empty street, and make their way home: the war, *their* war, for too many, following on behind.

———

People and things seemed solid and real and well defined in the town where I grew up. It might have helped that there was so much space in which to see so clearly. For my town was set at the bottom of an expansive canvas: a ribbon of buildings beneath a wide sea and horizon, all overhung with a huge sky. We looked out onto Bass Strait, the stretch of sea that separates Tasmania from the mainland of Australia.

Some days it was almost an assault upon the senses, breathtaking, the different shades of blue magnificent, the air a soft caress. Other days greyness came, and the salt air turned heavy and damp. On those days the wind off the sea would sting, and the sea would foam and break, hurling at the beach seaweed dredged up from the deep. You always knew you were alive in my home town, a town with the name, whimsical yet fitting, of Penguin.

Along this ribbon beneath the sky, a straight main street featured, lined for the most part on one side only, with shops that faced out to sea; the narrow road and a small nature strip and a row of pine trees to one end all that stood between the shops and the beach.

Yet it was not a town that saw itself as a 'beach town', a term from a later era. It was, instead, a town by the sea, which earlier in the century had featured an impressive and, for a time, well-used jetty of some length at the western end, just over from where the railway line skirted the town and close by a small bump of land which perhaps, several ages ago, had been the earth's offhand attempt at a hill.

Away from the beach, not far behind the jetty and railway line, up a small rise and over a bridge with a pretty creek beneath, in which swam trout that were plentiful and big, where trees clung to the sides of many of the bends, their knotted roots protruding from the grass and chocolate-brown soil acting as memory points for the children – men too – who came looking for where the lobsters hid; near to some beautiful houses with orchards and old-world gardens, and close to where Oscar Mather had chosen to build his little house for his wife, in which to raise his daughters and where he kept his horse and dray in a stable; and underneath the wide and dark green mountain range which cradled the town from behind with swathes of eucalypts still spreading – the town with houses, some large, with smoking chimneys dotted throughout the squares of the neat and diverse country fences, in amongst all that, not far back from the beach, and not far down from the cemetery on a hill, there stood a small church, made of wood, like most of the houses. We called it the Church of England as we grew up; its proper name, St Stephens Church. It is a church of a design seen often in Australian country settings, picturesque and charming, and, here in Penguin, white with a shingled roof. When I was a child it had soft green willow trees behind, for the creek ran there – trees which grew perhaps too well, we now know from a later time; back then they were graceful and magical. It was a place, I always thought, of beauty.

I never attended that church, my parents sending my brothers, my sister and myself to Sunday School at the Methodist Church along the main street instead. But my thoughts of my town and my childhood arrive back always to one particular memory I have of St Stephens Church in Penguin: men, many, gathered outside that church. But it all begins, as such things do, much earlier.

3

A soldier's firstborn

My father, Max Butler, was a gentlemanly sort of bloke for an ordinary man, even though his occupation of wicker worker placed him a hand span or two outside of ordinary.

For *wicker worker* was from another time, one wafting in from across the sea and belonging, surely, to pre-industrial England. It was an occupation that to my mind called up yeomen, Masters and indentured servants, artisan guilds as well. Even smocks. The quaint term, one strange with its use in the modern day, managed to survive somehow, here in Tasmania, tucked away in small places like Penguin. And it confused a young woman whose birth certificate read as if her father lived eons ago.

But Max lived in a much later time, in a very different place, and was without question a man of his own time.

He was as Australian as a third generation could be: his ease of being; relaxed movements; his open, generous and soft-hearted face, one ready to smile at any moment; along with his love of mischief, which he retained throughout his life, he was just another *colonial boy* now well and truly established.

The trade he plied in his backyard workshop – soaking the cane for his craft as needed in his homemade trough, creating the frames, weaving the cane work, listening to the radio as he did so, knocking off at precisely five o'clock after a good nine-hour day – was perfect for a man happy to make of life what he could in such a small place where there were not many jobs on offer. He had created his own work, a necessary strategy for many who wished to make a living in a town far from the larger cities.

He pencilled his orders and sales in a soft-covered notebook in his neat and well-formed handwriting, ensuring his numbers and columns were small and straight, an achievement that in its attention to detail, among the clutter of the cane and the wood cut-offs, obviously pleased him.

He was a man who made his furniture with care and in the small-town world he inhabited, and enjoyed so much, he had quite a reputation along the coast. His chairs, bassinets and prams lasted for decades, many still in existence and in use to this day.

He joked with his mates in his own quiet, contained, gentlemanly way; he played cricket with the home mob, just to fill the team; took his place on the footy field for the Two Blues, the local club (his left-foot kick still remarked on decades later); and, like many in the town, he enjoyed a beer and a smoke. All without an artisan smock in sight.

Later he took part in the community as a more responsible, settled man, by then one with a family. But by the time I came into his life there was a quietness there, a shadow, a darkness not found in many other houses, so I discovered as I grew. It made me fearful. Many times we, the children, felt that fear – but we did not really know what it was.

We would watch our kind, patient, gentle father – and understand only a little. Something was there. Memories. We did know that.

Our mother shielded him. As best she could. She tried so hard. Heartbreaking – we saw all that.

Max had been born in September 1918, far away from England, in Tasmania, where no-one ever thought about pre-industrial yeomen and guilds. He was born in the front room of his parents' rented farmhouse, on a heavily treed holding, many miles up a winding and bumpy track which headed up into the mountains, deep green and shrouded – and often damp – at the back of Penguin.

He was a baby who grew up in a time of peace (the end of that Great War coming two months after his birth), yet he was, in fact, a baby of war, the firstborn of a soldier who came home to Australia desperate for life and for living

Morton Linthorne Butler, a man with shock upon his face and a look of unspeakable sadness in his eyes, had been sent home from his hospital bed in England as soon as he was well enough to cope with the rigours of a journey by sea. He was a man who – even with the numbness that he couldn't shake – was scrambling to live. Somehow. For Mort had known the Somme, and Pozières, and Mouquet Farm on the Western Front in France. He had seen, and known, slaughter.

With a haste that came from pain and despair – and hope – Mort had married his sweetheart, Ruby, just three months from the date he disembarked, his baby son then born exactly nine months after that. And although the time has now passed for the full significance to ever be truly known, he gave that son a special name: one intended to rise above the battlefield and all that Mort had seen, the name he gave one that spoke to him of the best in men. For even though Mort was never destined to be a man fortunate to have privilege, or money, or great power, he was a man with ideals. Mort, a man who had little, was a good man.

There was comfort to be had in the fact that he had made it home at all with that name to give – for this was a time when young men from poor rural families who had volunteered to join the army had become infantrymen. And infantrymen in the Great War were never guaranteed of anything. Especially living.

———

. . . [T]he true role of the infantry was not to expend itself upon heroic physical effort, nor to wither away under merciless machine gun fire, nor to impale itself on hostile bayonets, nor to tear itself in pieces in hostile entanglements . . . but on the contrary, to advance under the maximum possible array of mechanical resources . . . to be relieved as far as possible of the obligation to fight their way forward . . .

So wrote Australian General John Monash, he who meticulously planned a different kind of warfare, and he who was concerned enough for the everyday footslogging soldier, the infantryman, to change the way battles were fought. His view that infantrymen shouldn't be sacrificed was almost heretical back then, when the image of dashing cavalry charges had been coupled with the concept of the glory to be had in dying in the mind of General Douglas Haig, Commander-in-Chief of the British forces; a concept exemplified, it seems, in Haig's mind by the surge of infantrymen racing en masse across any terrain, no matter how many times they were – every man – mown down. It was the wearing down of the enemy that mattered. For surely one man would get through eventually. And there were – it was only to be expected, was the reasoning – bound to be casualties on the way.

General Haig had at his disposal men – lots of them – to use for dash and glory. In fact, he had a seemingly endless supply for the asking – just send the word to the Empire:

millions of men for the despatching, wave after wave to face the bullets, the bombs and the bayonets. For those at the top of the Empire's tree had the view that men like Mort were there to be used in such a way: their bodies – and deaths – for the taking, if that was what was needed, in the service of something higher than them all. And Haig was intent on continuing with such a plan. For the Empire. But the question always remains: who in the Empire receives the benefits when soldiers fight and die?

The British Empire was a thing of wonder: men and women believed in it; loved the idea of it; volunteered to fight for it – that is, if they were Australian. (Other countries – Britain itself, Canada, even New Zealand – had to resort to conscripts to fill their respective quotas, the word 'quota' suggesting they were produce or sheep to be delivered.) In Tasmania towards the end of the Great War, when lambs to the slaughter were in far less supply (and by then far less than willing), recruiters desperate to fill the state's quota found one man hiding in a wardrobe. This was one agreement this man had no intention of making.

Mort Butler and two of his brothers had been among those who volunteered to fight, the three of them becoming infantrymen. It was true that the idea of Empire may indeed have appealed to them, as it did to many who answered the call, but it was just as likely the Butler boys went because they were poor.

Many men were even forced to go by employers who set

rules of exclusion – who refused to employ single men, for those single men were decreed by men in comfortable jobs to be eligible to fight. And the men went in droves: men with little education, no social standing, and often no jobs to be had. Conscription there may not have been, but compulsion was there. Volunteering to be a soldier would get you a job; for many, the only job there was. So Mort and his brothers went to war. They had given themselves, for whatever the reason, to the Empire.

It was General John Monash's views that helped bring about the great victory of 8 August 1918, the day that really put an end to the war. From that date onwards, it was a downhill slide for the Germans, day after dispiriting day, their generals in despair. Until it was over, the Armistice signed. Just like that.

For there had been 'developments' in warfare. On that day of days, 8 August – *der schwarze Tag*, the black day, as the Germans called it – sweeps of lively, confident and swiftly moving Australian and Canadian soldiers delivered a magnificent victory to the Allies at Amiens. It was a day when a massive military dance took place: tanks, aeroplanes, armoured cars, cavalry, artillery and machine guns. A day when ammunition was parachuted in near forward posts just when needed; when pioneer parties remade roads and attached themselves to each advancing brigade to help it over trenches; when engineers were on hand for the wells and bridges that the Germans had not had time to destroy,

SALLY DINGO

transport arrived precisely when needed with working materials, when quartermasters with food and drinks appeared on cue. It was a day when 'the staff work, timing, and road work were perfect'. And Charles Bean, the Official Australian Historian, said of it that 'the sight of the various services streaming up when the mist rose never passed from the mind of the 50 000 Australians who saw it. Their admiration for the enterprise of tanks, artillery and aeroplanes is outspoken in scores of narratives ... But the almost perfect co-ordination of all the services was the outstanding feature.'

'It was a *très bon* stunt,' wrote Sergeant FF Clausen of the 59th Battalion, a public servant from Newport in Victoria. 'I wouldn't have missed it for worlds!'

What a difference it had made, when General John Monash had been given command of the Australian forces and took his part in the whole well-planned scheme.

When General Haig met the three Australian divisional commanders several days after that watershed day, he 'spoke a few words of thanks, then said: "You do not know what the Australians and Canadians have done for the British Empire in these days."' It was reported that then 'tears rolled down Haig's cheeks'. But it appears his gratitude knew some bounds. For in his communiqué and press reports Haig presented 8 August as a 'British' victory! Charles Bean complained; Keith Murdoch too. But Bean was told by General Brudenell White that Australia had to make sacrifices 'for the whole'.

So it was that the Empire won on that day. And each Dominion in that Empire, it became clear, was to know its place. It was also clear that each individual man in that Empire was a means to an end. And each footslogging soldier was expected to offer himself: to the Empire. A perfect circle.

Hundreds of thousands had already sacrificed themselves 'for the whole'. An Empire seems an insatiable beast.

Unfortunately for Mort the infantryman, the footslogging soldier – and all who fought on the Somme, and in other parts of France and Gallipoli – Monash's style of warfare came too late. They had been withered away the old way. And Mouquet Farm, one mile out of Pozières, one part of that whole awful mess was a 'grinding out', Charles Bean called it, 'through mud and blood for a few yards of useless advance'. And Australian casualties, thousands upon thousands of them. Mort came to know all about that.

The Australian Divisions, the 1st, 2nd and the 4th, to which Mort's 52nd Battalion belonged, were marched up to near where the Somme River ran, through Picardy and Albert, towns where life continued, cafes operating, small bars or *estaminets* doing a roaring trade, so close to the carnage, not many miles from the front line. The men who came out of battle passed through these towns on their way back; and it was in these towns that those who came out of Pozières were seen.

'They appeared,' wrote Sergeant Rule, 'like men who had been in hell. They were drawn and haggard and so dazed they appeared to be walking in a dream and their eyes looked glassy and starey.'

He continued: 'And they were strangely quiet, far different from the Australian soldiers of tradition.'

Except for those further behind who were jabbering – those soldiers who had lost their minds. Lance Corporal Roger Morgan had seen the soldiers in that battle at Pozières at even closer hand, at the 2nd Battalion aid post in July 1916. He wrote home: 'It is awful to see crippled men staggering back with the help of a shovel, stick, anything, just crawling along until either they reach help or fall exhausted on the road, some to be picked up later or buried where they fall.'

Mouquet Farm, where Mort was headed, was perhaps worse: 'If you are killed, you are left there and your pockets or disc are not even looked at, and you are known as dead by being missing at the assembly after coming out of the trenches after being relieved,' wrote Lance Corporal Arthur Foxcroft in a letter home, telling of the fight for that small patch of farm ground. 'If [bodies] were buried they would only be rooted up again by shells – for as far as you can see all around us to the horizon is torn up, over and over again. When we get the Hun a good way back, the cleaning up parties will bury the dead and pick up all the matériel off the field.'

———

There had been six 'pushes' for the once picture-postcard Mouquet Farm, with its stone buildings and green fertile fields, and its underground cellars now bunkers with Germans in them – all of it considered by the British 'heads' to be crucial. So beautiful once, but now a wasted mudland with bits of splintered timber sticking out, those few sticks stubbornly clinging to the idea of the farm they used to be, refusing to believe what was happening – that is, until a bomb struck that spot and they were splintered even more. And craters, well, there were no shortages of those, shell holes now filled with bodies, or mangled parts thereof. Everywhere. And now a seventh push had been ordered, a continuing strategy of 'wearing down the enemy', a gem of an idea when you are not the one to be worn down, the idea from General Haig that, according to Charles Bean, resulted '[in] even more quickly wearing down the numbers – though not the morale – of his own army'.

Mort Butler and his two brothers, Charles and Herbert, were ready for the new fight, the three Butler lads all in the 52nd Battalion together, transferred over from the 12th.

Battalion after battalion had been sent in, and the 52nd had already been in among the fighting. The new stint was about to begin. Charles Bean, in one of his diary entries, wrote of the very story which would mean so much to Mort.

'I stayed,' wrote Bean on the afternoon of 2 September 1916, covering the story from behind the lines at Mouquet Farm, 'to have tea with Duncan Maxwell. He had his CO

[Commanding Officer] Captain Littler there, the man who for the whole time we were at Anzac was in charge of beach parties in Anzac Beach [loading and unloading stores of equipment, Littler's work parties consisting of many troublesome soldiers put on beach fatigues as punishment].'

> [Littler] wore a beard – a short grizzled beard – at Anzac. He was an elderly man – and two of his sons were serving as officers here, practically the same rank, the two sons and the father. The third son could not get in because he was blind in one eye . . . [Littler] was ill with lumbago and rheumatism and Duncan told me the night before that they were having to go in [to battle] without their C.O.
>
> 'It means a lot,' he said, 'because the C.O. is a grand man – the men would do anything for him. Captain MacNamara [who would be replacing him] is new to the work, and therefore more inclined to get jumpy' (very naturally).
>
> However on this evening there was Littler back. I didn't recognise the frank old face when first I saw it because the beard had gone. But something in the calm bluegrey eyes which looked at you so straight, and the kindly weather-beaten smile under the tawny moustache reminded me of the man on Anzac Beach.
>
> . . . He wasn't well at all, but he had come back in spite of doctor's advice, to take his part in that battle, and I felt more confident because I knew he was a man. As a matter of fact he was a much better officer than any of his seniors in the regiment, and they would have been a better battalion if he had been the Colonel . . .

He said this would be his last fight. He thought after this he would retire right, out of it . . . He was cheering the other officers. 'Well Maxwell — you'll come out with a nice little "blighty" — a bullet in the shoulder which will give you three months in London — and then you'll go before a board and they'll say, "Take another two months, my boy, and come back here again." ' And so on — wouldn't let the conversation get too serious for they all knew what they were in for.

'They won't let us wear boots like yours,' one young officer said, 'we have to go in in putties — boots would mark you as an officer and you'd be sniped at once.'

'They don't tell you not to carry a revolver,' retorted Littler.

'I reckon I'd carry a rifle,' said another youngster.

'Well, I'm going in with a stick,' said old Littler. 'I've never carried anything except a stick in any fight I've been in, and I'm not going to begin now.'

He had a talk to his officers (I left before this as I didn't want to intrude); and an hour later, as dusk was falling they went in. In the first charge in the morning — just as the sky was reddening — Littler was hit by a bomb thrown by a German as they neared the German trenches. He dropped to his knees, holding his chest, and went on directing his men.

'At them boys — go along — give it to the beggars!' he said — and he was hit again. He was hit a third time by shrapnel I believe, thru' the head as he sat there — and that killed him.

MacNamara was killed and 'Little' [Duncan] Maxwell (Little Maxwell is 6'3" but his brother Big [Arthur] Maxwell is 6'5") assumed command and took control of his battalion for 48 hours until they came out.

One of the men from Morton's 52nd Battalion, Sergeant Joseph Footman, wrote of that day that 'the only thing that surpassed all horrors was walking over the top of our dead and wounded comrades'.

And Lieutenant Duncan Maxwell, upon discovering a hundred-yard trench nearby with every one of the men either dead or dying, took three courageous Canadians with him and with continuous bombing, and smoke, and moaning of men – the stench and the mud and the blood – they 'carried out all . . . they could find who were not so badly hit to be past saving. The dead and the dying they left, as it would put them behind the barricade.'

At the end of this stoush Charles Bean, behind the lines, walked up to see if Duncan Maxwell and his brother Arthur had come out with the 52nd Battalion. He wrote in his diary: 'Only the first ragged remnants had yet turned up and was sitting around the cookers.

'"Lt. Maxwell – I tell you, he's a hero sir!!" they said – "he deserves a V.C. if ever any man did. You should hear the men speak of him." Every man . . . said the same.'

Bean walked further, worrying and wondering about the two Maxwell brothers of the 52nd Battalion. And then he saw Duncan coming towards him on a horse, seeking out his brother, exhausted, nearly tumbling off: 'He was wide eyed, and his eyes looked straight at you solemnly as if he did not understand. He spoke very slowly, and lost himself occasionally, and had to pull his thoughts together before he could go on. His cheeks were sunken and his eyes big, round and half tearful. His voice was down in his boots.

'I walked on,' Bean continued, 'I was going to the ... HQ at Pozières to find out what they knew of Arthur. It was pretty tiresome walking in the mud in my heavy boots – and I was immensely relieved when ... I saw a very tall gaunt figure coming down [the hill] covered with mud, tin hat a little on one side ...Well thank God – two chaps of 6'3" and 6'5" to get out of the thick of a scrap like that one – two of the best men in Tasmania when almost every other officer was hit. It was almost past hoping for.'

CEW Bean wrote in his diary alongside his notes about that battle: 'This has been a very stiff fight – much the biggest the 4th Australian division has had.'

There were more than 29 000 Australian casualties in the fighting at Fromelles, Pozières and Mouquet Farm. More than 21 000 of the casualties were wounded or gassed.

———

At Harefield Hospital in England, Mort answered all questions put to him by the Red Cross 'searchers' who had the task of trying to ascertain the fate of each and every soldier. They did their rounds, and asked and asked some more. All of it reminding a man again. Mort answered as accurately as he could, but with brevity. For there was not much else he wished to say. What more could he add? What more could they need to know?

The searchers noted what he had said:

> 52nd Batt.
> Butler
> A.I.F. H 3126
> Missing 4/9/16

> He was my brother as was also Cpl Butler 3119 the name just above his. My brother H Butler was blown up by a shell at Mouquet Farm, I was with him at the time. We were both A. Co. My people have been written to.

> Reference:- 3126 M.L.Butler
> 52nd Batt.A.I.F. Harefield Hospital 8.2.17

Herbert had died that day of the battle, wounded in the morning of the attack, then again by an HE (high explosive) shell in the afternoon.

'I was with him in the front line trench at Mouquet Farm,' Private SG Bauld of Staples, South Australia, reported to the Red Cross. 'A shell came over and wounded both of us. He was badly wounded and was still in the trench when I was helped out. That is the last I know of him.' But Mort knew. Mort had been there.

And Charles was missing.

'Informant stated,' so wrote another Red Cross worker after interviewing Mort, 'that: "On Sept. 3rd 1916 at Mouquet

Farm, I was in the same charge as C.H. Butler, who is my brother. I have since heard that he was wounded . . . [and] left . . . in a shell hole just behind the trench. Lieut. Penn told me that they had to leave him [there]." '

And yet, hope: yes, there was hope somewhere in all the carnage, of a real kind – with prospects – not just the wish for it among all the madness. For from his bed in hospital, Mort discovered that Charles's name had been removed from the list of the 'missing'. Could it be that he'd been found? It was, he knew, possible for his brother to still be alive, for others had come out later after battles just as bad, men who'd been as badly smashed. Maybe Charles was simply in another hospital somewhere, wounded but recovering, and wondering. Just like him.

Mort wrote letters. Then wrote again:

> I enclose copy of letter I sent you a short time ago, the original of which I presume you did not receive. I shall be very much obliged if you could let me have some information about my brother.
>
> Yours faithfully, M.L. Butler Cpl.

But a letter came back explaining:

> Dear Sir,
> . . . [W]e beg to inform you that we wrote to you on January 4th in answer to your letter of January 2nd. As you have not received that letter we will repeat the reasons then given you for removing the name of your

*brother No.3119. Cpl. C.H. Butler, 52nd Battn. from
our Enquiry lists.*

*Since Oct.3rd, we had had his name on our lists
of Officially missing men for whom there was no
inquiry. When he was reported killed in action by Head
Quarters, we removed it with many other similar no
enquiry cases. On hearing from you we re-added this
name and our searchers are again endeavouring to get
some news which will throw light on his fate. When
any such reports are received, we shall at once inform
you as we realise your anxiety for news . . . With
sympathy in your anxiety. Yours faithfully.*

Mort found, to his sorrow, that a bed in a hospital somewhere was not where his brother had been. Charles's name
was added to the already full list of the dead. And a cobber
of Mort's, and of his brothers', reported to the Red Cross
searchers:

A.I. F. 52nd Battn.
BUTLER Cpl. C.H. 3119
JEFFREY J. 3710
WOODWARD Sgt. C.C.G. 1003
MORRIS Sgt. J.C. 310
ARMSTRONG D. 2675
'KILLED IN ACTION 4/9/16'

*They were all mates of mine (and all Tasmanians,
except Morris who I am not sure of). They were all in
attack at Mouquet Farm on 3/9/16. I never saw any
of them in enemy's front line trench, they have been
missing ever since. It is generally understood that they*

were killed in the attack. I have heard that everyone of them had been killed. I visited the field of battle on 20th March 1917, I saw remains of soldiers who had been killed in this action, the water had dried up out of shell holes leaving remains uncovered.

Informant: – Sgt F.J. Fairbrother 2691
52nd Battn, A. Coy., Prisoner of War

Charles was buried in Pozières right beside fellow Tasmanian Captain Littler, the CO whom Lieutenant Maxwell said was a man the men would do anything for. So Littler, the father figure to the lads; and Charles Butler, a young man, twenty-eight years old, were together. There is consolation in that. And Private HJ Butler, a cousin from the same battalion, spoke to the Red Cross about Charles: 'I could not find out that they had got his disc . . . but he has a cross on his grave.'

Lieutenant Duncan Maxwell, the 24-year-old from Hobart, Tasmania, who had taken charge and inspired all his men, his actions earning their heartfelt respect – who had rescued men who would surely otherwise have died – was awarded the Military Cross. And Mort came home to Australia to settle in the town of Penguin. He gave his own name, Morton, to his second child (who died the same day he was born); his firstborn, though, was given the name Maxwell, the name of the lieutenant of his battalion, the man who had cared for men. Those qualities mattered to Mort.

4

Back to business

Mort didn't last long on the farm at the back of Penguin. He tried. Oh, he tried. But although he was only thirty years old, and before the war had been a farm worker at the small rural settlement of Gawler – where he had grown since a boy, and where he could go the distance with any farm-bred lad around – he found he was no longer able to manage the physical work, regardless of how hard he pushed himself. The long days, the damp and the cold, the strain on his body were proving too much. And too much for his lungs as well. He was spending half of every week in bed, ill and weakened, getting thinner by the day. For Mort had been gassed at Mouquet Farm.

He had chosen his partner well, though, a definite advantage for a saddened and sick man. Ruby, his wife, worked beside him, understanding his needs and helping with all that she could. Her husband's weakened condition was not the only one she knew, for the war had grabbed two of her own farm-working brothers, Tom and Jim, as well. They were now back home from France, one of them an 'Original' from the Gallipoli campaign, who had – a miracle surely, it must have seemed – managed to survive the whole war. They had both returned in a condition similar to Mort's, pretty well knocked about.

With so much grief already there, and now a more extended suffering to endure, Mort and his family would never need anyone to tell them about war and all it brought. They saw it in front of them every single day.

Now that he was ill, and the realisation had to be faced that life no longer resembled anything he had imagined or once had foolishly dared to hope, Mort was forced to make some changes, and he arranged a swap with Harry Whittle, moving his small family down to the house where Harry lived in Braddon Street, close to the centre of town. And Harry moved his own family up to the back of Penguin, to the house just under the mountain. Once this was done, Mort the country boy had become a man who lived in town. He was never to have a paying job again, which he found embarrassing. The kind-hearted sad man was distressed at the lack he now faced, the having nothing, the having nothing to give, and his inability to change it. He was granted a pension – a pittance the pensions were back then – which eased the burden a little, but not much, and life was a struggle from one day to the next. Determined to stay steady in the face of such an unforeseen life, Mort set about finding ways that would allow him some self-respect. For he was still young, only thirty years old, and needed to know that his life amounted to more than the constricted existence offered by a life on a soldier's pension. He needed to know that. That is, on the days he wasn't in bed.

However, he was grateful for the pension, for even though it was small – impossibly so – it came in on a regular basis. Mort would go to the post office and sign for it. It gave him and his growing family stability, a defined and known poverty to work within. And they would cope. Somehow. Both Mort and Ruby had lived with little in their lives before this. Bare, unadorned houses were not that unusual in rural Tasmania. Food would be grown; Mort, already skilled in the garden, would see to that. Fish could be had in Penguin as well, just a few yards down at the beach, there for the pickings on the mornings when the tide was right – garfish, too slow to catch the tide, could be found caught in the stone fish traps. Struggle it might be, Mort knew, but this was a town where the same difficulties were faced by far more people than just his family. And for many amongst them there seemed no way ahead.

———

Before Mort had moved to Penguin, some veterans had attempted to interfere with the way things were run in the town. Perhaps from despair; perhaps from pensions not granted, and facing the very real fear of how they were to cope in their lives ahead, they'd spoken without prudence and earned the animosity of many. The local branch of the Returned Soldiers and Sailors Imperial League of Australia, the RSSILA, had put a proposal to the local council in January 1917, before the war had ended. It was a proposal from men who had been sent home medically discharged:

> *That in view of so many returned to Penguin from the front incapacitated and unfit for manual labour, we desire that the office of council clerk be filled by one of these men at the end of the present year, as we consider the present clerk eligible for active service and think at least he should offer his services for such before again being elected.*

They had gone to war, the men explained, and suffered in a way most people would never know. The councillors replied with barely concealed rage that the 'tone' of the letter was not appreciated. And, they continued, the council clerk had indeed volunteered three times, had a reject's badge, and his two brothers were at the front. It was an exchange that revealed the veterans' bitter belief that they had been used, and misused, in the war; that showed how little people back home, far from the battlefields, knew of what the soldiers had been through. And it was a salvo from men whose fates had now been sealed. For they were unskilled and undereducated; their proposal, in fact, a plea (clumsily put) from men who had now seen something of the world, seeking opportunities beyond those available to them, from a town which could not provide – so few jobs on offer even when times were good. These men had injudiciously made known their resentment towards those men who, for whatever reason, had escaped the horror of the trenches. In a small town such ill feeling would probably never be forgotten. The ex-soldiers were back where they began, only more so: at the bottom of Australia, now unemployed. And sicker. But at least the Empire was grateful.

———

Towns and cities across Australia were slowly returning to normal, the memories of the war receding. There were houses, though, where photographs of men, sometimes boys – all from a time when flesh was on their cheeks and their eyes were still alive – would look down from mantelpieces for decades to come. Those photos carefully framed, placed often on a lace doily, that homespun spiritual cloth hand crocheted with love. In those houses women cried quietly for years, and some fathers never recovered from the grief. In other houses young women were beginning the lonely years in which they would grow old alone, their young man or fiancé not coming back. In still more houses people scurried back and forth to attend to the ill and ailing ex-soldier in bed. In others, wives and children coped – or didn't – suffering with moody, disturbed men who had taken to drink and to bashing, their anger and confusion about life, and all they had seen, far too great. In so many ways the war was still there.

For the rest, well, there had been so much strain it was a relief it was all over. The conscription issue that had divided so many people was now forgotten – except by those who remembered the bitterness. Strikes were no longer such nuisances, those stoppages which for the people on the north-west coast had caused threats to farmers' livelihoods – vegetables, entire crops, were rotting on the wharves. Gone too, thank goodness, were the strident women taking it upon themselves to deliver white feathers to young men who, so the women had decided, should be at the front, those women not knowing a man's circumstance and causing such stress. And gone was the need for comfortable men in comfortable businesses and jobs, those men of influence who attended the ceremonies and made such wonderful speeches – or sent their employees; gone was their need to think up excuses about why they were needed at home, and therefore, sadly, couldn't enlist. Yes, it was such a relief it was all over and gone.

In Penguin the war was no longer mentioned, apart from the service on Anzac Day, with its heartfelt and lengthy march that snaked along the main street in front of the sea, over the creek and past St Stephens Church, up to where the stone memorial had been placed, just down from the hill where the cemetery was. Nearly everyone attended. And then that, too, over for the year. The people of the town went about their business.

5

A safe, sheltered town

There were benefits to be had from living in the main street, all of them evident to young Jack Gandy. Jack (who'd been named John when he was born, and thereafter not called it again until he was twelve) saw the whole town as a playground. His father was the saddler and harness-maker in Penguin: Bill Gandy to some; Mister Gandy, though, to those children who were afraid of his direct and unflinching manner, of the quick summation he would make, for he was a man who'd seen a child or two around the world.

'What are you up to, Deverell?' he would growl in greeting to Hedley's young son, Bill, as Bill walked past, those few words able to put the wind up a less robust child. But Bill was the son of a veteran, and he knew what lay below the surface of things. Bill liked Mister Gandy and would answer politely. For there was a kindness in there, he knew. You just had to learn to see it.

William Gandy had come to Tasmania from England via South Africa. He'd left home when he was just a young man, reaching South Africa too late for the imperial frenzy of the Boer War. He witnessed a Zulu uprising in Natal in 1902, completed an indenture of three and a half years and then sailed for New Zealand and Australia as a qualified saddler and harness-maker. After having seen Penguin from trading ketches he sailed on, and deciding that it would be the beautiful spot where he would spend his days, he had set up his business only to discover that the world had changed. So suddenly.

Businesses like his were spluttering and dying; the blacksmith a street away the same. Cars, trucks and buses — all were slowly but surely making their way into daily life. And even though there were few cars yet in Penguin, there weren't many horses now either. Bill Gandy was almost as poor as Mort, and he was — with two daughters as well as Jack to support, and now on his own since his wife died several years before — a man who had a few things on his mind. He ran his ailing business from his saddlery shop, which was to the side of his house there in the main street, and would take part in the popping in and out of other people's premises, which happened in the street. Everyone knew everyone. He would stay for a short while, joking and chatting about events in the town, simply being sociable – which, he had found, was sometimes to his advantage.

It was Richardson from the Motor and Cycle shop who'd run behind him that time when Bill had heard someone say, 'Where's that fire?' and then the reply: 'It's at Bill Gandy's place!' Richardson bolted after him and saved his young son's skin by holding Bill back and cautioning, 'Now don't you go in to that boy, Bill! Bill! Now you wait till you calm down!' Jack had been under the bed cowering, at the same time in awe at how well his experiment with the old, crumbly lace curtains in the kitchen and the match had worked. Bill left the damage for a good twelve months or more before he painted and fixed it. He was a strong man, someone who'd made his own way all across the world; someone who had a sea chest and all that that implied; someone who knew life was full of hardship: a man who wouldn't let himself be broken. But there were times when it was tougher than others. Jack felt guilty for years. And years.

Penguin was a safe, sheltered town, and Bill allowed young Jack freedom to wander. There were boys to play with – Jack's special mates near where he lived – if Spud Hall was home from Devonport High School for the weekend, and different groups he would join with scattered in different areas of the town, most of them playing near their own houses; so much land and space for each. All the boys played variations of the standard games: cowboys and Indians, chasings and cricket. There were times when Jack would break out, go with his friends Elvin Ling and Spud – both mischief makers of whom Bill Gandy didn't approve – and walk eastwards on the road towards Ulverstone, past where the Jupps had a farm on the corner: and go 'parcel fooling', a game they had named themselves. This was a game of such thrills that their excitement was hard to contain, and a game so good they were willing to risk the consequences. It was also a game which couldn't be played near the town.

The old boot box had been wrapped to look like an ordinary parcel and set in the middle of the road – which at that time, the early 1930s, was still dirt. And rough. They lay in wait in the grass at the side, holding the string. This game never failed! The car owners would see it, stop the car, hop out, saying, 'Oh, a parcel. On the road!' By the time they walked around to the front of the car, a quick pull on the string and there was nothing there. The car owner was left scratching his head. Such fun! However, sometimes the best of plans can go awry, and there was a degree of consternation when for the first time it was not a car that approached. How could this happen? A bus instead. When buses were not frequent services on the road! And then another from the other direction. Then another! All three buses stopped, and all drivers were out. Talking to each other. Looking for the parcel, which had by now, with the speed of light, suddenly vanished! The three very brave boys took off up and over, right over the top of a sizeable hill, and slunk along a back road, South Road, heading home, hearts beating. A long walk, wondering all the way if they would be gaoled. It took quite a while for Jack's heart rate to return to normal.

After ventures like these Jack wondered whether hanging around near his home was perhaps the wiser way to spend his time. For him that meant the railway station just along the road, which took up a large chunk of street just past the Methodist Church. A railway station with its engines hissing and clanging, and transferring one train from one line over to another, then held there to let another through, then shunted back, noise and movement in the still air, sometimes people coming and going – all of it was activity that held a strong lure for a boy. Jack would find himself waiting – just seeing what was going on. And there would be Oscar Mather, one of the World War I veterans.

Jack had never been told about the war; he was born in 1919, the year after it ended. But he knew about it. All the boys in town did. And whenever he saw any of those men going about their lives, just doing what everybody else was doing, he would notice. And wonder. For the boys all thought that they were men apart; there was something about them. At the railway station, every working day through the week, Oscar, together with Charlie Ling, would pull up at the platform out the back on the seaward side, each man with his horse and dray, collecting their goods to be delivered throughout the district, Mr Ling collecting and delivering to a different part of the town. Jack would hang around. A man who had seen as much of men as Oscar had, knew what a boy loitering near a carriage meant, and after Jack had hung around looking inconspicuous long enough, Oscar would give him the nod that a lift was being offered.

Jack would wait until Oscar was ready. When Oscar had finished stacking his goods and parcels he would climb up with his well-practised movement onto the board that served as the seat and begin his rounds, reins in one hand, the horse moving off in response to the slight pressure, out onto the road which these days was lightly metalled in the short strip in the main street, with Jack standing on the side of the dray, looking in.

There were times when Oscar had a delivery for Jack's father. Bill would order a side of leather from Genders in Launceston and Oscar would drop it in to the workshop at the side of the house, say a few unhurried words to Bill, then go back to his rounds. Sometimes Eastalls Drapery, the shop next door to Bill's, had a parcel of clothes arrive on the train, sent from D&W Murray in Launceston. And here Jack was, a short ride with the parcels and an even shorter word spoken – maybe one or two – by a man amused by, tolerating of, boys, and a boy in awe, admiring of men. Oscar would pull the horse to a halt outside Jack's house in the main street, wait for him to alight then, with a flick of the reins, continue with his deliveries, Jack watching.

There was another veteran Jack noticed and found himself

wondering about. He wondered how the man managed to survive in these tough times, as Jack knew the veteran didn't work. This man often looked so ill, so very sick. He and his family lived up the opposite end of town. Jack didn't set out to have him in his sights when he and Elvin and Spud decided to go knick-knocking up there; it was just less likely that their fathers would see them. The distance from their homes would surely help them stay undetected.

Knick-knocking was another from their armoury of such good games, and even better after dark. Hard to top the satisfaction of this one. They'd been 'working' the different areas – the evening before was somewhere else, and now a new night, a new area.

They had arrived at Dooley Street. Then Jack remembered who had recently moved there: Mort Butler! Oh, this would be fun. It was such a harmless game. A bit of a chuckle; a feeling of satisfaction; the person who answers the door is puzzled for a while, and then everyone goes home, a great night had by all. This knick-knocking was going to be especially satisfying because there was a vacant block nearby, from which they would be able to clearly see every reaction.

They went to the door – *Knick-knock, knock, knock* – stifling giggles. Then they raced back, slid into position on the block – a heck of a good slide, for that was half the thrill – and watched Mort come out, come out *all* the way onto the street. He looked both ways, then went back inside again. Magnificent! They were so good at this. And it was so funny!

It was time to move to a new house, although Jack and Spud and Elvin were covering their tracks – because you never know. So it was time to move to the other side of the street. *Knick-knock, knock, knock.* And more giggles. They raced back, slid once more into position, watching. Oh, this was great.

Suddenly, *wallop!* From behind, from out of the dark, on Jack Gandy's bum, a flattened hand – one meant to give fright. Which it did. There was Mort. He'd been standing, watching them. Mort Butler, not ill in bed on this day, won the battle for the streets. It was the only time Jack Gandy was ever caught.

6

Never enough

When Ernie Eastall took possession of his new car, an Essex, and drove his own children – as well as Bill's son, Jack, who lived next door, and one of Mort Butler's sons, also named Jack – to Ulverstone he covered the seven-mile distance in only half an hour! It was an unbelievable feat, but they had been really flying. It was obvious to all that there were great changes happening, and probably more on the way. And those changes were finding their way right down to the bottom of the world, and out into remote small towns. Towns like Penguin. This was not even Ernie's first car; there were some people in the town who were managing to get ahead.

That car trip was astounding to Jack Gandy. The only times he had been to Ulverstone before was when he had walked over with his older sister, Millicent, when she wanted some variety in her life and was looking for something to do beyond the confines of Penguin. It would take all day. Now Jack had been in a car! Thrilling for a boy, but disheartening for a saddler and harness-maker. For even though Bill admired his neighbour's new vehicle – and certainly didn't covet it – he was a man sufficient unto himself, no matter how little he had, always insisted on paying fully for everything, no keeping accounts at shops and stores around the town, there were many thoughts that Ernie Eastall's car brought to him: the world was changing in ways he had never dreamed possible. That car was pointing to further poverty for him, perhaps worse than he now knew.

Bill did what he could to bring in an income. He bought himself a heavy-duty sewing machine, second- or third-hand and, at night, with Jack and the two girls helping, he would mend canvases, the bulky and cumbersome cloth needing additional hands to hold it straight and flat as he sewed. Jack hated the work, the canvas so thick and tough, and there were reams of it to negotiate. But his father, he knew, needed the help. Bill also plaited belts and whips, and mended boots and shoes, even though there was already a bootmaker with his own small shop elsewhere in the town. And regardless of how poor they were he would insist on making boots for Jack, for the leather was there on hand. Jack pleaded with his father to be allowed to go to school barefooted like most of the other children in town, but Bill Gandy would have none of it. And so Jack suffered great embarrassment every day. For not only did he stand out because his feet were shod, but his boots were too heavy and high for a young boy's taste, his father a proud saddler with a liking for his products firm. There were, though – Jack had to admit – several other children at the school whose feet were covered, but at least their shoes did not shine with quite the same bulk. One of those boys was Max, Mort Butler's son. Jack knew Max and sometimes played in a group with him, but Max lived up the end of town towards Ulverstone and therefore neither was part of each other's domain. Jack, though, was always aware of Max. Because Max's father was Mort. And Mort was a veteran. And was so thin. And, often, looked so very ill. Jack always wondered how Mort and his wife managed, for Jack knew about his own father's precarious state. Mort always seemed to have so many children around his house. How did he feed them? How did he keep going? Jack knew pensions were never enough.

7

The toll it took

Soldiers look so different out of uniform, especially loose-limbed casual blokes who haven't been near an army route march in well over a decade. And, over time, the only people who seemed to remember who these men had once been were the families. And the children. Who watched.

In Penguin Hedley Deverell, of the 26th Battalion (but who finished the war in the 12th), another of those miracle blokes who had gone the distance, survived the whole debacle, from the first landing at Gallipoli right through to the Armistice — was now the father of four children. And by Christ, he would do what he had to do to look after them all. He'd always been a man who pushed himself to the edge, if that's what it took.

His mates from his battalion would get together on Anzac Day each year, meeting down at the pub after the Dawn Service, heads all leaning in towards each other, beers in their hands, laughter booming out then subsiding as the stories changed; getting half shickered before the next service and topping up again when that one was over – after all, this was a big day. It was during those times that the subject would come up again: Hedley, they all agreed – shaking their heads at the injustice of the omission – should have been awarded the VC, his forays into those trenches something to behold. But, they all lamented, a high-ranking officer hadn't been there, hadn't seen – and the wrong man . . . Oh, but they wouldn't say. And not one officer to verify Hedley's courage, selflessness and disregard for his own skin on that day. The men all knew and remembered, though. They remembered the day; they remembered watching him. And they all knew one of the truths of the battlefield: there are those who deserved the awards they were given, and those who didn't. Some men were even embarrassed to receive them, knowing what had actually gone on out there.

Then there were those blokes who should have been recognised, but never were. But – they rationalised, knowing how the world often works – they were just ordinary blokes, and you learn in life: sometimes you win, sometimes you don't. It was a bloody shame about Hedley. What he did, the man he was, deserved to be known. Now those who had not seen would never know. Back in Australia he, like all the others, was just another returned digger – a nuisance, if the truth be told, according to many now the war had been over so long. So you got on with life. They all did, as far as each could manage.

Hedley was doing all right. He had a job, a family, a small house. His health was a bit iffy, but so far it was holding. He'd be buggered if he was going to give in yet. But it wasn't easy.

'Don't forget to let the dogs off, Sylvia,' he'd call over his shoulder to his wife every Sunday night as he started his trek, by bike, to the timber mill at Hampshire, forty miles away up in the hills, making sure he would be there ready to start his working week first thing Monday morning.

Those dirt tracks with all the bumps were rough on a bloke's body, and the old rattling pushbike didn't help matters either. Sometimes the weather was a bit on the bone-numbing and wet side, especially when the rain ran down in icy streams out of those overhanging trees. Hedley didn't complain, though. Nor did he mention his gammy arm. That arm was now so weakened he had to give it a lift, reach over and pull it up with the other one, a distinct disadvantage when you work with heavy logs and timber – and cutting and lifting and stacking.

The war had left its mark. Every year he was reminded, and sometimes he would mention those hospital stays in England to his son, Bill. *Who would credit it, son? Three wounds.*

Three Christmases. One arm still worked, though, and he knew a lot of blokes didn't even have that. The three Naylor boys, from just over the way near where he and his family lived in Penguin, those poor lads didn't even get to come home. Alec Oliver down at the pub had told Hedley about the trench he'd hopped into, and there they were in front of him, all dead, in the mud: three brothers, gassed. So Hedley kept going, kept pushing. All the blokes he knew who'd been through what he had did exactly the same. You did what you had to do. No whingeing. Never once did his family know if he thought it was all, perhaps, too hard.

Bill knew the toll it took on his father, though; he saw how exhausted he was sometimes. And he would watch, amazed, when Hedley, arriving back late on a Friday night after his long bike ride home in the dark, would reach and grab for the jar of mutton bird oil. To Hedley it was an elixir, that globby, thick, mucous-like stuff bought directly from the men along the coast who worked the mutton bird season and who had drained it, then sold it to him just as it was. 'Unrefined' was an understatement. Hedley would take huge swigs, seeking relief. Its silkiness put the flame out for a while, eased the burn in the tissue as it made its way down to his gut.

All the blokes he knew – well, just about! – who'd been there on the Western Front in France had received their own dose of gas, some worse than others. And now they wheezed, those men with his dad – every one of them, Bill noticed. He could sense, almost feel, the effort in each breath. And the mutton bird oil, Hedley's own idiosyncratic home cure – well, Bill couldn't help but notice that either. The oil seemed to hitch a ride out of his father's body, sliding on the back of the sweating it caused. His father reeked at those times, his blue worker's singlet soaked in the stuff. The smell was merely another thing about the war that no-one mentioned at home. Bill, his mother and his three sisters all knew and understood: no need to speak of it; just help Dad if you could.

So when Hedley shouted about the dogs, they all knew what they had to do. 'Tomorrow night!' he would remind them, despite Sylvia having no need of such a prompt. For by now it was all routine: Monday night, let the hunting beagles off the chain. That gave the dogs enough time to race away from Penguin, head inland, up country, free and excited, following the same route their master had taken – in their meandering, exploring dog-like fashion – first passing some cleared paddocks with the stumps that still remained, the embedded roots waiting for a bullock team (or for the struggling farmer to find the funds to employ one). Then onwards into the bush, miles of it, thick and black in the night – and all through the next day and another night, with a few excursions and adventures as they went, until their destination was just a few whiffs into the air away. The dogs would arrive at the timber mill the same time every week.

Hedley, at work, would keep an eye out for them all

morning; as usual, it was lunchtime on Wednesday when they arrived, panting and pleased with themselves, and happy to see him. By geez they were reliable and he, in turn, was always pleased to see them. He would greet them, give them water, tie them up and let them rest. Then he'd work until knock-off time, when the wallaby hunting would begin, Hedley grabbing the 12-gauge shotgun he kept up at the mill, striding out, ready: his one good arm, his spot-on eye, hunting dogs at full stretch tearing after wallabies at dusk – all of it heart-thumping, all of it essential: wallabies were food. They helped a working man's pay last longer.

On Friday night, bounty secure in a hessian sugar bag and slung across his back or tied onto his bike, and dogs following happily behind him, they would travel the forty miles back home together, heading down towards Penguin and the sea. And in the Deverell household in the coming week – to add to the vegetables picked and dug from the home garden – wallaby stew was on the menu. Or wallaby patties or wallaby steaks. So many ways! And some would be given to his good friend Mort. You always helped if you could. And you helped a mate.

———

Mort Butler of the 12th Battalion, then the 52nd – and, these years later, a bloke whose body was slowly packing it in (but if he kept going there was a chance it might last) – now had a sizeable family too, only Mort had one more child than Hedley: five in all, three surviving boys and two girls. Proud of them all, and devoted and, like Hedley, determined to look after his family – even though physical feats, and a job, were just a hope from a lifetime ago – Mort did what he could. He taught Max, his eldest son, fishing and rabbiting, Max in turn teaching the others. Mort helped them get their sugar bags, their nets and lines ready – and watched his boys set off together, heading down to the creek or onto the rocks at the beach.

At home, when Mort was out in the small vegetable garden, young Max was often beside him, helping his father as far as he could: the two of them steady in their approach, always calm – sometimes talking, sometimes not – working on until Mort would have to have a rest. They dug and turned the soil in preparation for planting, each row dead straight and neat, the tall, skinny man and the shorter thin boy satisfied with their work, proud together of the laying out of the beds. All that, at least, was still within Mort's capabilities. He just had to breathe a lot to do it. Max adored his father, his kindness and care, admired his will to live as normal a life as he could manage. And Max told his sister Althea that he aimed to become a man just like their dad.

Mort had always been a tryer, a man with ambitions: not the unattainable, but a life larger than the one he had been born into. His parents were illiterate farm people, his labourer father, Joseph, a 'marksman' – a man who drew a cross, his mark, for a signature, and his mother, Sarah, had finally perfected writing her name, *SButler*, in a shaky hand, her concentration evident in every penstroke, her nervousness heartrending. Before the war Mort had been making headway towards such a life. He and Charles and Herbert had joined the citizen militia (the Citizens Military Force) to step into that bigger, more varied world; and they had each been promoted. Plus they knew how to read and write, had attended school as children. After such achievements – as small as they were in the wider scheme of things – there was a confidence there, restrained but hopeful, a recognition that they were capable young men. Perhaps one day . . . Who knew what they could do? Mort with a mate, on pushbikes, had frequently ridden down from Gawler, through its farm settlements and bush still being cleared, and its houses here and there – some visible, some hidden in valleys around the district – into Ulverstone, that much bigger town on the coast. Perhaps he would move there one day. Maybe to a different town. Maybe take a role somehow, be part of the happenings in a community. Maybe he could find a young lady, the right one, and love her, and she him; have his own family. Be special to someone.

Mort was friendly with the Dunhams, who lived in Preston, not far away. And in that family – one from better circumstances than his own, for they owned their own farm – were three fine young women. One of the girls, Pearl, was a trained teacher as well as a pianist and singer, with a voice that soared and trilled. An artistic spirit with a leaning towards the dramatic flourish, and with independence sewn, it seemed, into the stitching of her modern clothes, she sang in concerts and often went away to Hobart for her music. She had no intention of settling to a closed-in farming life. When he was away at the war, Mort and she wrote regularly to each other, Pearl offering a comforting voice from home. For they were friends and two of her brothers, Tom and Jim, both of whom Mort knew, were serving in France as well.

The eldest sister, Ruby, stayed on the farm, helping her parents, driving her pony and trap to all of the neighbouring farms collecting for various war appeals and for Red Cross. It was Ruby – the kind one, the one with some shyness, with the sense of humour that bubbled and burst forth at sweet times – it was to this sister whom Mort wrote 'darling' over and over, on one of his postcards sent on his way to the front. And it was to Ruby, during his time in hospital in England, on another of the cards he sent, that he had even included an exotic *Au revoir*, squeezed the two small words in at the last minute, angling them between the tightly packed sentences, up in the top left-hand corner, amusing himself – and, hopefully, her – with his audacity. Him, the humble farm boy from Gawler. Speaking French. His knowledge and experience now went beyond the confines of his small region in Tasmania.

Mort wrote to Ruby from Heliopolis. 'Well darling', it said on the card – which featured, in ornate script, *With love to my dear girl* and a soldier gazing longingly at a letter, the soldier seated under intertwined imperial flags and a royal crown behind him – 'my hands are too cold to write much this time'. Casually, as if it didn't matter, as if it wasn't the purpose of this card, he just happened to mention – with pride showing – that he was now the Battalion Orderly Sergeant, and was writing while all the boys were out on a march. He was a man with a future, declaring himself to her; a man on the move. 'I will close now,' he wrote, 'with fondest love darling. I am yours.'

And he signed his full name: *Morton Butler.* Perhaps in case she had forgotten his surname.

Back home, the man who had once been on the move had been brought to a halt. He faced it, knew he had no choice, but it was hard to push that fundamental tenet aside: men worked, earned a wage. Even while growing up – for him and all he knew – working had always been part of his life. It couldn't be any other way. He and his brothers and sisters had been sent out to the woodheap, to do fencing or to the vegetable garden from the time they were old enough to pick up a piece of wood, milk a cow or scratch around in paddocks gathering potatoes when a farmer's crop somewhere was ready to be dug, unearthing them in rows, making small piles, then shoving them all into sacks. Any money earned had gone straight to their parents' purse and helped the family keep going until the next cheque could be earned. It continued that way as Mort and his brothers grew to become young men. Money – survival – was a family concern.

Working had always enabled Mort to assist his parents. When Sarah and Joseph's boys had first signed up for the Australian Imperial Forces (AIF), sailed away to the other side of the world, Mort and his brother Charles arranged for six shillings per day to be deducted from their pay and sent home through the paymaster, to their parents. Just about all the fellows did the same. Across Australia widowed mothers, elderly fathers who were no longer able to work – frail parents who had no hope of earning any money, many and all who were struggling to keep poverty from the door in an era when pensions were almost nonexistent – were supported by an allocation from their sons' daily pay. Distress and hardship were caused when there was an administrative mix-up, when it didn't arrive or wasn't received in time. Those shillings, which amounted to pounds over time, were heaven-sent lifesavers.

Until those sons were killed, and then the money no longer came. In houses in towns and cities, in little cottages on small, remote holdings where the odd jobs were mounting because the sons were now gone, 'impoverished' became a well-used description in documentation, in appeals – frequently unsuccessful – to charity. Or it was never mentioned: too embarrassing. It was simply endured, the despair and suffering and privation hidden as much as possible. Another layer, a terrible addition, to the grief. Behind closed doors.

In Tasmania, when Mort's two brothers were finally, and officially, reported killed in action, Joseph and Sarah were notified that they would be sent the remainder of their sons' outstanding pay and that they were entitled to a gratuity payment for each – in 1920, four years after their boys' deaths. But first, forms were required. And then some more. And signed permission from Sarah. Even then it would not be paid in cash, but bonds. Bonds! What were they? Such foreign things – of the well-to-do! It was times like these when life seemed hardest, confusing, for a man who could neither read nor write, and his dead sons reduced to a figure on a page. Joseph had the postmistress write a letter for him, explaining his situation – for he had his pride, as much as he could muster. He was not in debt, but paying his way as he went:

Gawler
25/10/20
District Finance Officer

Dear Sir,
I received today your notice telling me that I was entitled to a gratuity bond for my son Charles Henry Butler. I asked for cash as I thought I was entitled to it. I am an old man of 65 and not able to do much and have been in failing health since the death of my two sons . . . both killed the same day at Mouquet Farm. In regard to investments, I have no investments or money and have been forced to use what money I did receive after my boys' affairs were settled up. All I

*have left is just about six or seven shillings in my bank
book. I cannot forward any bills or documents but you
can refer to Mr Frampton or _ all of Gawler for the
truth of my statement . . .*

*As I would not be able to cash the bonds with the
tradespeople without buying a lot of furniture that I
don't require, I would be very thankful if you could
see your way to give me cash for one and a bond for
the other. Hoping you can oblige and thanking you in
anticipation.*

Sincerely yours

Joseph X Thomas Butler

After agreeing to that which he didn't want – one of the
settlements in the form of a bond – for he did not wish to
appear unreasonable and demanding, he had the postmistress
write again soon after, begging their pardon, hoping they
didn't mind, telling them how grateful he was for any
assistance they could manage, powerlessness, poverty and
knowing his place on the social scale having done their work.
Whatever they decided is what he would accept, no matter
what difficulties they presented him with.

In 1921, the War Services Unit sent Joseph a form,
explaining they were no longer able to find the last resting
place of 'your son, the late No 3126 Corporal H Butler,
52nd Battalion' and asked to have on loan any letters or
information which could assist them. Joseph had someone
answer for him:

*There was a soldier told me that 3119 C.H. Butler
was buried along side Captain Littler and 3126
H. Butler was buried by a shell as far as I know. I had
a letter from Corporal Denny and he said he had seen
him in a shell hole but could not help him as he was
holding a position. I am forwarding two letters I got
and that is all I know about them.*

Yours faithfully J. T. Butler

It never seemed to end. Shell holes, burials, sadness.

Joseph and Sarah were sent the pamphlet *Where the
Australians Rest*. And Herbert's grave was never found. He,
like so many, was remembered on a list on a memorial in
France. And Mort – the son who had been to school, who
had not long ago had plans – was on a war pension now, no
longer in a position to help his aged and grieving parents.
It was hard enough to help himself. There are many ways in
which a man is shamed.

But there are ways to deal with that as well. His children
watched. And learned. You can find pride. You can.

8

Simply getting by

The Depression was taking hold. More blokes were out of work; those who had steady jobs were almost the upper crust. Hedley battled – boy, did he work for his money; Oscar had his carrying business and a small farm at Carmentown up the back; Spud Hall's dad had a carpentry business which brought in little jobs, and he made the coffins for the town as they were required; Elvin Ling's dad, Rupert, delivered for the River Don Trading Company, the largest shop in town, taking the orders in a truck filled with goods to all the farms up in the hinterland; the postmistress was set; anybody who had a shop of their own which managed to cope with people constantly asking to 'put it on the account' was doing all right, and the railway stationmaster was okay too. Then there were people like Bill Gandy, and the blacksmith round the corner; and those on a small pension, like Mort. And those who were out of work. There was some government assistance, sustenance, but mere shillings a week for a man and his family, no matter how many children he had to feed, didn't go far.

Along the coast many an anxious man travelled from town to town seeking any possible work, only to face disappointment and have to return. The Penguin Council kept a list of registered seekers for work and finally in 1931, when a federal grant was allocated to the town, they organised for a large party of the unemployed to make footpaths in East Penguin. It wasn't a job that would last long, but many families had some relief for a while, could pay something from what they owed at the Don. Probably before booking up more groceries again. At the next town along, in Burnie, thanks to a small federal grant the council organised a weekly pick-up of the unemployed, preference given, they stated, to the most 'conscientious' cases – a baffling term, it must have seemed, to many of the men. For there is many a man who keeps himself to himself, who won't admit his true circumstances. And who really knows what another is going through?

There were soup kitchens for ragged-clothed children and worn-out mothers in Hobart, in all the Australian cities, their husbands out searching for work, distressed, despairing.

In Perth, in Western Australia, a wharf labourer had been sent away, had to go if he wanted the sustenance road work, his wife staying behind, washing and scrubbing – and then some more – rather than beg for food for herself and her children. She was taken to hospital after collapsing at the wash tubs. In Wagga Wagga a young boy, Allan Bertram, saw men 'jumping the rattler' – a dangerous practice, one best completed before the train gathered too much speed. And he saw men push others off, attempting to prevent these rivals getting to the town, taking the jobs (if there were any) before them. In Victoria Frank Power saw people who 'were not hobos or tramps', he wrote, 'they were poor people endeavouring to reach Mount Buffalo, where [they believed] "there was work". They took enormous risks. I saw them under the carriages and cattle trucks, riding on most uncomfortable axles – less than feet from the tracks and wheels.'

General Sir Harry Chauvel, who had been the commander of the Australian Light Horse in the Great War, came across a camp of men in the Black Spur area in Victoria while he was out taking some friends on an enjoyable trail ride: the men were former light-horsemen, unemployed and living in the thick bush, old mates supporting each other. It was all still a battle, for so many, from one day to the next.

In Tasmania Mort, involved in his own struggle, didn't know exactly what Doctor Hamilton had written down and sent on to Hobart. What he did know was that sadness descended too often, the weight of it all pushing on his nerves. His father had died the year before, which had been a time of reflection. But he had got on with it. And he did have love in his life, that was not the problem: he loved Rube and his children deeply, and they him. But some days were hard to move through. How could he shift this feeling? What could he possibly do?

A letter came:

> *8th May 30*
>
> *Dear Sir*
> *Arising out of a report recently received from Dr.*
> *Hamilton, it is considered advisable that you enter*
> *Hobart Repatriation General Hospital. If you wish to*
> *enter Hospital please report to Dr. Hamilton to whom*
> *the necessary warrant has been forwarded to enable you*
> *to make the journey to Hobart.*
>
> *If you do come . . . kindly report direct to Hospital,*
> *Davey Street, where arrangements will be made for*
> *your admission.*
>
> *Yours faithfully*
> *Deputy commissioner*
>
> *(J. F. Humphris)*

And Mort made the full day's journey, changing trains as was necessary at Western Junction, south of Launceston, his morning train unable to continue. Mort and all the other passengers traipsed over to where another engine and a row of passenger railcars waited in position, ready to take them down to Hobart. Then the driver of his morning train did what he did every trip, turned and shunted his engine around, then backwards into position, clanging it onto the back of the passenger carriages – which had now become the front – and, procedure completed with its usual noisy, hissing ease, headed back up to the north-west coast, travelling along the railway line where it follows the edge of the land, just next to the rocks and the sea, a clear, uninterrupted view on offer for the driver and those seated to the right in the carriages. And Mort took the different train with its different smell, different seats, a different feel from home, travelled inland straight down the midlands of Tasmania, through its flat, dry sheeplands, to Hobart.

His ticket was paid for by the Repatriation Department, the term 'Repat' one which had by now entered the Australian lexicon, well known in the houses where returned men lived. It was a term which in other residences, if it was known at all, did not resonate with quite the same urgency or disdain – or relief, when a pension was finally granted and often tearfully, thankfully, received. For Repat – overburdened, and a system still in shock at the magnitude of what it had to deal with after the war – had its problems. It had to decide, case by case, which symptoms were war related and which weren't. Many times Repat got it wrong – records were incomplete, for a start, with many Army records containing no entries for ill health during war service; and on their return many men did not report all their problems. Gassing, in particular, was not mentioned if the men thought their dose slight when compared to their mates'. Men like Hedley struggled to keep working to support their families when pensions were denied or only part thereof approved, with the result that people soon came to know the term 'burnt-out digger' too.

The department did as well as it could within the constraints confronting it; the cost to the country so high, and becoming greater every year. For the men were getting sicker: 'aggravation', it was called in the department – that is, ailments that became worse over time. And that applied to so many of them. When Mort had been in hospital in England he had been diagnosed with a 'soldier's heart': a disordered action of the heart, DAH, caused by strenuous service. Mort always had tried too hard.

Mort was admitted to hospital in Hobart on the thirteenth of June, 1930. The medical superintendent noted on his report that his patient had a 'Nervy and irritable heart. Mixture prescribed.' Six weeks later the report noted, 'Heart still irregular has put on a little weight is feeling better ...' And then – Mort's secret desire – 'wishes to go to South Australia as he feels better in a warm climate'. Mort was 'discharged accordingly to own home', to face again the fact that, as pretty as Penguin was, he had wanted to go, but the cost for him to up and move his family interstate was prohibitive – out of a poor man's reach. A dream which would never be. He was having enough trouble simply getting by.

Mort did, though, have a roof at least – a very plain one – over his head. And he was managing to feed everyone: there was the catch plucked from the rockeries, the stone fish traps, to help – so much so that Althea, his youngest daughter, was heartily sick and tired of fish at so many meals. And there were rabbits Max and the boys caught, ferreting down the creek with the small nets Mort had bought them from the Don in the main street. And there was wallaby from Hedley as well. Mort had the most basic needs of life covered, even if the quantities were never large.

But a man's a man, sick or not. There had to be a way to do more. So Mort did the unthinkable: he took to doing the housework, Ruby acquiescing in the unusual domestic arrangement. Many tongues clicked in horror, and there were whispers from the unkinder quarters of the town. Some women, it seemed, decided that Ruby – who must be lazy, for there could be no other explanation – should alter her ways, reprieve her husband and allow him to rest, the poor man. It was *all too dreadful*.

Devoted to her dear Mort, Ruby refused to bend to the gossip. And, accordingly, refused to explain. She allowed Mort to sweep and busy himself, to help her deal with the children, until – as she knew would be the case, after several days of pushing himself – exhaustion would set in; and then, weakened and breathless, he would be back in bed.

And when he had recovered sufficiently, he would do it all again. Mort, a labourer and a man from the land, had never expected this to be his lot; and he, just like Hedley, would do whatever he could. If it meant housework for a man to be useful, to care for his family and give him a purpose, that is what he would do. Ruby resumed all those same duties whenever her help was finally required. His Rube knew, and understood.

Althea and Valerie though, Mort and Ruby's two daughters, felt the effects of the gossip at school. It hurt. Those mean people didn't know the full story – what it was like for their mum, how she was helping their dad. No-one seemed to know about the war anymore, and what it had done.

The gossip was the poor speaking against the poor, resentment and jealousy from people who had little, directed against those who, it appeared, received an unfair advantage. For as poor as Mort and his family were, his children still managed to have shoes, had their books paid for, received financial assistance for their school needs, the Soldiers' Children's Education Scheme providing what many families in town could not afford. No-one had much, but some, it occasionally seemed, had a bit more than none – and it was noticed.

The gossipmongers didn't know of the many times Mort was embarrassed, almost humiliated, at having so little, at being unable to provide. Or the times when he wanted to be one of the boys, to meet up with his cobbers, Hedley and Oscar and Alec, and whoever was down at the pub for the company, and have a few laughs and tell some stories; times when Ruby would watch him place a nail or two in his pocket with a halfpenny or penny before he left. He would jingle it for her, his hand slapping in his pocket against his thigh so she could hear the clinking sounds they made. *Almost convincing, eh, Rube?* And they would share the joke; her funny husband. But it tore at her, watching him, how he tried. Oh, how she wished he had more money – just for himself. How wonderful it would be if such a joke never had to be made; kind, considerate Mort pretending he had money to spare. Pretending he had any money at all. So many of the diggers in town were the same, the having little, the embarrassment, the need to get a grip and carry on.

9

Toc H

Just about all the soldiers knew about the Ypres salient, twenty kilometres long on the Western Front, just over the French border. It was another of the killing fields, claiming over one million casualties. From the latter part of 1916 up until October 1917 all five divisions of the Australian Imperial Force (AIF) were involved in the fighting there, with thousands of poor Australian lads copping the horror, the mud and the blood. Those who headed there knew where they were going, and it could make a bloke feel despondent. But there was a place you could go, call in, feel as if you were home, either on the way to the front or on your dazed return, and it made all the difference.

Eleven miles west of Ypres, in the Belgian town of Poperinghe (the town known as 'Pop' to the blokes), Queensland-born Army Chaplain Tubby Clayton – the Reverend PB Clayton – opened a soldiers' club, a haven to the tens of thousands of British, Canadian and Australian troops who fought nearby. It was a place of equality. One of the signs hanging on the walls inside read 'All rank abandon ye who enter here' (with a nod to Dante's inferno). But it was the sign hanging out the front which made the club's purpose clearer:

Talbot House, 1915
Everyman's club.

Talbot House, known to the soldiers as Toc H, its initials parleyed into signaller's code, was one of those places that gave you faith in mankind, helped you know there were places you could go in the midst of turmoil, where someone, somehow, was looking out for you. Or it simply gave you a feeling that all was right in the world, for a while. At Toc H soldiers would enter through the ornate iron-grilled doorway and be washed with laughter and music and cheer; greeted by the sight of bunches of soldiers, all just men facing the same circumstances, all together. If they felt in need of communion with a guiding hand there was the Upper Room, in the loft on the fourth floor, where many a captain, a private, all ranks, knelt side by side in the chapel in front of the carpenter's bench (which had at one time been found in the garden) before facing what was to come. Twenty-five thousand soldiers were recorded to have visited that room.

One young soldier left a note, just before he left for the front line:

> *Will you pray earnestly for me that I may have strength given to me to do that which is right and to make an effort to help others; not so much by what I say, but by my whole life. I have wandered away very far, but I want to put things right; and the prayers of Talbot House will mean much to me.*

Toc H meant so much to so many that in 1925 a Toc H movement had emerged worldwide, grateful soldiers wanting to ensure that the ideals of Talbot House carried on. In 1929 Talbot House in Poperinghe was bought and preserved – and before the German occupation of the next world war the people of the town hid the contents, including the carpenter's bench; and, after the war, put everything back in place. Just as it had been.

Members of Toc H were meant to work quietly, to seek out people who needed assistance, to be of service to others. Be a friend. And Mort Butler, a man who understood men in need, became one of the founding members of Toc H, Penguin Group – his memories, all that he knew to be of value, the quality of men – none of his war had been left behind. And you live with it however you can. Mort had chosen how he would live with his. Toc H, its ideals – Mort's ideals – all were part of that.

—

Ruby and the children giggled when Mort told them all what a chump he had been. Mort and his family were gathered in the big kitchen at the house at Crescent Street where they had recently moved; the owner, Phil Hales's dad, had approached them and told them it was vacant. This most recent house was bare like the others, but the rooms were good sizes, and it had a long passageway where Ruby hung maroon curtains at the arch and placed a tall stand with a pot plant there. It almost looked posh.

Everyone felt better here. It had a verandah out the front, perfect for sitting in the sun, listening to the sea and watching the train go past several times a day – always an invigorating time, with the track right there in front of them, trains rumbling along between their street and the shops, which were just over the line and through the white gate. It was also ideal for chatting to people who went past, or sitting with them when they dropped in. Many of Mort's mates – old Army cobbers as well as ordinary mates from around the town – dropped by for a yarn if he was up and about. This house was in a good position. And today, again, Ruby and the children were giggling. What Dad had done! They couldn't believe he had said it, and they loved him for it, Their dad, his little stories, how he made fun of himself.

'Do you mind if I put the light out now, Frank?' he had said, ready to turn in for the night in the hotel room in the pub where he had been staying with his friend, sharing a room, and being considerate of his friend's comfort. Frank Marriott, a federal president of Toc H and a member of the Tasmanian Parliament, as well as a commissioner of the Boy Scout Movement, had paused – a startled moment – then turned his sightless eyes to where the voice came from.

'Oh, I think that would be all right, Mort,' he'd said. And laughed.

Mort, reminded, could just about have slapped the palm of his hand against his forehead. Oh, the things you take to be normal. How much you forget. For that was precisely why he'd been there: to be Frank's eyes. Frank, the former captain from the 12th Battalion, the same battalion Mort and his brothers had first been in before their transfer; Frank, who had suffered bullet wounds to both eyes at Bapaume in France in February 1917; Frank, the man who could no longer see.

Francis Marriott had been fortunate that he had been a settled man before the war had taken his sight. He had a loving wife and a family who could look after him; he owned a farm at Elliott, and he was well educated. At first he had fought against the shock and fear his blindness had caused him, and he had refused to accept his life as it now seemed to be. There must be possibility, somewhere. In 1919 he sailed to London with his family, and re-found a purpose – hope – for himself at St Dunstan's Hostel for Blinded Soldiers and

Sailors, where he learned Braille and typewriting, joinery and poultry farming. While there he made quite an impression at Windsor Castle in 1920, when he was received by King George V, the Patron of St Dunstan's, who enquired whether Frank sometimes hit his thumb with a hammer during his carpentry work. On hearing the affirmative, the King continued: 'And does that make you swear?'

'Well, I *am* Australian, Your Majesty!'

When he had come back home Frank was approached to stand for Parliament, and was elected in 1922, his wife reading aloud any Bills which were to be debated and his memory doing the rest. Mort knew his friend to be a man of integrity and compassion, with a willingness to go the distance for what he believed. Frank's voice, it has been written, was resonant, and he was forthright in his speech. The Frank Marriott whom young Jack Gandy saw enter St Stephens Church in Penguin on a Sunday on a regular basis – Jack watching, as he did, from his seat near the back of the vestry, having just completed his job of ringing the church bell to call the congregation each week – that Frank Marriott who was guided by either his wife or one of his sons down the coir matting over the wooden boards in the aisle, a hand softly placed behind his arm, nudging him sideways into the wooden pew to face towards the altar, was a man who was gentle, another of those whom Jack knew to be a man among men. Mort would have agreed.

Here, now, Frank was travelling, with Mort's help, along the north coast of Tasmania to speak with and listen to the needs of many of the returned men. Those men were in need of someone like Frank to hear them out, to speak up for them: many Australians had given up listening, long ago.

'I was born in 1913, and some of my boy and girl friends are thoroughly sick of war pictures, and especially sick of anything relating to Australian soldiers,' a young man was reported as saying in the *Labor Daily* on 25 November 1931. 'We see nothing to interest us in these plays and talkies. What we actually see every day till they have got on our nerves are crippled, blind and battered wrecks, with brass badges on, begging in the streets, howling about pension reductions, while their women and children are in dire straits, so if there was ever any honour and glory in the whole wretched business, it vanished before I grew up ... the general opinion among fellows like myself is that Australians were very foolish to let themselves be lured into going ... none of my friends like returned soldiers.'

And the men weren't seen as much better in the less populated climes of Tasmania. The Returned Sailors and Soldiers Imperial League of Australia stated it as they saw it in *The Tassie Digger* in 1922:

> ... *The false glamour which surrounded men on their return to Tasmania made almost certain a swing in public opinion to one side or the other — on the one hand that none but returned men were worthy of*

anything and on the other that (as one so often hears
in business houses) people are sick of the name of
returned soldier . . .

It hadn't helped when newspaper reports had appeared over the years, highlighting how much had been paid to the 300 000 returned soldiers and their dependants (64 million pounds by 1927) for it seemed so much for all of them doing so little – or so the attitude was. And it certainly hadn't helped when it was in the paper that one of the returned men who attended a scheme for training – a digger being a digger, a bloke with a sense of humour – 'calmly bespoke his desire to be taught to watch the roses grow in Sydney Botanical Gardens', and another aspired, he said, 'to be taught to hold down a job like that of Mr W. Hughes the Prime Minister'. Readers of newspapers don't always laugh in all the same places.

Oh, those bothersome men and their bothersome problems, untidy irritants that they were. The blinkers in Australia were firmly on, so many refusing to acknowledge the existence of such a difficult plot line in the everyday Australian story, the part where just under the surface, out of view, a whole other thread was playing out in people's lives: grief that never ended, despair that no-one saw. SAPPER HEALY DIES: 13 YEAR ORDEAL said the headline in *The Sydney Morning Herald* in 1928. Frank Healy, who had been paralysed at Gallipoli, had lain 'helpless on an aircushion' since 1915, said the news report, and had, these many years later, finally died. In 1933, VC winner Hugo Throssell committed suicide. The chaplain at his funeral stated for all to hear that he 'died for his country as surely as if he had perished in the trenches'. But it made little difference. The days of the glorious lives, and deaths, had finished, it seemed, the day the war ended. There were few, apart from those to whom it was happening, who knew about this story.

In Tasmania, in that hotel room, a veteran doing whatever he could to make a worthwhile life for himself and help a man helping men like himself, turned out the light, embarrassed and amused, with Frank Marriott not noticing the difference.

And Mort had another funny story to tell his family. Oh, what a chump he could be.

10

Time passing

Frank Marriott had to work hard in Parliament, in the House of Assembly, to get that fifty pounds allocated to the Boy Scout Movement in Tasmania. Talk about having to deal with the animosity that flowed! But he had fought and pushed it through, and the Boy Scout Movement – at a low point with not many more than 1000 scouts in the whole state – was grateful, though the amount was less than Frank had hoped for.

Perhaps it was the appearance of the uniforms that created such bad feeling; perhaps it was the manual *Scouting for Boys*, with its pages (as interesting and useful as they were) which featured stories of colonial campaigns Baden-Powell had been part of. Whatever it was, it seemed anything which could be interpreted as fuelling militaristic tendencies was on the nose these days. The Western Front was perhaps responsible, although no-one would admit it; the whole military destruction drama had been a tad excessive, not to mention outside the realms of understanding. And maybe if everyone just kept their heads down and refused to look at it, it would never happen again.

Some of the returned men were getting a bit pushy too, fed up and making demands, some of them downright communistic. And apart from that, all the countries were still working out how to pay for it, nearly thirteen years later. Soldiers, the military – no-one wanted to know.

Jack Gandy and all the young boys of the recently formed Penguin Scout group – who in 1931 were camped out near Lobster Creek up at Hobsons Flat, in a grazing area out the back of Ulverstone – couldn't have cared less one way or the other. A Scout camp was just plain good fun. They'd constructed a bridge over the Leven River, each of them conspiring to end in the water as spectacularly as possible, amid laughter and splashing, the Scoutmaster too. They'd built their own beds out of forked sticks and saplings and, using a chaff bag, had slept on the ground. It had been a bit cold – freezing, in fact – and when Bill Gandy came to see how his young scamp of a son was faring, he came bearing a priceless gift: an extra blanket.

In Penguin the Scout group hadn't been going for long,

but nevertheless it had been necessary for Jack to wait until his father had enough money to pay for the uniform before he could join. And now, fully kitted out, here Jack was, thrilled to be with so many of the boys from town. Phil Hales was there, Spud Hall, Elvin Ling, the Yaxleys, and Max Butler too. And Mort! Mort was his Scoutmaster! Jack admired him for being there, for taking time with all the boys, being patient and tolerant, teaching them, making the effort Jack could sometimes see Mort needed to make to get through each day. Here he was: Scoutmaster Butler – the first Scoutmaster in the town, conducting the camp without a uniform of his own; probably learning from the manual as he went along; coping with the cold too, for the boys. And he did know about camping and roughing it, as he and his two brothers had been in the citizen militia together for a couple of years before the Great War. And sleeping and living arrangements during the war had never been a picnic either. Here, now, only his son Max would have known it had only been six months since he had come home from his stay at the hospital.

When Jack's father came visiting at the camp, Jack's sister came too, bringing her camera. All the scouts lined up for a photo, tall and skinny Jack standing sentinel-like, proud in his new uniform. Spud Hall was unable to stop himself looking like the head parcel-fooler and knick-knocker that he was, mischievous and cheeky; Elvin looked on in admiration at Spud's face-pulling and contortion act, while Max looked

. . . well, obedient. And Mort, steady Mort, stood fatherlike over them all.

———

Over time at the Scout meetings, Jack noticed that Max was someone content to merge with whatever was happening, someone who, while willing to join in and have some fun, was not one to push himself forward. More a member of the pack than a leader. And yet in life there are times, it seems, when that which is least expected can occur, and when it does it leaves a bloke almost speechless. Here in small-town Penguin, something was about to happen which would be remembered and mentioned with amusement and awe for years: a challenge issued which, in a surprise move, was about to be taken up.

A new town hall was being built in the main street of Penguin, positioned straight over from the beach. The new building was a welcome modern addition to the town, and townspeople of all descriptions were helping in whatever way they could. The Scout group volunteered to lay the foundation, because Phil Hales's dad was a builder. Laying the foundation was not too daunting, and it shouldn't take too long if everyone did their bit and chipped in, for the bricks were the larger grey cement blocks – a stretch they certainly were for a hand to hold, but easy and quick to lay.

'I bet,' said one young Scout to the group at large as they

worked, the young lad no doubt inwardly congratulating himself at having thought up the ultimate in bets, one he was sure to win, 'I bet you can't carry one of those grey bricks in one hand, all the way to the top of Mt Montgomery – no stopping, no dropping the brick, no changing hands or position. And fingers on top, brick downwards. Bet you can't!'

And Max Butler, the boy who'd never declared himself or openly shown his hand – Max, the unknown – accepted the challenge.

A gaggle of Scouts followed behind – noisy, animated, amused – up Ironcliffe Road, up the steep slope of South Road, round the big bend and then straight ahead until they reached the winding, thick bush. Then through the rough scrub and native prickly plants with the scents that waft as you pass; through the eucalypts; lots of legs tramping along on the thin dusty track, all the sweating way up to the top of the smallish mountain which stands behind the town. Max made it, carried the brick one hand, brick down, fingers on top, all the way. Max, the quiet, determined unknown; that grinning imp. It seems no-one knows what you can do until you choose to show it.

———

The years were moving on. Max and Jack – all the children in Penguin – were growing older. Life continued in its uncomplicated fashion, not much to grab your attention except a hungry belly – although for Jack that was attention grabbing enough; the gnaw – ever present, it felt – in his stomach. There was, of course, the constant speculation about how much biffo there would be in the footy matches in the coming weekend competition along the coast, especially if the boys from the Two Blues, Penguin's local team, were playing Ulverstone. But apart from that, not much at all. Except . . . now, in Mort's house, Ruby's brother had come to die. It was 1932.

———

It had been obvious for a couple of years that Tom wasn't going to last much longer. He had tried, and they had all thought he could do it, just battle on, at the Repatriation Hospital in Hobart. Every now and then he'd come up to Penguin to stay with Ruby and Mort and the kids, and Ruby would take care of him while Mort popped in and out of his room, did a fair share of the housework and helped. But Tom Dunham, of the 12th Battalion then the 52nd, an 'Original' – a bloke who hadn't dodged enough of those bullets at Lone Pine because a couple had got him there (and he had written to his mother saying, 'Yes Mother, I am very lucky to be able to write to you. Poor old Tom was near done for, this time'); Tom Dunham who, after his stretch in hospital, recovered then marched on over to France and found that a new companion, pleurisy, lurked around in the trenches, and then found that pleurisy could clear a path in a debilitated body and lead the way to tuberculosis. Now, Tom Dunham of the 12th, then the 52nd, after all that, was at the end of his road.

It was a sad time, the decline: him smiling at them when he could from his bed, at his dear sister Rube and her family; his lack of flesh, his shrunken face; him talking, when he had the strength, to his nephews and nieces, young Max and his playful brothers and sisters as they controlled themselves and stood by his bed, being with Uncle Tom, just being there. The watching as he declined – Ruby and Mort easing him towards what was to come, helping him as much as they could. Knowing the effort Tom had made over the years. The knowing of it all.

There had been a time for Tom when life had looked as if it would smile on him for a while. He and his brother Jim, another 12th Battalion man, had attempted to go back to the work they knew: back on to the land, taking up one of those soldier-settlement holdings – theirs in Penguin, up Pine Road. Back to life as it used to be. But it hadn't worked out.

'[T]he landowners . . . in many cases must have seen the soldiers coming,' so said Mr G Bell, the local parliamentarian, in 1927, 'and "got in for their pound of flesh"', the *Weekly Courier* reported. By then it was obvious to all and sundry that so many of the lads were under terrible pressure: rents were too high; they had to pay for their own buildings even though they didn't own the land on which those buildings stood; equipment and farm implements had doubled in price after the war; many of the blocks were too small to make a go of it for anyone, or the land was terrible and unproductive; there was a drought in the early 1920s, and there were punitive fines from the authorities when the soldier-settlers were late meeting any of their payments. And their bodies were crumbling away. On a regular basis an inspector would show up, write a report, decide whether a man was a 'trier' or not. Many a soldier-settler walked off his land with spirit, body, hope all broken, all gone.

Another of Ruby and Tom's brothers, Jossie, came back from interstate to help him on the farm — left the best job he'd ever had to try to help (and was never to have such a job again, his one opportunity gone now too). But even he, a healthy man, found the work hard and rough. Then Tom's back went on him.

It was all over. It's curious how it's not always the most obvious thing that gets you in the end, the one that tips you over. So Tom was off to Repat in Hobart. He never got back to the farm.

Now he was here in town again, as he had been so many times before. Kind, tolerant Rube was the one everybody came to when they needed care. She arranged for Mort and some of his mates to fill in part of the verandah so Tom would have a room of his own — 'the sleepout', it was called. It wasn't flash, and the walls were pine and thin, the floor still the cement of the verandah. But it was with family. And it was a home.

Tom heard the trains pass several times a day: a passenger train once a day, the others all goods trains carrying freight. The room shook a little when the trains rumbled and clattered along the stretch of line right at the front of the house, and sometimes he was awakened by the multi-toned whistle the driver blew as the train neared the crossing at the main street. All of it friendly, life-filled and vigorous; all of it so close to where he lay. The world was continuing, people were working, travelling to other towns; even Mort's homing pigeons for his races would be on some of those trains. The sun came in the window and when Tom's head was propped up a little he could see some of the town. Ruby put flowers in a vase for him; and he was fading away.

His faithful fiancée, Sister Dorothy Ward, a nurse he had met at the hospital, came to stay as well – in another room, of course. She had waited, all these years, yet knowing the truth of it: that they would never marry. But she would not leave him.

Tom died. He was buried in the Penguin cemetery, up on the hill which looks out to the sea. Only then did Dorothy allow herself to marry. She was one of those who knew, who understood: the drawn-out heartache; the pain they tried to hide; the lost lives of so many men of Australia.

It was January 1933. It had been just a little over fourteen years since the war had ended.

11

Change coming

There were lamentations galore, complete with wailing, and quantities of robust shouting bouncing off the walls in the Gandy house right there on Penguin's main street – the uproar between father and son lively enough to rattle the whips and tools and saddleware in Bill's workshop just outside, and loud enough to be heard right down at the beach if someone had been sitting and fishing over on the rocks. Sound carries in the quiet in Penguin – not that Jack cared right then. But Bill Gandy would not budge: his son was off to boarding school, no matter what.

Bill had been ready for a day such as this, and had been prepared, had something he could draw upon – the bonds his own dear father had sent him as a wedding present from England all those years ago – laying them low in preparation for an occasion serious enough to warrant cashing them in. And that time was now: two thousand pounds in Dover Corporation Bonds available, which had matured and increased in value. After all these years of difficulty and lack, never cashing them in through it all (for he had been determined to keep them to provide for Jack's future), the childish notions his son was declaring now – to leave school and become a telegraph messenger boy here in Penguin (*Even if a vacancy existed right now, Jack, which it doesn't, if you would just calm down!*) – well, it would not get a look-in. Or a hearing.

There had been disappointment the year before when Jack had been so close to gaining a cadetship to become a midshipman – as was possible at the age of twelve – to the naval college in Melbourne. He had been one of the final lot for selection, the eight boys from Tasmania even taken to Melbourne by a Chief Petty Officer. It had been exciting for them all at home: the waiting, the going. And also for Jack: the trip across on the boat, being put up at the Victorian Coffee Palace and then, after the interview, being left on his own to wander Melbourne, as he did with Jack Lockrey; catching the cable tram, the last one there was, on the Brunswick line to the zoo; looking down and seeing the cable running under the slot in the ground. Then it was time to find their way back to the boat – young boys, twelve years old, first time in the city – *thank you all for coming, now find your own way there.* And then such bad news for the Gandys: even though Jack had done well to be one of the boys chosen from each state, he had been unsuccessful in being selected in the final lucky thirteen.

Bill had been terribly disappointed. And that was when he decided: no matter what his son had to say on the matter, he was going. To Launceston Grammar School. The Penguin headmaster, Bob Thorne, was called in to add weight, and, having persuaded Jack to give it a go – just try it for a year – a deal was reached.

Jack agreed, though secretly planned a speedy return to his town and friends and freedom, when he would then get that desired job. Until he found how much he liked it all. And food! Well, quantity anyway, which the other boys left nonchalantly on their plates. Unbelievable.

Jack stayed. And with new circumstances, new people, and the school referring to him by the name on his birth certificate, he took on his given name. So Jack (a name he had never liked) became John. John Gandy. Which pleased him.

—

School life carried on in Penguin as usual. The children muttered about who was going to cop it that day from the teachers – one boy in particular, they agreed, was targetted and picked on in a cruel way, the girls finding it hard to watch. A fair percentage of the boys were regularly lined up for the 'cuts' on the hand: a cane whipped down hard, each slash delivering a sting as sharp as a knife cut, each 'cut' capable of bruising the boy's flesh to the bone. The boys were just as regularly confused about what they had done this time to deserve the same old treatment.

There was a day when Mort – who had raised his children without laying a hand on them – found he had to walk to the school just near to where they had once lived to make sure there would never be a repeat performance of his daughter Valerie's head being continually banged hard against the blackboard, accompanied by the words, 'Can you see now, Butler? Can you see?'

The Anzac Day sports came around again, anticipated, talked about, the heady excitement not easily contained. It was held each year after midday when the service and march, in which the whole school participated, was over. It was on at the Rec, the recreation ground just over the fence, behind Mort's house. Max and his brothers and sisters loved living in that prized spot – one Jack Gandy had always envied – because they could slip through a secret gate and there they were in at the footy, or the sports – whatever was being held.

For the Anzac Day sports, children had been brought in by bus from all the schools in the area: Cuprona, Natone, Riana, South Riana and Penguin too; the shouting, wriggling, boisterous mobs mixing freely, and all determined to win. Maurice Jones came in from Cuprona, and it was a mad dash against John Midgeley of Riana and Max Butler of Penguin. There would come a time when Maurice would no longer be able to run as well, but that was in the future. None of the children present, nor the adults, knew what was heading their way, what the years would soon bring. For now the children squirmed and tussled and shouted from the grandstand, and partook of the afternoon tea booths if they had a few pennies, a marvellous spread provided by the mothers.

On the footy field, which today was pegged off into racing lanes, with bunting and flags and fluttering colour, Bill Deverell had a hell of a competition against Morris Ling of Penguin and Digger (Roy) Ling from South Riana. Bill could beat them at seventy-five yards, but after that it was a serious, lunging fight for the tape. Even more so in the two-twenty and four-forty. Digger, it seemed, could run for a week! Everything about the day was remembered, wondered at, relived and re-enacted the next day at school. Nothing else could ever be of such importance.

The following year Max went off to the Technical College in Launceston, and had to board; he had no other choice if he was to attend school beyond the Merit Certificate. Other children as young as nine and ten left school: some wanting to leave, some regretting that they had to go – especially girls – as soon as they had passed that exam, their formal education was at an end, many of them needed at home to work on the family farms. And there were other families in different circumstances but with the same end result, their children forced from school, because they could not pay for the books. Max's education was covered, otherwise he would have left school as well.

Max came home on the train from Tech each school holidays and would be one of the Penguin lads again, a lad like many along the coast. So many of the children, living in similar conditions to Max, had grown watching their parents battle on, witnessed how tough they needed to be, the strength life sometimes required. Many children imbibed the post-war lesson: you continued. It's what you did. But if you could find a way or two to live life a little, revel in the freedom of the air and space and the country living, you'd do that too.

Max fished at the beach with his family and his mates as he had grown up doing; played footy and cricket in the local teams; helped his dad with the racing pigeons in the homemade loft at the back of Crescent Street – pigeons were cheap to buy, and from those you bred your flock. Max bred some of his own and every night, when letting them out for exercise, with eyes peeled skyward father and son would watch the whoosh of the birds swooping and circling. When they entered several in a race, sending them away on the train, there was a pang of pure excitement at the sight of a home-bred champion coming in from on high after a release miles away, liberated from its cage by a stationmaster somewhere along the coast. And there was always the thrill of coming close to beating Hedley and Bill Deverell. Pigeons lived in many backyards along the coast.

Max and his mates and brothers would head off towards the hills some days, Max's ferret retrieved from the cage kept in the backyard on the opposite side to the pigeon loft. Safer that way. It had been upsetting for all of them, especially for Max's little sister Althea, when the animal had escaped that time and found its way into the hutch that housed her white fluffy pet rabbit – a present it had been, from Mum and Dad – and it had then ripped the pet to bits, leaving the evidence for Althea to find in the morning, blood-splattered white fur spread all over the back lawn. But Max had grown up with ferrets, and squeamishness about their purpose didn't enter his head. Many boys and men along the coast had them, for ferrets all possessed the same hunting instinct which caused the ferret fiasco in the Butler backyard – the very trait which, when successful, provided an adjunct to the family finances and tea table: the meat a ferret could bring a family was welcomed and heartily consumed.

So Max would set off lugging a sugar bag containing the springing, unpredictable descendant of a polecat bouncing around and protesting as was its habit. He would release it near where too many rabbits had taken hold, underneath the blackberry bushes along the creek. And with his ten or twelve small nets – one placed over as many of the burrow openings as he could cover – he would retrieve the terrified prey, wring their necks as he'd learned as a little boy, skin them on the spot, dress them and take them home, skins as well. Then he would sell the pelts to a skin buyer – mostly to Billy McCarthy when he came in to Penguin from Riana, buying pelts from all the locals from his truck at the back of the pub.

Then, after weeks of being with his dad and his family and mates at home, Max was back on the train to Launceston again. At least he had been home in town, not yet sent to Tech, when Penguin won the football premiership in 1932 – an event so momentous it rivalled winning the Melbourne Cup. Well, it felt like it. Penguin floated in its glory. It was like that, Penguin: it felt like every bit of it belonged to all.

The town was certainly changing. Electricity had been connected five years before, and town water too; a couple of families had wirelesses now, and music arising out of nowhere – songs featuring Peter Dawson's dulcet tones – could be heard floating and bobbing in the air out of people's side windows. More cars were rolling in over the stretch of metalled road which had been laid just in front of all the shops. Those cars and buses and trucks were still only for the lucky few to own, but nevertheless were now an accepted part of the scenery. And there were changes brought to the families, too, with the children who had been born after the

Great War now leaving home, or leaving school. The younger children who remained noticed a shift, a reorganisation in their families, about who now fitted where.

It was certainly noticeable at Mort's house. Althea, the youngest child at about five years old, now found she could trail her dad, hang around even more. Always seeking her father out – wanting him near her as much as she could wangle – had proven embarrassing for Althea one time when she had been so excited to discover him standing talking to some men in the main street. She had gone up to him and tugged hard on the bottom of his jacket. And he had turned around – a man she didn't know! She had been mortified.

And traipsing after her dad, hanging around like a shadow, had also caused a terrible event to take place which had never happened before – something so out of the ordinary she had never imagined she would ever see it. It still caused her father guilt and grief. And it had been her fault.

Mort had been bending over in the hallway, just slightly, picking up something, and in her attempt to attract his attention – she was going to make him notice how funny she was – she swung her foot, intending to playfully kick him up the backside. But he had turned around – and she had connected with a hernia. Oh, he had raised his voice! Almost a yell. Chastised her! Only a sentence or two – but she had never heard him utter such words. She had cried; howled. And her dad had shed his own little tear as he hugged and tried to calm her, as he attempted to cope with the realisation that he had behaved towards one of his children in such a hurtful manner.

———

She bounced back, though. And there were times when she did manage to play happily by herself around the house. But everything was changing by the year, it seemed, especially with the boys away. Her brother Jack, Mort and Ruby's third son, was now at Tech too, up in Launceston learning to be a telecom technician. She was growing older and now, at about eight years old, knew many of the latest hit songs which were played on the wireless, their house having joined the list of fortunate townsfolk who had one; Ruby's brother Jim, who had a shop, had arranged a short-wave wireless cheaply for them. Althea would roar away in the backyard at some of the songs she liked – more volume than tune – and thoroughly enjoy herself and her performance. Until her mother would send her across to the shop to buy some milk, over the railway line and through the white gate next to the post office, and into the first shop there. The three Miss Lettes, the owners of the milk bar who lived on the premises in the rooms above, would tease her and let her know the one fact that all townspeople knew: sound travels.

'We love hearing you sing, dear,' the sweet ladies would say. And Althea would vow to herself to never roar again, the burning in her cheeks so great. But the commitment wasn't there, that big open sky simply begging for a voice to fill it, even one as blatantly untuneful as hers.

It was probably fortunate for Mort, with eager Althea on the loose, that he was now involved with several community organisations that kept him as occupied as he could manage on the days of the week when he was out of bed. In addition to those activities he and Harry Whittle had started up the bowls interest in the town, learning as they went along, playing on the green developed on a block of land which had been donated by one of the men of the town. Mort loved this new game – the slow, leisurely concentration it required fitting perfectly with his temperament and the state of his health. It also meant he wasn't always on hand to be his daughter's comedy sidekick.

Hedley Deverell didn't have as much time on his hands as Mort did. The Depression still had a hold in Tasmania, and with the timber mill at Hampshire now finished and the area 'cut out', Hedley had been faced with the prospect of no job – and, therefore, no money coming from anywhere – and so had gone squaring railway sleepers up at Riana. This was tough work, all right, especially with his useless arm. But it was work for which he could earn at least some income. Dressed in his ubiquitous blue singlet – for he was a practical man, no pretensions – he would keep on going, doing whatever it took, for that's what he expected of himself. He would cut the wood – it had to be dry – in long lengths with a crosscut saw, then pay Harry Whittle, who ran the largest carting business in town, to come up in his truck and collect the lot, deliver it all down to the railway yard off the main street, and Hedley would then stack it. He greased the ends thickly, as was required if they were to be considered suitable for the Railway to purchase them, and would stand and wait for the verdict when the inspectors came, when they (in the pedantic manner of the powerful over the man with a need) would look over each one in the pile there awaiting them.

Their decision was final. The top price for a sleeper was one shilling and threepence; for those they classed as second rate Hedley would be paid eleven pence. And if any had any splits or knots, they would be rejected and he would have to replace them. It was a nerve-racking, hard way to make a living, especially for a man with an easygoing nature, one who was fair to the bottom of his boots, who bent to what the inspectors said.

Hedley was starting to feel the strain; his wife knew the pressure he was under. A war pension, even part thereof, would ease his life, his breathing and his body a little. But so far with Repat he'd had no success.

There was some relief in Hedley's working life, though. He had saved and bought an old Triumph motorbike, his lungs and general health no longer up to the long pushbike ride he used to make. And with the Triumph he was able to come home to his family every night, a degree of comfort now present in his week. On Saturday mornings his son, Bill, was able to go with him too, then be dropped off at his friend Morris Ling's farm while Dad went to work, Bill riding on the back, clinging to his dad, even managing to stay on. But not so successful at stopping his jaws from playing a merry tune of their own devising, opening and slamming shut, the bumps in the dirt road and Hedley's bike's suspension a combination in a class of its own. It was a wonder, Bill always thought, that he had any teeth left at all.

———

The local papers were bringing unsettling news these days: headlines and reports about Europe and Germany. Japan too. *The Advocate*, the local paper along the coast, had been reporting on Japan since back in 1931, when its troops had entered Manchuria and Britain had protested for a while. And the news on the wireless now was no cheerier.

Mort and Hedley and the men were aware of it all. There would be a comment among them. Just that. A few nods. And no discussion.

Mort worried on his own: he had three boys. There were so many boys in town.

12

A serious turn

The wireless was a marvellous invention. The sounds of the wider world crackled, sometimes faded for a while; then, when the right place on the dial was found, burst into sound, booming and clear. And Adolf Hitler's funny voice, strange and disturbing, was far too clear for many a fellow; so, too, the speeches he made and the processions he oversaw.

The wireless brought all this into people's homes. And gave John Gandy reason enough to join the militia when he finished school and was back along the coast. A young man now, he had completed his four years at Launceston Grammar School and was working as a bank teller in Ulverstone, staying back home in Penguin with his father, who was now happy to be occupied with his new role as the superintendent of the Penguin Fire Brigade, with Spud Hall's father as his deputy.

The wider world was changing dramatically; at least the changes at home were more familiar – except now John paid board. In that wider world, to John, and to many people who heard what he heard, Hitler meant trouble. But it was not certain yet that there would be war.

Max Butler had also returned to Penguin, and he had managed to get a job in the opposite direction, over in Burnie: an apprenticeship of sorts at Fred Price's, where he was learning to make cane furniture. He, too, joined the militia, and every Friday night he would wait for his old running rival, John Midgeley, to turn up – John riding his bike the eight miles down from Riana to make sure he could go too – and they would travel over to Ulverstone in Percy Whittle's old Chev 4 truck, and do their three or four hours in the drill hall. John Gandy, who would take the bus there instead, travelled with plenty of other local lads, belting out bawdy songs all the way. Each of them returned home with not quite the same energy as when they began.

When Max arrived home late at night, without fail he would go in to yarn with his father, tell him any news, just be with him for a while. If Jack and Col, his younger brothers, were home as well they would all gather in their parents' bedroom, a few words and laughs together before saying goodnight. Max told his father it had been decided: he would go if war was declared.

Mort was finding it hard to believe; it had only been a little over twenty years since he and all his cobbers had returned. But he carried on, in those troubling days, living his life as if all was usual. Or so it appeared. He was proud of Max, so much so that Ruby and he hung a large framed portrait photo of their eldest son in his militia uniform in pride of place in the sitting room. It was high up, and all eyes were drawn to it. It was the most ornate thing in the room.

Mort's heart had been playing up on a regular basis for some time now, and the doctor would have to be sent for, usually by one of the boys if they were home. They would run over to the post office, knock on the door and raise the operator, ask her to ring up for them. Or sometimes they would run hell-for-leather and fetch the doctor themselves. The doctor would arrive at Crescent Street, hurry up the short pathway, come in through the large entrance with its heavy front door and turn left into a big bedroom at the front of the house. A tall clock always ticked away loudly in the cavernous space. It had done so for years from its spot on the mantelpiece above the fireplace, the rhythm interrupted only when it chimed every quarter of an hour with a longer ringing melody on the hour. All sounds echoed in this room with its high ceilings and lino on the floor. But when Mort was sick no-one noticed any of it. All they wanted was for Dad to be up, feeling well.

Mort had had many 'turns' over the years, and it was true, he spent much time in bed. But he was still in the land of the living, each episode a relief when it was over. And he probably would be here for many more years to come: if he had lasted this long, he could last a while longer. The doctor would see to him, make sure he was comfortable, check that he had what mixtures he needed and go away again.

———

It was a shock for Ruby's brother Alf when the cottage in which he and his family had been living burned down. He had just managed to get his boys out. The incubator for the chickens had been in the room right next to where his young sons had been in bed — and that was the place where the fire had suddenly burst into flames, right near their sleeping heads. So it might have been that. Or faulty wire. It was hard to know for sure. What was known was that the worker's cottage Mr Groom provided for Alf Dunham and his family, while he worked there on the property at Grooms Corner, was now completely destroyed.

Alf had tried and tried. He had saved the boys but not much else, just a small wardrobe from another room. And so he and his wife, Linda, and their young sons, Barney and Trevor, left the charred shell and came to live with Rube and Mort. Which meant Althea and Val had to let their uncle and auntie and young cousins take over the large bedroom they had previously shared, the one opposite their parents, and move into the smaller sleepout out the front.

Althea enjoyed the new arrangement and refused to believe that her older sister really did want her to shut up every time she pleaded, 'Let's play guesses!' And she also refused to believe that her sister actually wanted to get to sleep, because surely everybody would want to be awake with her. For young Althea had come to believe that if she fell asleep before midnight she would not be able to wake up in the morning. It would be impossible and, as a result, she would die! It was obvious, really. Mort – who checked on his daughters nightly anyway – now had to make sure his timing was correct, so that he would save his daughter's life. And when he came checking, making sure she was asleep, she would ask the time: *Is it twelve o'clock yet, Dad?* One evening he came at eleven, and ummmed and ahhhed when she asked her crucial question. But her father could never lie; she knew that. He had to return at twelve.

Max was now spending months at a time away with his militia battalion, the 12/50th, and regardless of Mort's attempt at appearing merely the proud, mildly concerned parent, it was causing Mort great worry. One day when he needed to give voice to what was on his mind, simply say it out loud, he pulled his nephew Barney close to his side when they were seated and just talked. Simply talked – not wanting a reply – about what it was like to be gassed; talked about canister bombs and men's lungs. About what it felt like.

It was 3 September 1939. Up the end of town near to St Stephens Church, Hedley Deverell, who had been listening to his wireless, came out of his house and threw a stone onto the roof next door to attract attention. Phil Hales came out to see what the devil was going on.

'She's on!' Hedley sang out. 'She's on!'

War had been declared.

———

Max wasn't going to wait any longer, no matter what they were saying. There was no guarantee that they could swing it so that the 12/50th militia could all be together in the same battalion. And Phil Hales was already in. They were, right now, forming units and taking recruits for the 6th Division. On 3 January 1940 *The Examiner* reported that there appeared to be a good deal of misconception and confusion regarding the name of the 2nd AIF and the 6th Division, since many people were of the opinion it was, in fact, the first division being formed:

> It was pointed out by the Department of Information in Launceston yesterday that actually it is the 6th Division of the Commonwealth Military Forces, as there were five divisions in existence before the outbreak of war. It is called the Second AIF . . . At present, the Second AIF of 20,000 consists only of the 6th Division. If more troops are enlisted for service

abroad, however, it might possibly become the Second
AIF, 7th Division, 8th Division and so on.

It was to be the sound of the name, the 8th Division, which would soon resonate in many men's hearts, in the pits of their stomachs, in the most complex corners of their souls – and in the silences their families would one day come to know. Other divisions would themselves know many of the same experiences; but the name of the 8th Division echoed with something beyond even all that. And it would haunt them for decades. But all that was to come. No-one yet knew, or suspected it could ever be.

Max arranged to enlist, and was, he understood, soon to be going to the Middle East – until someone got hold of him and persuaded him to wait. Several of the bigwigs had been pushing for a whole battalion from Tasmania, just as there had been in the First World War – the 40th Battalion to continue, the colours to go on. But it hadn't been finalised, and Max wouldn't wait. He resigned from the militia, enlisted in the AIF and took his final leave before his new army life began.

He travelled home by train. Colin and Jack were also home, all there to spend time together as a family before Max left. Max was doing the right thing by joining up; everyone knew that. Colin would soon follow; Jack though, far too young.

—

Although this wasn't the final night of Max's leave, there was something odd Althea thought. But she had no idea what it could mean. Her father came in to check on her.

'I wish you were a little tidier, dear,' he said, his voice warm and forgiving, as was his usual tone, and he picked up and folded her clothes. Nothing unusual in that, either, but somehow there was . . . something strange.

It was Friday night, and that meant late-night shopping, which in Burnie was almost a social occasion. People milled about in the street, and a party atmosphere pervaded. Max and Colin had taken the bus over so they could catch up with some of their respective mates, and now they were back home. They called in to have their customary pre-bed talk with their father in his bedroom. Then everyone went to bed.

It is not known if Max discussed with Mort what had happened that day, July the first, when word had gone out to all the militia boys from Colonel Youl that all the 12/50th men shouldn't wait any longer for that all-Tasmanian battalion: it wasn't a done deal. They could just enlist individually, go ahead and someone further up the chain – he hoped – would take it from there, apply the pressure, make it happen.

Surely that piece of information couldn't have been what finally stretched everything too tight; there was nothing in that news that seemed worse than before. Perhaps it was the sound of so many young men all heading off in a mob, enlisting in a rush together. Perhaps dying. But no-one would ever know. For, whatever it was, just after midnight on the second of July, 1940, Mort had another 'turn' – one which they all knew was serious.

Ruby raced from her room down the passage to the room at the back of the house where Max was sleeping. And Max went for the doctor. It was too late: Mort died as the doctor walked through the front door. The doctor had walked down from his house, which was up the hill towards the war memorial. This outcall to Mort's was quite normal procedure; he had come so many times before. He apologised for not rushing over, was terribly upset. But Ruby and the family understood: there was little that could have been done. This had been the one – the big one for Mort. Auntie Linda went in to the girls in the sleepout to tell them; and the whole house was now awake, Ruby in shock.

In the morning, when nobody was looking, young Barney, unable to help himself, opened the bedroom door a little and peeped in. He'd never seen a dead person before. Uncle Mort didn't look any different: he was just lying there. Waiting.

———

The RSL moved into action. By the time Althea peeped in a trestle table had appeared, and a coffin in which Mort had been placed. Althea knew she wasn't allowed to go in, that it had been expressly forbidden – but this was her dad, her dad who looked in on her every night, who called her *dear* in that kind Dad-voice. She had time to rise on her tiptoes, peer over the side in wonder, see her dad, see that he looked as if he were just asleep – *Oh, maybe he's just asleep!* – when she was grabbed by the scruff of the neck and taken out. But she had seen him! It wasn't long enough, though; could never be long enough.

She wasn't meant to watch the procession either but, seeing the hearse out the front of her house, and the cars ready to follow it to the service at St Stephens Church – and no-one nearby to stop her – she darted out and took a spot right near the front hedge, peeping again, her only chance to see. She needed to see. Mr Gardiner from round the corner came and noticed her hiding there, saw her tears, her all alone there, and chucked her under the chin and spoke softly to her, telling her everything would be all right. It was kindly meant, she knew, but she wasn't sure it was true. She stood and watched the line of cars move slowly away. Oh, those tears. If Dad were only here to call her *dear*!

At the church four returned soldiers, including Hedley, headed the cortege; another four – the fitter ones, Oscar Mather among them – carried the casket, which was draped in the Union Jack. The last post was sounded; and the local member of Parliament, Mr JH Chamberlain, read the RSL service. Mort's obituary in *The Advocate* said that he had been 'in very indifferent health' for some years. It also said that 'he appeared to be in his usual good spirits and [he had that day] attended the weekly Homing Society meeting. Always very popular he took an active part in many ways, having been president of the football club (senior and junior), bowling club committee, Boy Scout movement, and Toc H and President of the Homing Society.' And it spoke of the respect and esteem in which he had been held.

Mort, the humble son of the 'marksman'; the son who was embarrassed about what his life had become – about the pension – had, in his shortened life, done himself proud. In a humble way. In the very best of ways: in people ways. 'If I can be just *half* the man Dad was . . .' Max said to his sisters. He didn't finish the sentence: his father was fifty-three.

———

Max called in to Devonport to see Althea at her high school to say goodbye. He, like all of the soldiers now seen in high-spirited groups heading off to the Brighton Army Camp fifteen miles north of Hobart on the train, looked handsome in the loose, casual way they wore their khaki. She was pleased he had come. There weren't a lot of words spoken. Not at a time like this. Just enough.

PART II

13

Cobbers

So much activity. Recruits were pouring in, especially since Dunkirk and the news that Britain was in a spot of trouble. John Gandy was in the Navy recruiting office in Launceston, after a friend told him he would be a shoo-in to be accepted because they were short of writers, and him a bank teller. Max was in the 2/40th AIF, which had now been formed, mainly of Tasmanians but with a small component of Victorians as well. Elvin Ling was there too. So many lads had enlisted from the Penguin area itself, including another bloke Max knew well – Tom Bird, whose father's allegiances shone through with the middle name he had given his son: Kitchener. Over half the battalion was from the north and north-west coast, many from small areas. Five young men from the tiny area of Wilmot alone and many from the Yeoman Football Club from the Cooee end of Burnie, who all joined up together: country boys going away, farms and small towns emptying again (for it wasn't just the 2/40th Battalion going), just as they had done only a little over twenty years before. But it was a different world now, with all the changes: mechanised, modern, with better communications. It would be a different type of warfare. Wouldn't it?

In June and July 1940, when the streams into the recruiting offices turned into a flood, many of the younger ones stuck to that age-old script about young boys in search of adventure: working out ways to be accepted; forging signatures of permission from parents if they were under twenty-one, and changing dates of birth if they could get away with it. Ray Barber of St Helens only had to change his by six months to make him appear twenty-one, but there were several sixteen-year-olds and rumours of a couple of fourteen-year-olds who'd managed to weasel in.

There was also the problem of working out what to call your job: if you came up with the wrong description they might decide you were Essential Services and march you right back home. Two brothers, Lloyde and Gordon Spencer, who joined the 2/40th soon surmised – after a wrong answer – that 'farmer' would get them rejected, but 'farmhand' meant they were in. If backtracking and quick talking and covering up had been a prerequisite for promotion, many would have been generals by the time they swivelled on their newly enlisted heels.

Then there were those like Ken Dolbey of Ulverstone, who, although he had been in the 12/50th with Max, ended up in the AIF only because he had been frustrated with the twelve months it took to be accepted into the Navy after applying, especially when you were rearing to go. When you're ready, you're ready! And Ken, who'd joined with his brother Cliff, was just one more lad with the minor issue of his age. Just a little tweak. Put it up a year.

The refrain 'You'll be sorry!' echoed in Army, Navy and Air Force depots all over Australia, those doing the singing-out thinking it a great lark, the new recruits arriving, smiling feebly – or scowling. Nobody had told them what being a rookie would feel like.

Max's battalion was made up of all kinds of blokes, and they came from across the top, down to the very south of the state and the east, and from Queenstown and Zeehan too. There were chaff cutters and rabbit trappers, butchers' assistants, fishermen, apple packers, bushmen and quarrymen. There were joiners and textile workers, a bridge builder, a railway shunter, a tramway operator, a shearer. And on and on. There were farm labourers, and then there were just plain labourers – heaps of those. Max, who'd been to Tech, was a wicker worker. And there were a few clerks. This was a hands-on practical group of blokes who knew – no two ways about it – which way a bastard of a spade was up. But whatever they had been previously, they were in the Army now. And training was about to begin.

Oh, how wars come upon you suddenly! At Brighton it was a shambles for a while, with so many recruits arriving, hanging around, waiting. What to do with them? More Non-Commissioned Officers (NCOs) would help. Where do you get those at short notice? Lloyde Spencer, a private, was promoted to acting corporal and didn't even have time to feel pleased with himself before he was promoted again to acting sergeant all in one go. The 12/50th men turned up in their militia uniforms with their stripes sewn on, and wonder of wonders, that was the rank they now held in the AIF. At least the militia men already knew about soldiering. And Max, who'd been a sergeant in the militia, became a sergeant in his new battalion.

It was probably fortunate that most of the men who were recruits understood cricket and football. It would have made it easier for them to recognise the schoolyard selection method used when assigning the men to either A or B or C Company within the battalion. Several officers from interstate (who had suddenly appeared from nowhere when the decision had been finalised to form the 2/40th from Tassie recruits) stood up the front, picking them in good old Aussie fashion. Max was placed in 7 Platoon A Company. It was, no doubt, an efficient method, because within half an hour they were all marched, platoon by platoon, into their respective companies.

D company was formed by using the two sergeants left over, then any blokes returning from leave, and anyone else who came to camp. No need for a manual to tell anyone how to get all that done.

At first some of the men wouldn't quite bend to Army procedure – or even just put up with the bloke next to him. A bloke's a bloke, after all. And who's gunna make me? Some of the NCOs became a tad frustrated with persistent insubordination. Basil Billett, fed up with one bloke, and fed up with writing out charge sheets, finally decided that there was only one solution: he sent his platoon off with the other NCOs and invited the bloke to fight, with the proviso that, whoever won, the bloke would change his attitude. The fellow backed down and Basil didn't have any trouble from him after that.

Sometimes it takes a while to learn a thing or two about Army etiquette when you come from a life where you've left home and you're the one in charge. Don Woolley from Glen Huon – whose father (according to Don) had taught him the only thing his father knew, which was work with a capital W – was a man whose childhood had included milking the cows before school, cutting the oats – or 'green stuff', as he used to call it – as well and after school, when it was apple pruning time, picking up rows and rows of cuttings, milking cows (again), feeding the pigs and young calves, all sprinkled with liberal doses of the leather strap. In the summer his holidays were weeks and weeks of twelve-hour days picking raspberries, because they were, as his father said, 'already droppin''.

During the Depression, at the age of seventeen, he left home with a billy can, a frying pan, a couple of blankets and a small tent, and went to Tarraleah to work on the road from the West Coast Highway into Tarraleah, living in the tent with a fire outside. Every morning he woke to find the roof a couple of inches from his face, the snow so heavy that his first action before he could leave his cold spot on the ground was to put his feet up and push and shake all of it off. He and the other workers were paid nine shillings a day by the bloke who had the contract to build the road, the work they were required to do so hard that many didn't measure up and were sacked the first day. Only the 'best' workers – those desperate enough to keep going to earn that income, as low as it was, no matter the conditions or how back-breaking the work – were kept on the job. Twice a week he and the other men walked three miles through a bush track to a makeshift shop to buy their food, which was mostly bread, butter, jam and saveloys. When that job finished he went felling trees with a long-handled axe on the Hydro line to Queenstown, then to bridge-building.

Then his life as a 'boss' began. He had gone to work for Dave Mansfield at the Denison sawmill in the south of Tasmania and, after learning how to 'head in and tail out', could see the possibilities for a solid worker like himself. He saved up and bought an old Fordson tractor, a spindle and saw, and an old bit of belting. And an old horse. He built his own sawmill, of the most rudimentary kind. And, a couple of sawmills later, the war came along. In June 1940 Don, twenty-six years old, decided to enlist. He turned up at Anglesea Barracks in the morning and by six o'clock that night was surprised to find himself on a train to the Brighton Army Camp with about six others. *Gee, they don't muck about, these blokes!*

And so the next morning there were a few things he knew which had been left undone and needed his attention. He had to get back to break the news to the men who worked for him, that they were going to have to find themselves another job. Well, he wasn't actually a backwoodser, he said; and he had been to school, topped his class all through, and passed the scholarship exam a year earlier than he could have; and he did understand he was an Army man now, a man of the 2/40th Battalion as of yesterday. And so he understood the procedure: he wasn't the boss here, and you asked permission for things. Sufficiently clued up, he sauntered in to see the lieutenant.

'What can I do for you, Private?' Lieutenant Harris said from behind his desk – Harris was a man from the other side of the tracks to most of the new recruits, from the family that owned *The Advocate*, one of the most successful newspapers in Tasmania.

'What about a bit of leave, mate?' said Private Woolley. After the initial shock of Lieutenant Harris's explosive response – 'Don't call me "mate"!' – which shook the room, Don Woolley was clicking his heels and turning and saluting; changed from a rough-and-tumble bushman to a disciplined soldier in ten minutes flat. He learned to use the word 'sir', over and over, for the first time in his life, and he never called an Army officer 'Mate' again. And he did manage to get some leave, travel home and settle up, and then return. It probably took him several days to stop blinking in astonishment.

It was obvious that there was a fair bit of getting into 'Army' shape required for many of the men who had never lived near enough to join the militia, or who had simply never done so. Therefore elementary training involved a fair whack of getting used to army life, learning to salute anything that moved, the shock of keeping their clothes and barracks clean, the having to contend with weeping blisters from route marches, and then there was parade ground drill – *left, right, left, right* and then again.

There were not enough uniforms for a while. And equipment? At one stage there were twelve rifles in the whole camp, six used by the guard and the rest to train half a dozen blokes at a time. The quartermaster guarded his few Lewis guns as the precious things they were, even if they were World War I vintage, and wouldn't let them out for men to learn all they needed in case he didn't get them back. Some blokes had to sneak them and tear off into a hut to practise stripping and reassembling, so that you could do it anytime, anywhere, in the black of night, learning how to clear blockages and all they would need to know one day.

Ken Dolbey and the new cobber he had just made, Shorty (Bertram) Rhodes, were assigned to 7th Platoon 2" Mortar Section and had no idea what a real mortar looked like. In training they used a short length of round timber and a flat piece for a base plate. There weren't Bren guns for the Bren gun carriers, so the blokes mounted Vickers machine guns but still called them Bren guns. And field training meant responding to firing instructions as in a pantomime and then crawling back to drag up more 'ammunition'. But they did it, these boys: threw their lot in; rose at dawn to do the serious soldiering; welcomed their issues of rifles and bayonets as if they were the very latest in equipment; did their relentless route marches all through the countryside, some starting not many hours past midnight. What else could they do? They would get their full equipment, full training, when they were finally overseas – so they assumed. For now they would be content with rifle shooting. Many of them were excellent shots; Les Richards, one of the five boys from the tiny settlement of Wilmot, was a crack shot even before he'd joined up. It was a serious affair out there on the range, the competition fierce. Private Ken Dolbey won a couple of trophies, which was pretty satisfying. He'd surprised himself with his skill. He might just take this up after the war, pursue it as an interest.

One thing they hadn't needed training for was having a few down at the Pontville pub. Many a group of mates could be seen a little worse for wear, doing a fair bit of leaning and staggering, making that long walk back to the barracks after dark. Don Woolley had become a bit of an icon in his platoon precisely because he *didn't* drink. Older than the others, with only Dennis Headlam being older again by three months, he came with a nod towards maturity – and the willingness to look after the boys when they'd had too much to drink. Looking after them – that's what mates were for.

Don was enjoying the Army life and training didn't worry him one bit. And he had made friends, as close as brothers could be. Comradeship had been emphasised in Brighton Army Camp, an important part of the training. Your comrade's life had to be as valuable to you as your own, and he and all at the camp were drilled and trained so that they would never leave a comrade in trouble, even at the risk of their own lives. Don believed in all that, believed it to be right.

For Max and his mates from up the coast, the pub visits in time off, the camaraderie, the soldiering – all of it was nothing new. They'd done bivouacs many times before, months of training at a time, and knew each other well. There was a trusting ease with which they worked together. One time out the back of Brighton they'd crowded in on each other for a photo, Max the sergeant grinning away in the middle, the boys all leaning in, lolling on one another – friendship, familiarity and the pleasure they were taking in this game written on most of their faces. Seated next to

Max had been young Thomas Robert Riley from Blythe Heads, on the coast road out of Penguin on the way to Burnie. His height had helped him succeed in his subterfuge at the recruiting office: he was only sixteen. He had enlisted in the full knowledge of and, perhaps, because four of his uncles had been killed at Gallipoli. Tom Bird – he with the Kitchener name – had hung his arm loosely over his cobber Max's shoulder, and Wally (Ernie) Wescombe was there with his great mate Jackie Moles; Dick Eastall too, who always wore his hat his own way, never turning it up. And Phil Hales looked on from behind.

There was something steady about Max, in the middle, which made him the natural bloke to lean on. For as he had grown, so had many of the same qualities his father had possessed. He carried his father's memory, all the values Mort had held dear, with him. George Lawson of Ulverstone, a signaller of the 2/40th, would later say that Max was a kind sort of man, easygoing. And nice. A real gentleman. He was one who would be with the blokes, not among the sergeants who wouldn't mix – all of which is a good rap for a fellow in the street, but not exactly Army standard. But before the war would be over Max's style, his manner, would be needed. So many different styles would be needed, not just his. And blokes leaning on blokes, as they did in the photo – that was one of the styles.

14

On the way to …

Max and the boys had settled in for sure. In fact, the men in the battalion were waiting. They'd been training now for several months, and other battalions seemed to be moving out before them. It would be soon. Surely. Many had been wanting to go since the moment they'd signed their papers.

Even Len Mallinson, a quiet, sensible married man who didn't ripsnort like the younger single blokes, was waiting to move. With the Depression in Tasmania still having a hold, men like Len had enlisted hoping to help their families — the regular pay most welcome — as well as do their duty. When he joined Len had left his wife, Veronica (whom he called Vie), and his two children behind in

St Helens, and even though St Helens on the east coast of Tasmania is not easy for a fellow to get to unless he arranges a couple of connecting lifts, Len had managed to travel home to see them. He wrote to his mother from there in August 1940. He had news: he might be able to come through all this soldiering with a good future ahead of him.

St Helens
Sat 28.8.40

Dear Mum,
Just a few lines hoping you are all well again at home . . . I have not been able to get up to Launceston to see you, we do not get much time off now. We only get two weekends off a month now, one long one from Friday night till Monday night, and one from Saturday at 12 o'clock till Sunday night if you are not on duty. By the time a fellow pays his fare home off a long weekend, he has not got much cash to go anywhere else. I go into Hobart occasionally, but it does not cost me much in there as I stop at Vie's Auntie's place. But I will try to get through on a short weekend to see you all.
They seem to think that it will not be too long before we get a shift now. Eric Dwyer and Colin Brooks are home on their final leave now, so it will not be long before they go. They are in a different Unit to me though. They are in the Army Service Corp and are not attached to the 2/40 Battalion. Bad Boy is in Hospital with appendicitis. Bowie and Bertha came up to Pyengana this weekend. Bowie is in the 2/40 Band now. All of them got fined 5/- the other week for being A.W.L. I bet Bowie was wild about it. I don't

see much of him and the others now I have been put in another Company. They transferred Doug Mitchell, myself and 5 or 6 others into the Signallers, but all except one chap and myself got transferred out again, they did not like it. I am going to stick to it for a bit longer to see if I can pick it up. It is a Specialists job and when you qualify you get extra pay. It is fairly hard to learn and there is not many like it, but it won't be a load to carry if I can learn it. If a chap comes out of it alright it gives him a chance of getting a pretty good job in the Railways or Post Offices.

When you write again, address my letters
Pte L Mallinson,
No. 1 Platoon
Headquarter Company
2/40 Battalion
Brighton

Will end now with love to all
Len

———

At last, things were looking up for them all. They might not have had the orders to move out yet, but in October they marched through the streets in Hobart — that was a start — and again in Launceston in December. Oh, they had been impressive in their full dress kit, an endless line of manly soldiers two abreast, bayonets at their shoulders, tin hats on their heads. They certainly looked as if they were ready to tackle anything right then. Smartly dressed men and women in hats and suits had stood four deep on both sides of the street, straining to see, and in the buildings above men and women risked falling from windows in an attempt at a better view. For the men marching in the uniforms, the view they were after was 'somewhere else'. And finally, the announcement: they were moving out.

Brighton Camp
1st Jan / 1941

Dear Mum,
. . . I would have liked to have come in and seen you all in there, but the time passed that quick that it was time to come back before I knew where I was. I did not go much on leaving Vie and the kiddies this time. It may be a good while before I see them again, and although I might not show it much, I think a lot of her and the kiddies. She has been a pretty good kid to me, we have had a few bits of tiffs at different times, but she would always do nearly anything for me, & I don't suppose I have been as good to her as I might have been but since I have been away I realize that she has been a pretty good pal to me . . .

Love to all at home
Len

They didn't go far: Victoria was only across Bass Strait, but most of the lads had never been out of their home state before, so there was novelty there. However, it wasn't the Middle East. Instead, they were at a camp at Bonegilla.

Here they trained with two other battalions, the 21st and the 22nd, the three battalions altogether comprising the 23rd Brigade of the 8th Division AIF. As one huge, immaculate, shiny bunch they marched in Melbourne, they marched in Albury; they trained; and the 2/40th blokes now had better facilities, better equipment. They were ready. Again.

Sun Feb 41

Dear Mum,
. . . All the troops from the camp left here thursday night for Melbourne, they marched in Melbourne Friday morning and they then got five days leave. A good few of the tassies were coming with them but I was too crook. I would like to get home to see Vie and the kiddies now. I get a bit homesick for them at times. I am lying out in the verandah in the sun writing this, it is pretty hot too. I have only been allowed out of bed this last two days I reckon I have lost dash near a stone in weight since I have been crook, still feel pretty weak . . .

Love to all at home
Len

Time to leave. Don Woolley – who'd been made corporal back in Brighton Camp – had now, in Bonegilla, been promoted to sergeant, which he thought wasn't much of an effort, since in his Machine Gun Platoon in HQ Company there were quite a few blokes who had come from the bush and who had no idea of Army life or Army discipline and had never seen a machine gun. So he didn't feel *that* special. But he wouldn't knock the promotion. It felt pretty good, anyway.

On leaving Bonegilla, though, there had been one annoying problem which the 2/40th had no choice but to take with them: Victorians. One was a nitwit, so one bushman wrote in his diary. One of them, Sergeant Bill Coventry from St Kilda, even smoked Craven As instead of full-strength Capstans. Bloody snob!

It was touch and go for a while. They didn't want Ned Kelly's mob with them — thieves and bushrangers! The Victorians retorted and told them the 2/40th needed some good troops to stiffen it up. It was all smoothed over in a while, probably helped by the Vics becoming familiar with the Tassie requests. Bill Coventry was on close personal terms with the request 'Got the makin's on ya?' having heard it so often. That particular piece of fine English etiquette was for those times when perhaps one of the blokes did at least have a cigarette paper, and just needed something to go in it. Like tobacco. Or the other request, 'Got a full?' when they were going all out for a bit of class, mate, a ready-made smoke. Preferably a Capstan. And Bill was soon used to recording in his diary the most important pieces of information for the week: 'Lent Munting 6 pound; Rainbow 10 pound.' Somebody else, 8 shillings.

A move finally began: a lengthy, irritating, dust-covered

trip – and maybe one day they might get to where they were headed. They went up through South Australia, the blokes becoming more restless by the day – even the calm, straight-down-the-line chaps. A fear was starting to take hold, that they had had the wool pulled over their eyes. Had anyone ever had any intention of using them as the soldiers they had joined up to be?

Terowie
March 4th 1941

Dear Mum,
. . . It has been pretty cold here the last couple of days. I don't like being here, it is a cow of a place, a chap is never clean, he washes and five minutes after he is just as dirty as ever. It is a terrible dusty place, you can't keep your clothes clean, and those a chap has packed in his kit bag are covered with red dust, it seems to sift through into everything. A chap would have to be washing and changing all day to keep clean. I don't know how much longer they will keep us here . . . When we first came here, they told us that our stay would be made as easy and as pleasant as possible, but we have had more work than we have had since we left Tasmania.
Well Mum . . . will end this scribble, just wrote to let you know I still think of you sometimes. I would a lot rather be home with my darling wife and kids than stuck up in this dam [sic] hole. Lord only knows when we will get overseas.

Love Len

When a fellow joined the Army – brand spanking new, enthusiasm on the boil – a fellow handed over his trust: the trust that the Army would use him well, that the contribution he was willing to make would be appreciated. He trusted that he would be given the opportunity to be a soldier. And that he would get home to see his family every now and then.

Trust, in just about everything to do with the Army, was now starting to disappear.

Borrow Creek
Friday 11 1941

Dear Mum,
Just a few lines hoping you are well. We were to move straight on again this morning but for some reason they decided to stay here a day . . . Not much of a place . . . it is alive with flies, they are like swarms of mosquitos . . . It is nothing to swallow a few when you are having your meals . . . None of us know for sure where we are going yet. It has been a pretty monotonous trip, biggest part of the country has been desert . . . I have got my doubts about us getting final leave from up here it is such a long way to send us. I wish the war would end. I am getting sick of this mucking about like we are. When I joined up I thought we would be over there long before this. I would have been better off at home than mucking about like we are. It is alright for a single chap, a great life, but when a chap is married he would like to be home with his wife and kiddies. I would like it only for that.

Love from Len

———

At last they were on their way to Katherine, pleased to leave the motor lorries behind, those hot sweatboxes they had been crammed into for a time, and even been bogged in up to the axles when they had gone through a swamp. The sandbagging hadn't done the trick. Max and all the blokes had certainly earned that half bottle of beer they were issued with at the end of all that. Now they were on a train, one which was even worse than the old north-eastern line in Tassie, according to Bill Rainbow. He was sure the engines and the line must be the oldest in Australia, and with fifteen miles an hour a good speed the boys, generous souls that they were, gave the engine driver the benefit of their advice and their encouragement. Perhaps it was a bit rowdy. All of which the driver seemed to resent.

At Katherine, a camp which was just tents (with two huts arriving later), Bill Rainbow ran in the mile race at the sports meeting on Anzac Day, but he was too far back to do any good. However, he had more success establishing the two-up school with 'Happy' Lowry, but then they switched to Crown and Anchor, which was a good decision because he cleared ten pounds out of the transaction.

It was all just filling in time.

Katherine
4th May

Dear Mum
. . . I don't know how much longer we will be here.
There is some talk about us moving nearer to Darwin
to be re-equipped and have <u>*Final Leave*</u> *. . . it is a*
certainty that we will have to be re-equipped and
reorganized before we leave Australia. So I reckon
we will get Final. Hope we do. I would not like to
go away without seeing Vie and the kids and all the
rest of you before I went . . . I wish I was somewhere
where I could get a decent feed. The tucker is pretty
light on here and a chap can't buy anything to eat in
the town. They got about 100 Pounds worth of lollies
into the canteen the other night & they were all gone
in about an hour . . .

From your loving son Len

———

Perhaps they weren't on the way to anywhere. How could all this take so long?

Sergeant Bill Coventry of D Company knew his boys were frustrated. These were virile young men, enthusiastic. It would be difficult to keep a lid on things if this show kept on being nothing more than day after day of finding work to keep them occupied.

All the boys coped with the discipline required for Army life; he was proud of them for that. They were good men.

He knew all their personalities by now, and felt for the ones whom he could see should never have been in the Army: too gentle, this life really not for them, even though they worked hard at fitting in. They coped, but it was hard to watch them struggle and be so out of step all the way. There were others for whom that wasn't an issue.

Perhaps he had let that stoush between Viv Atkins and Bill Rainbow go on for too long before pulling them up, as Reg Haye reckoned he did. Yeah, maybe it should have been stopped. But they were bored, and it was a sport for everyone to watch as they had tried to get a rise out of the other, to pretend, for everyone's entertainment, that they hated one another.

22.5.41

Dear Mum,

Just a few lines in answer to your welcome letter. I received it last night and also four more with it. Two from Vie . . .

. . . The latest yarn is that we are going to the Dutch East Indies don't know if there is any truth in it or not. Probably none . . . They had us out working on the pick and shovel yesterday . . .

It was at Noonamah where Bill Coventry saw the makings – not of a cigarette, but of the men and all their capabilities, of how extraordinary these boys really were. Bill Coventry himself had grown up working hard, beginning with a paper round at four in the freezing Melbourne morning. He had watched his adoptive father come home every evening after his job collecting money from gas meters in people's homes; a joyless task his father had with his bag full of pennies, and each night he would line up the little piles of coins and sit at the table and count them out.

In these couple of months Bill had watched, awed by the Tasmanian boys' capacity for work, and by the skill, the physical prowess, these bushmen showed. Oh, they could work. And clever! They would put a small stick as a marker in the ground and the tree they were felling would fall *exactly* where they wanted it to be. They always knew precisely where they were, where the sun was, and they could track the bloomin' pants off you. When they had to build huts – which was what they were doing instead of being soldiers, that and roads and guarding anything, just to keep them at something – they would head out after trees of a certain height and, no problem, back they would come. And blokes like Bill Rainbow – you'd never lose them! Bill Coventry knew that if you had any sense as a sergeant and your blokes knew more than you, let them teach you – they'd get the trees while you were thinking about it. And all would be done. But always give them something to do – preferably something which actually meant something.

In the meantime, same old, same old. And they were over it.

8. 41

Dear Mum,

. . . we were going into Darwin on leave on Wednesday but some of the boys out of one of the other AIF Battalions ran amoch in there last night, wrecked one of the Pubs and a few shops so it has been put out of bounds to troops till further notice. They are sick of being up here and reckon they will wreck the place every time they get in now till they send them away. It was a silly thing to do . . .

Dear Mum

. . . We might be on our way home in a few more weeks if we are lucky. We have been up here seven months or over, [and] over four months in this camp and three months or more at Katherine now . . .

You are wrong about gambling and betting being the two worst things out, there are plenty of worse things. If a chap did not have a bit of a gamble at times up here, he would go nuts.

. . . I hope we do get sent home before too long. I would love to see the kids and Vie again now. Vie said in her last letter that John is getting a real lad now, and that I am missing the kids at the best time. Cheerio and best wishes to all.

Heaps of love, Len

20/10 41
TX 3787 Pte L Mallinson
H.Q. Company 2/40 Bn Darwin

Dear Mum,
Just a few lines in answer to your welcome letter. Was
pleased to hear from you and also to get Lucas's letter.
He seems to be the same old stick & having a good
time making the best of things, which is the proper way
to do over there, because one never knows when a little
messenger with your name on it is coming along. Things
are pretty serious in Russia at present if he beats them
Lord knows how much further he will go. england and
America will have to wake themselves up. I hope he
can't beat the Russians, but am afraid that they will
want a lot of help from Britain and America to hold
him. there's no doubt he has every thing wonderfully
well organised and working like a clock. All of us are
counting the days now . . . There were more troops
arrived here yesterday, came into our camp . . .

   We were all pretty dirty and tired . . . I had the
biggest wash I had for a long time. One has to change
pretty often up here on account of sweating so much
. . .

You're in the Army; you wait. You go. Pearl Harbor had been bombed; America was in the war. The boys were off. And so was final leave. They hadn't been home for eighteen months. However, this is what they had joined up to do.

At battalion parade on 7 December, the troops were told their orders for embarkation on the *Zealandia* and *Westralia* the next morning.

They were told 'they were sailing to a destination unknown,' wrote Bill Rainbow. 'But we know it is war.'

'I've been up all night very excited', Bill Coventry wrote in his diary. 'We were ready for the train at 6.30 a.m. but didn't leave until 9.30 a.m.'

They were off overseas. Somewhere.

———

On 12 December 1941, 81 officers and 1505 men of Sparrow Force landed in Dutch Timor. The 2/40th Battalion made up the bulk of the men in that force. Other Sparrows – as they termed themselves – were 268 men from the 2/2 Company heading towards Portuguese Timor, as well as 126 members of the 2/1 Heavy Battery, 52 of the 2/1 Fortress Engineers, 46 2/1 Fortress Signals, 26 in B troop, 18 Anti-Tank Battery, 36 from 2/11 Field Company, six members of the 23rd Brigade Signals, 2/2 Field Ambulance, some Army Service Corps and 10 from the Light Aid Detachment. All Sparrows. All off to war. Most sailed on the *Zealandia*.

On the *Westralia* – on which Lieutenant Harry Medlin and B Company, among others, sailed – an instructing officer explained the procedure all the Sparrow officers were to follow if they were shelled: they were to stay where they were, because they would have no 'effing' idea what the shells were, and therefore no idea which was the safer side. Harry thought the lesson most instructive – unforgettable, in fact.

They didn't have a great start: they'd had to jump into waist-high water from barges, holding equipment above their heads to wade ashore. They were also largely without communication equipment because the wharfies back in Darwin had dropped and broken many of the boxes. 'Are they Irish? Are they on the same side as us? Or do they just want a pay rise?' Ron Cassidy had said.

And it wasn't a great discovery that the Dutch, whom they had been sent to assist, didn't seem to be taking the whole thing seriously at all.

15

For the Empire

Empires are such wonderful possessions, if you can keep them. Or create them. An empire allows one such feelings of power, of invincibility. Of absolute might and superiority. And it provides such economic, not to say military, muscle. Plus, if your empire is big enough, there are endless men you can call upon.

Britain already had one. And surely there could be no doubt that the British Empire loved its subjects well. In Winston Churchill's maiden speech to Parliament in 1901 he even referred to Australia and Canada, 'where the people – down to the humblest farmer in the most distant provinces – have, by their effective participation in [the

Boer War], been able to realise, as they could never realise before, that they belong to the Empire, and that the Empire belongs to them'.

A comforting thought for all Australians, surely. And comforting for those on their way to war: the might of the British Empire would be with them.

The Dutch too had an empire – albeit on a smaller scale – which gave them oil and economic benefits. Timor was part of that empire. Japan wanted an empire, too – a new one. And they were having quite an easy time finding recruits to the idea of a benevolent Japanese empire. Their plan, so they claimed, was to create a Greater East Asian Co-Prosperity Sphere which would benefit all Asian countries, lift them up, and they would all live in peace and happiness together – with Japan, of course, as the leader (as they had already proclaimed themselves to be) of the 'Asiatic peoples'. The Asian countries, so the argument went, were to be released from the humiliating and exploitative colonial slavery to which they were now subjected, and there would be nothing but glory . . . under the Japanese.

'Co-prosperity' was such a fine word. Although it was not one which had been of much use, or even considered, among many in the British or Dutch colonies. Perhaps if it had received a hearing – or, more to the point, imple-mentation – the Japanese would not have found such an easy pathway for their deceptive and destructive plan. It had not exactly figured in the top of the British and Dutch priorities. In the far-flung colonies of those empires, the most striking priority was the social exclusion and snobbery seen as essential to upholding standards. So too, it seems, was suppressing peasants harshly. In Burma, a country which prided itself on being happily interracial, the Burmese were not allowed into any of the main metropolitan clubs in Rangoon. Singapore had its tea parties and leaving one's card, and English women becoming parodies of themselves, taking British identity and lifestyle in the tropics to a new plane altogether. Being apart from and excluding the local peoples – except for your servants – was good form. All of which may not sound politically harmful. But it was, gravely so. The local peoples who welcomed the Japanese into their countries with such open arms did so because those social conventions, those race boundaries and exclusions based on birth that were embedded in the British upper-crust psyche, were used to determine who had access to wealth and power, or even a decent living, and who did not. And those who did not were most of the Asian people from the colonies within their own countries.

'Poor whites' received a dose as well. Australian soldiers who arrived in Singapore in early 1941 'were not permitted to enter the sacred European clubs and hotels. The people they were sent to defend did not wish to know them socially.' And when the Aussie men fraternised with the local communities, which they did easily and readily when they first arrived on the Malay Peninsula – at one stage joining in a festival at

Batu Pahat to commemorate Remembrance Day in 1941 where 'the gayest of them all were the Australians, who delighted the crowds by dancing the *ronggeng*, a sensual Malay rhythm' – their behaviour was used to condemn them. Their egalitarian spirit was not acceptable, was lowering standards. Well, what could be expected? Churchill himself said that Australians came of bad stock.

Reports were sheeted home to Australia that 'the Orstralians' were not behaving well, merely having a holiday, not soldiering as 'professional' soldiers should. A well-placed story or two in the press could help bring many a free-spirited problem back into line, public opinion could be swayed, and the people would decide. According to historians Christopher Bayly and Tim Harper some Australian soldiers then received white feathers in the post, sent from home. Many of the soldiers were left feeling sick at heart. Betrayed. And the Indian officers, from the Indian troops who were there in great numbers also to defend the British Empire, and who had also fought for the British in the trenches during World War I and had never received even the acknowledgement of a guernsey, were not allowed to join the local club either, or ride in the same carriages. They too were humiliated. One troop rebelled, peace finally restored by the Argyll and Sutherland Highlanders, and 'the whole business hushed up'. There are those who ruled in empires, it seemed, and those who were ruled. And there were many who did not like it.

———

When the Japanese assault – and it was brutal – hit Penang on December 9 and 10, 1941, 'Japanese radio broadcasts taunted the British: "You English gentlemen. How do you like our bombing? Isn't it a better tonic than your whisky soda?"' There were those from the Empire who knew how damaging the treatment handed out to the local people was. In the terrified panic following the Japanese attack on Penang, many British were horrified at what they had to do: all Europeans were under strict orders to leave. They gathered at the Eastern and Oriental Hotel, disgusted and appalled at having to leave their loyal staff and servants.

And in the panic of the evacuation to escape the terrible onslaught, any non-European was refused assistance. Senior Asian civil servants were turned back; however, 'the [European] fortress commander still managed to get his car on board . . . J.T. Quitzow, like many single women, had demanded to stay but was ordered out. The manner of the British withdrawal, she wrote weeks later, was "a thing which I am sure will never be forgotten or forgiven"'.

———

In these countries where dissatisfaction bubbled away, fifth-column activity was deep and widely spread, and the Japanese were heading their way armed with crucial local knowledge and a determination to teach the West a lesson, and take their rightful place as one of the leaders of the world. Japanese soldiers heading out were issued with a pamphlet: *Read This Alone and the War Can Be Won*. 'Once you set foot on the enemy's territories,' it said, 'you will see for yourself . . . just what this oppression by the white man means . . . These white people may expect, from the moment they issue from their mother's wombs, to be allotted a score of natives as their personal slaves. Is this really God's will?'

They were out to destroy and conquer. And ultimately demean. They were heading to Singapore.

———

Halifax, Canada: Lieutenant Fred Ransome Smith of the 5th Suffolks had never seen anything like it. All focus was on the massive American liners the *Manhattan* and the *Wakefield*, each as big as the *Queen Mary*, and each one not so long ago gliding swanlike and serene through the water to some idyllic carefree locale somewhere, bearing a crowd of well-heeled holidaymakers on its decks. Both liners had recently, hurriedly, been transformed into the battleships before him, and both now floated – or, rather, loomed, immense and solid – at the quay, their purpose evident in their newly slapped-on coats of grey. And they were being loaded, if that was what it could be called.

With such a deadline – Lieutenant Ransome Smith and

the 5th Suffolks had to be trans-shipped overnight – what else could it be but bedlam? The shouting and thudding, the din which resounded at the wharf, was anything but swanlike or serene. Cranes roared, swivelling backwards and forwards in the dark, and in the blind panic to get it all done – for everyone knew the gravity of what they were doing – ammunition and boxes of equipment, and containers filled with he didn't know what, were dropping, smashing, into the sea. A terrible sight for a soldier to witness.

Fred stood watching, he and his men confused about such a sudden change of plans when their initial intention had been so clear. The 18th Division had been on its way to the Mediterranean, to the Middle East, crack British division that they were – *the* division – confident in their preparedness for what they had been about to face. They had fully trained mobile units; they had every piece of whatever they would need to fight effectively in the desert terrain and the climate. And now it was all being taken from their ship and loaded into these two cruise ships lent to Churchill and Britain by Roosevelt and the United States, a surreptitious and above-board way to give support from a country whose people wished that their President, and they, could stay right away from that war over there, for it was none of their concern. And Britain certainly needed the ships after the devastating losses in the Battle of the Atlantic.

From all this activity there was one thing Lieutenant Ransome Smith knew: something was amiss, very much so. The panic, the no time for care. Was it going badly for Britain, again, somewhere?

By the time they got underway, about four people had made a run for it while they were in dock – the small number though reassuring.

The ship's horn blared twice into the air, and they were off, crawling – crawling! – down the coast of America. It was understandable, though, because German submarines were active and seemed to be everywhere, and not long ago had done over the French Navy. There was a short stop at Trinidad, where they drew lots as to who would go ashore. And then a decision had obviously been made: to make a break for it, to *go! go!* out into the open seas, a desperate tear for the convoy straight across the Atlantic; head, it seemed, straight to the middle of Africa. Surge forward and hope. 'Air cover' were words little in use these days.

They saw their first destroyer about a quarter of the way into the journey, the Suffolks and the 18th Division convoy zigzagging, evading; saw too many U-boats for anybody's liking, and kept on, the only relief from the tension the sight of each other, ludicrous and large in their Mae Wests: huge yellow life jackets, too puffy for comfort, which they lived in the whole way. And too risky not to. And just try to sleep in a bunk in those damned things, no matter how familiar and enticing the name!

In the Sunda Straits the Japanese bombers came. They lost their transports and one ship, which was blown up completely when a bomb went down its funnel. As they continued, the newly created battleships put out their para-veins, huge attachments on steel cables out the front of the vessel, which collected mines as they touched the wire and slid them along, exploding them away from the ship. They were now in a different war from the one they had expected. And this war was one which Churchill and many – especially in Singapore – had refused to believe would ever come to much. For the Empire's might was daunting and Singapore was impregnable – a fortress.

There'd been too little, too late, despite Australia pleading with Churchill to increase Singapore's air defences, despite Australia – those jumpy people, according to Churchill – receiving assurance after assurance that all was in hand. And while Churchill's eye was on Europe and defeating Hitler first; while the good people of Singapore kept up appearances, dining and dancing, and endeavouring to ensure that any defence works were neat and unobtrusive, the well-equipped, well-trained, underestimated powerful invader was steaming down the peninsula. And Japan had air power. And now control of the sea.

The Malay Peninsula stretched to the north of where Lieutenant Ransome Smith and his men were waiting. Up there in the jungle and the mud and the slush, exhausted troops were fiercely fighting and dying – a desperate battle, three Australian battalions of the 8th Division achieving the only noteworthy successes against the Japanese in the whole campaign. And civilians were pouring in, taking refuge on the island of Singapore.

Lieutenant Ransome Smith was ready, as ready as he could be, he and his men inured to what would come. But all of them unaware what was about to steamroll through – for there were no defences on the north side of the island, apart from a strategy to blow up the causeway that connected the mainland to the island. Yes, it was all too little, too late. And Lieutenant Ransome Smith – all the troops – and the civilians were soon to pay someone else's price. The wait was harder for some.

'But I'm married, sir! I've got a kid at home!' one man said, in the waiting. And Fred Ransome Smith, twenty-two years old, known as 'young Smudger' – because he was an artist – knew what was on the soldier's mind, knew the strain it was for men like this, the worry the married men carried.

'You come with me,' he said and took the man who, even though he was older than his young officer, needed someone, some reassurance. And they joined in one of the patrols, a dozen men sent at a time, a different group every two hours across the muddy flats there before them, in case the Japanese were making movement; the whole thing for them, they knew, soon to begin. The young officer and the older soldier beside him fired off a few rounds at a small disturbance in the distance and, in that, some comfort was given.

Comfort, though, would soon be gone. The impossible about to take place.

16

Japs coming

February 15, 1942: Singapore was in chaos. The dead were lying in the streets; trucks were roaring around, picking up bodies; ambulances struggled through the traffic to take the latest casualties to the overflowing hospitals; volunteers were fighting fires; the bombing and fighting were continuing. Black smoke was rising over the city, billowing up, constant, telling all that things were not as they should be. But many continued efficiently, without overt panic, for this was what war was. It was a fight which would go on.

'We loaded four big trucks of the wounded, about eighty blokes, some with their legs cut bad. And an officer, Captain Snelling – he had both his legs riddled,' says Allan Bertram of the 2/19th. 'He was sitting in my truck, poor bloke. We tried to get over the bridge to take them to hospital in Singapore. And I drove up on the bridge. Captain Snelling asked the Japs if we could take the fallen back. They said no. "But if you surrender we will let you through." We weren't gunna bloody surrender. But the men couldn't fight. They were wounded. The Jap said, "Don't move the truck. If you move it we'll open fire."

'Anyway the bridge was leaning. So at night we put our brakes down. Anyway I got them back [as far as I could]. I said to Captain Snelling, "What are we going to do, sir? I can't leave you here – four truckloads!"

'"Listen, Bertram," he said, "you were told to go yesterday. If you don't go I'll court martial you for disobeying orders!"

'So I went to the trucks and said, "Anybody who can walk, we're going."'

He recounts what the wounded were saying: '"Don't leave us. Don't leave us."'

'But what are you going to do?' Allan continues, his voice shaky. 'Anyway, with about thirty of them it took three days, and we, the blokes who weren't wounded, carried some. Some of them had minor wounds. And there was one English guy. He was only about twenty-one. He was a lieutenant in the English Army. And he had his arm bandaged up. And the maggots coming out. Everywhere.

'"Don't knock 'em off," I said. "Let them eat the flesh." So anyway I gave him a hand. Ooh! He smelled – ooh! You've got no idea of the smell.

'I was sort of carrying him along. We had our spell. And I'd leave him and go up about twenty yards because of the smell. And then come back for him. I used to look around hoping somebody else would catch up. But nobody did. I was alone.

'I had a pair of overalls, boots and bayonet. He said, "Leave me, and leave the bayonet." I said, "What do you want the bayonet for? You wanta go like this, don't ya?"' Allan makes a slicing movement across his neck then continues. '"Not on your bloody life. I've carried you long enough – I'm gunna get you back to Singapore."'

'I got him back. Went another day, and then there were about five or six trucks working. Put him in there with the Australian wounded.

'I got back then. We fought on in Singapore. Then we were all taken prisoners because we had nothing to fight with. No aeroplanes.'

And so for troops who were freshly arrived, who were trained and willing to fight for as long as it should take, there were some sights too shocking to see. Lieutenant Fred Ransome Smith had stood and watched them, the small party of men coming his way. And couldn't believe it. Just couldn't believe it! A party of men with a white flag had walked along the road, past where he and his men were still fighting. His company commander, Captain Bill Oliver, pulled his revolver – concerned, as they all had been, about strange fifth-column activities – and went straight up to them. 'What the hell are you doing?' he demanded.

'I'm Brigadier Newbigging!' said the officer, who was on his way to Japanese headquarters to arrange a capitulation. General Arthur Percival surrendered the whole British forces on the island of Singapore.

It was over. Singapore's water had been cut across the Jahore Straits; it was being bombed comprehensively twice a day. And there was the ever-pressing air cover problem. There was so little of it. Yes, it was over. They were now all stunned to find themselves prisoners of war.

———

Max and the men on Timor had been doing what they could. Some of the officers and sergeants had been carrying out unofficial reccies to see where an invasion would come if it did. But they were such a small force to cover so much ground.

It was 19 February on Timor when a sergeant from the Signallers had asked for volunteers from his platoon to man an observation post on Semau Island, just near the entrance to Koepang Bay, and with no hesitation Jimmy Bock stepped forward and said he would go. None of Sparrow Force had any idea of what was coming. What Robbie Clare, Jimmy's close mate, did know, though, was that he wanted to go to the island to be with his mate. 'No, Bobby,' said the sergeant. 'You stay here and relay his messages.' And he sent Joe Grant to be Jimmy's signal partner instead.

Robbie waited anxiously, but only received part of the signal before his battery power ran out: '. . . there are thirteen ships in the harbour' was the part of the message which managed to come through, and Robbie made a desperate sprint three miles there and back to retrieve his 'flashers', his light signals. The rest of the message then came through: the ships were Japanese, and they were invading. He relayed the message on to the command, and waited anxiously for Jimmy to return. He didn't come.

———

Lex Milne of Red Cliffs in Victoria – who had become part of Sparrow Force at Bonegilla when he was assigned to the 22 Dental Unit and found himself suddenly a dental orderly – was woken by a sergeant, an unwelcome intrusion so late in the night. Word had come about thirteen unidentified transports in Koepang Bay. Lex was to take another soldier and head to the observation position they had already been using. He protested.

'But I've been there three days,' he said to the sergeant. 'It's not my turn.'

'Son,' said the kind old sergeant, stoically staring into

what they were all about to face and not willing to accept any resistance, not now, 'they reckon you're the only bastard who can find the place in the dark!'

From his place with his partner up high, Lex could see all the land spreading out. He could see all 'our people'. And he could see the paratroopers floating down. He could also see, about a mile away, twenty-seven transports, and planes and troops. He and his mate there had counted them, one by one; knew they definitely weren't Yanks. Lex could see the big red spots on the side of the transport planes. And Zeros, lots of them – they certainly could see those, circling round and round, and landing on the transport ships. None of this was good.

Lex knew they were a longer distance away than his brain was registering, but looking down from where he and his partner were, on top, it appeared as if the Japs were just *down there*. Right there! And here they were, just the two of them camped on top of the hill. The battalion was some way back he knew. Some were spread along the beach, some near Usapa Besar; the battalion spread out over miles. They had to be! With so few men. There were a couple of beach defences and aerodrome defences. Well, that *was* the reason they were there: to defend the aerodrome, even though it had progressively become an air base without planes and without air cover. And now it was an empty aerodrome.

But Sparrow Force hadn't been the only ones in this position. Before their own strife loomed, the other two battalions at small outposts, Lark Force (2/22nd) on Rabaul and Gull Force (2/21st) on Ambon – which, with Sparrow Force, made up the 23rd Brigade – were also garrison forces assigned airfield defence. All three were undermanned and underequipped. And all three were essentially there to put up a show. Lieutenant Colonel Roach of Gull Force was well aware what sitting ducks they were, and had notified the senior military leaders in Australia that his small force could 'not hold vital localities more than a day or two against a determined attack from more than one direction simultaneously'. The reply, from the deputy chief of the general staff, Major-General Sydney Rowell, had been: 'put up the best defence possible with the resources you have at your disposal'.

Colonel Roach sent message after message to headquarters in Melbourne, pleading for more men and equipment, but none was sent or considered. Instead, Roach was replaced. The British General Archibald Wavell, who was in command of the area, said, 'As far as I can judge position at Ambon not critical and in any case I am opposed to handing out important objectives to enemy without making them fight for it. Quite appreciate feelings of lonely garrison but am sure Australians will put up stout fight what ever happens. No doubt it is wise to change commander.' An Australian officer who was in Java, General Lavarack, was aware of what was close at hand and cabled the Australian prime minister, stating that all Australian troops should be withdrawn from the Netherlands East

Indies immediately. But his recommendation was ignored. The British commander's decision held instead.

On 22 January Rabaul fell to the Japanese, and no-one would know what happened to Lark Force until the end of the war. At Tol Plantation on the Gazelle Peninsula, the Japanese rounded up and massacred 158 Australian soldiers. Sydney Rowell commented, 'It's not the first time a few thousand men have been thrown away and it won't be the last.'

Years later an Official War Cabinet memo would reveal the terrible truth: 'They must be regarded as hostages to fortune,' it said. 'They must not be reinforced, withdrawn or re-equipped.' On 31 January it had been Ambon's turn. And now Timor was left.

———

Down at a palm grove close to the beach, near to where they had camped with the Dutch forces in case the Japanese should attempt a landing, Harold Cox had stood-to all night, Arthur Beattie, Bernie Haywood and John Cunningham with him. It was, so many of the men claimed, practically the last time a Dutch soldier was seen. However, Tom Cunnington of the 2/1 Heavy Battery did at one stage see a Dutch colonel and four of his troops carrying his big bed through the low hills and flat, swampy ground. Priorities. It's what Army life is about. The Sparrows, though, hadn't been concerned with luxuries like beds for a while. And certainly not now. Harold was a new recruit, and in B Company under Captain Roff. What a battle of wills it had been for him to keep his itchy fingers and jumping nerves under control. He'd only recently arrived, one of 145 reinforcements who'd been in the Army just ten weeks. Some had never fired a rifle. Harold had: he'd done the compulsory training that all men were now called to do since the spread of the war to the Pacific region. And he had then enlisted.

Nearby, Max Butler was ready with his men at the beach at Usapa Besar. He had watched, Private Fred 'Lofty' Smith [a different Fred Smith from Lieutenant Fred Ransome Smith] had too — they all had, as the paratroopers had floated down from the sky; all the different-coloured chutes. Different colours for different sections of their army, the Australians thought. It had been a terrible sight. No specific thoughts had gone through Lofty Smith's head right then, though. He had begun the process of going blank, getting ready. It was the same sense of shock spreading through them all.

To some of the old hands — the original 2/40th who'd gone the whole distance, endured the months of boredom and frustration while they waited (and many times this whole caper had felt years longer than the eighteen months it had actually been) — it was hard to believe this was about to happen. A full-scale invasion might have been seen as likely not long ago, but too many months of inactivity had dulled any feeling of reality about this. It had felt – they had almost taken it for granted – like life would continue in its uneventful way for at least another year and then, probably, they would be sent home. Now they were dumbstruck.

George Lawson had been ready to fight since the first day he'd left his job as a teller in the bank, enlisting when Max Lloyd, the accountant, had announced he had joined up ('I'll come with you!' had been George's instant reply). He had been convinced, especially after the whole Noonamah episode – when there had been so much filling in time, making work for the boys – that nothing would ever happen. And Timor was such a beautiful place for a young man from Tasmania. George had had a lovely time, fishing and playing around since he'd arrived. He had gone into the villages, generally had a good nosey around. He had, though – he and the signallers – kept up his training.

There had been bombing raids almost daily since 26 January, and there were times where there would be up to twenty-seven planes on any raid, flying low in formations of nine, strafing and bombing but they were unable to offer any resistance. Some of the soldiers had thought that hadn't necessarily indicated a full-scale invasion. Bill Rainbow, an infantryman, was just one of so many of the boys who had hated not being able to hit back, though; to return some of what was being flung at them.

There were, however, those who had known from the beginning what was likely to come. They knew they were a ludicrously small garrison force just sitting there with no air cover, no sea cover; knew they had antiquated equipment, and not enough of that; and all of them now had heard the news that the reinforcements Lieutenant-Colonel WW (Bill) Leggatt, the commander of the 2/40th, had requested time and time again, and who had set out from Darwin – the 2/3 Pioneers, some artillery, with an American crew on its way as well – had suddenly been ordered to turn around and go back to Darwin. They'd been attacked by 35 Japanese bombers and nine flying boats on the way.

Sparrow Force was alone. They knew the position they had been placed in. Left in. Now Darwin had been bombed, that very day. There would be no aircraft coming to assist them.

———

It had been a mad dash for young reinforcement Fred 'Lofty' Smith. The battalion had been involved in skirmish after skirmish. They'd go a short way, get past that lot and then have to fight again. Fred had kept going – they all had. The enemy paratroopers had spread all over the island. And the 2/40th boys just had to keep going, fighting as they went. Because no-one knew what was really coming. No-one knew where the Japanese were.

———

The Japs were coming in. And Lofty Smith, of A Company 9th Platoon, and his section were doing two-hour guards, near a church with brilliant moonlight overhead. Night noises echoed, putting him on edge as he squatted, peering in each direction. Little pigs ran through the jungle; sticks cracked, and it was hard to tell which was a Jap and which just another jungle noise. Fred couldn't be sure, and he was downright jumpy, for the Japs had managed to creep close by and they were only about 200 or 300 yards away. But he didn't think for one minute that he and Sparrow Force couldn't hold this.

The paratroopers had taken positions up in the palm trees, sniping Fred's platoon as they had come in with Captain Roff to retake Babau, and bullets had been flying everywhere. It was hard for Fred to believe he hadn't been hit. Especially when he couldn't tell where the bullets were coming from, or see who was firing them. One of those snipers' bullets had come too close for comfort, but Pop Taylor had seen the puff of blue smoke from up the palm tree. 'Give us a tommy gun!' he'd said. And then he had let him have it, the Jap tumbling straight out of the tree.

At one stage Ron Cassidy, with a load of beer on his truck, had picked up men from A Company. There was not a drop left by the time they hopped off.

More skirmishes had continued the next day when they had split up and gone into the jungle. It was difficult – an understatement – with no communication equipment and men sent with messages between platoons. Each section had gradually advanced to Usau (Oesaoe) Ridge to try to get back to Champlong. They fought all day to try to get past, but on the bare hill the Japanese were dug in with machine guns and mortar. And their land army had come ashore and was circling. This ridge was the only way through. The men were weary, thirsty and hungry, but would have to fight on. A decision was made: there would be a bayonet charge at 5 p.m.

Fred stood waiting, ready, on the river bank; Lloyde Spencer was nearby on the mortars. They would be wading through the river, which today was only ankle deep – not too bad considering what it could have been. Up until recently there had been huge wet-season tropical storms. While he'd been on the island some of the thunderstorms had thrown off lightning so forceful and bright you could nearly read a book by it. Heavy grey clouds always rolled in to bring those storms, and only a few days ago rain had been pelting down in bucketloads. It hadn't been particularly comfortable for him and quite a few of the men: he hadn't had a tent to sleep in, and had had to rob the fly off somebody else's to get some protection – which the fly had failed to deliver in all that rain. Today, though, and ever since the Japs had landed, the weather had stayed clear. It was *hot*, and the sun was beating down.

Like all the boys, Fred was wearing their Army-issued uniform for the tropics: shorts, which had already proven to be a problem. There were so many unforeseen problems they had encountered up here. Malaria was one. And that had really done many of the boys over already, some severely. But there were also the tropical ulcers that came from nowhere, it seemed, a tiny knick or a cut and suddenly it would spread, eating into your flesh. Many had already developed them and they were hard to heal. If the men had had long trousers, or breeches and puttees, they would have given some protection, stopped the small abrasions, which, up here, were bad news.

It didn't matter right now in the heat of the battle, but another of the orders they had been issued with was to keep their shirts on, regardless of how hot they were – to keep up the standards in front of the native Timorese. More British baloney. It never mattered to any Aussie bloke: if it was hot, you took your shirt off. And standards! Whose standards?

It had been at about 4 p.m. when they'd first been told they had to stand-to. Ready. And now they were all in position right along the river bank. Viv was here – Viv Jackson, who with George had been sworn in that same day last November in Hobart – and that at least felt good. George and Viv had become such good pals after that. They were such trustworthy blokes, and Fred had enjoyed the three of them palling up and travelling together. That was only three months ago, and now here they were, Viv beside him in a bayonet charge. George wasn't there right then; he'd been sent back to Babau, to guard it.

Corporal Herbert Butler, who was killed in action at Mouquet Farm, France, on 4 September 1916.

Corporal Charles Henry Butler, who was killed in action in the same battle, on the same day as his brother.

Morton Linthorne Butler (my grandfather) and his wife, Ruby (my grandmother). Mort married his sweetheart three months after he disembarked and Maxwell, my father, was born nine months later.

Hedley Deverell, a World War I veteran of the 26th Battalion and close friend of Mort's.

Hedley's son, Bill Deverell, who grew up in Penguin with my father.

The first Penguin Scout Group. Scout Master Mort Butler is fifth from left in the back row. My father, Max, is in the front row, sixth from left. Next to him on the right is John 'Jack' Gandy and on the left of Max, looking mischievous, is Spud Hall. Elvin Ling is fourth from left in the front row.

Sergeant Max Butler, my father, of the 2/40th Battalion.

Alex White of the 2/19th Battalion.

Alex White (*right*) with his older brother, Bill. Alex survived Mergui Road.

Allan Bertram (*top left*), was in the 2/19th Battalion

Bill Coventry (*top right*), a sergeant in the 2/40th.

Fred (Lofty) Smith (*left*), of the 2/40th. 'I talk about it,' Lofty would say decades later about his war experiences, speaking of those who were never to come home, ' 'cos *they can't* talk.'

6 December 1940: the 2/40th Battalion marching in Launceston.

MADDOX.L.A.J. WELLS.M.G. TERRY.K.S. PLAISTER.J. DAVIDSON.G.G. HANSON.C.B. JACOBS.R.G. YOUNG.J.R.
McLEAN.B. WICKHAM.L. O'BRIEN.S.G. SMITH.I. JONES.H.H. GILL.T.M. SMITH.E.G. RUSSELL.H.H.
HARRIS.I.CT.
BURN.H.F. KEATING.M.S. WALKER.A.C. TUNKS.A. KERKHAM.A.C. B.LLOYD.G.A. BUTLER.M.L. BAILEY.E.
ELMORE.W.J. RUSSELL.M.J. KINGSTON.R.L.
SALTER.T.E. DOLBEY.K. MUNDAY.V.L. KEATING.O.A. DOLLIVER.T.H. DWYER.L.A.

'7' Platoon, A Company 2/40th. The names were written by one of Max's mates.

12 March 1947. My mother, Bessie, and my father, Max, on their wedding day.

Sgt. Max Butler, a Tasmanian who demonstrated under-standing leadership during days of adversity on the Mergui Road

My father was featured in the book *Comrades in Bondage* by Frank Foster. It told of the diggers' experiences in prisoner-of-war camps. My father never looked in that book – he knew too well the stories within.

Lorna Bertram, Allan's wife. Lorna says they have only been speaking about the war in the last couple of years.

My mother (*right*) at the Penguin RSL Club with Edna Mainwaring (*left*) and Betty Dazeley (*centre*).

The Butler kids: a proud older brother, Robert, holds our newborn sister, Elizabeth. Mark (*back*) and me (*beaming on the right*).

Ready to go anywhere: Robert, Mark, Elizabeth and me.

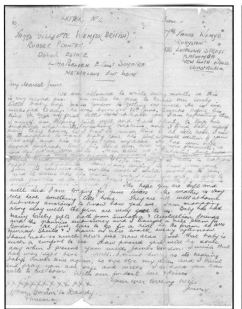
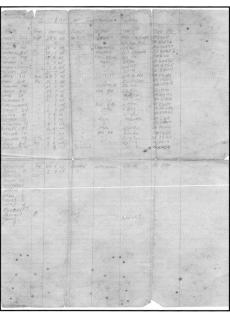

The letter (*left*) that at first shocked my sister and myself. And the reverse of the letter (*right*). The list of Australian dead, in my father's handwriting – it took my breath away.

In 2009, Fred 'Lofty' Smith returned to Timor. Here he is at a service to remember those who died there. 'I thought of all my mates, the fellas. It was very emotional.'

When they'd been among the 100 new recruits sworn in on Armistice Day 1941, Fred and Viv and George had all just finished saying the oath of allegiance, and were outside on the steps in Hobart, when the announcement had been made – 'On the eleventh hour of the eleventh day' – and they had all stopped, every one of them, and stood to attention in their civilian clothes and saluted. It had seemed so natural, because they all knew what they had just signed to do. And it was serious. So standing and saluting when no-one had ever told you to felt perfectly right. Fred, whose English father had been wounded at Gallipoli, had, like so many others, joined up after hearing about Dunkirk. He'd been nineteen. His mother had signed the papers, thinking she was safe and he would be refused because he'd had rheumatic fever as a baby. But even if that had been still likely to affect him – and it didn't seem to, for he was now a healthy six-foot-three young man – the armed forces were desperate. Soldiers were soldiers. And there was a war on. One deaf man was now a member of the 2/40th Battalion.

A bayonet charge was part of what they had to do. He didn't think about it. Fred had already noticed that something happened to his thinking in a skirmish, or a stoush of some kind: he wasn't really there. He did things because that's what he was there to do. He was not his normal self. But before it . . . that was different. Just waiting, knowing he was going in, and he had the time to think. That was terrible. Because one never really knew what was coming.

Fred stood with his rifle with the bayonet fixed and thought about his parents, and his brothers and his sister. He wondered if he would see them again. It wasn't good, he knew, to think of those things, because once you started – well, it got to you. And right now he needed to be right here. But at least he didn't think he would be killed. He really didn't think he would. Somehow it just wasn't going to happen.

The covering fire came from R Company behind with Bill Coventry in charge, when the boys were told to move off. But a Bren gun carrier came, driven by Tom Uren of the 2/1 Heavy Battery, who was to push through and crash all the fencing wire across the bridge. Fred and Viv and their platoon were then forced to move out onto the road, as a steep culvert was in their way, which they couldn't cross. That was when they discovered that the Japanese had a machine gun lined up on the road, positioned securely behind a lantana bush. For this charge to succeed, to give all the boys a chance to take this ridge and then move on from there, that machine gun had to be removed. They knew it. D Company were already moving resolutely, and with absolute courage up the hill, moving abreast right into where the Japs and all their heavy guns were. And they were copping it.

The boys were all in this together; you kept doing what you had to do. By the time they took out the machine gun nest, walking along yelling to one another 'Are they over here?' – 'No, further up' and so on, and the Japanese were chattering and calling from their dug-in position, there had been many casualties: Sergeant Chocko Smith, who'd suddenly said, 'I know where they are!' and had raced down and was halfway there when they got him in the back; Corporal Billy Milne, who was from the next platoon to Lofty but who was in the search, knowing it was crucial, and had said, 'Ah, right!' and with Lofty and five others raced to go round a prickly pear bush to get to the enemy, but ran straight into the machine gun. Billy died first, then Pop Taylor, who was shot through the head. Viv Jackson and Beswick had small wounds, and Lofty – loaded down with magazines for the Lewis guns, in deep shock – kept going. It's what you do.

They rescued Chocko Smith, who'd been shot in the back and who died two days later. They pulled out Fitzy Maurice – EF Fitzmaurice – who emerged laughing, even while his throat was hanging down, mortified that the medical orderlies said he should stop. 'They want me to go on the truck!' he complained. Fitzy would die a couple of days later. And they kept pushing.

Private Fred Smith took some field glasses off a dead Japanese officer, and was peering to where he knew more Japanese troops were in some huts down below, when he was joined by a chap from the heavy battery unit who was there to assist. Their unit had not fired a shot from their weapons, as their guns were facing out to sea. They had now spiked them so the Japanese could not use them.

Fred heard the *crack, crack* and had time to think, *They're bullets*, as they flew past his ears. But by the time he said, 'Get down', to the fellow from Heavy Battery, the man was dead at his feet. So many of Fred's blokes . . . but the machine gun nest behind the lantana bush had been dealt with. It was only later that he noticed someone's brains on his boots.

The battalion took Usau Ridge. There are those who claim it as the last bayonet charge. Those who witnessed it were astounded. One British soldier from the 79th Anti-Aircraft Unit, who had themselves impressed the Australian men with their cool, claimed he'd seen more courage that day than anything he'd seen at Dunkirk. Against incredible odds these ordinary men – this small group of men on Timor – had a victory.

They planned to retake the town of Champlong the next morning: a crucial battle, for all their food and ammunition were stored there. With little radio equipment, and no communication with other sections, they did not know that the paratroopers weren't there. They could have gone straight in.

But it was too late anyway.

'We were on our way to retake Champlong the next morning,' Fred 'Lofty' Smith would say many years later, 'when a stream of tanks with a white flag came up. Many of the soldiers thought the Japanese had wanted to surrender. The Americans must have landed. But the next word we got was they wanted *us* to surrender.

'Then they gave us the ultimatum. They said we would be bombed from nine o'clock. We were just about out of ammunition, we hadn't had any food for four days, the only food I had had was one can of bully beef I'd grabbed the first morning, and we'd split that between eleven men.'

'Oh God, you could see what was happening,' recalled Harry Medlin. 'They landed on the south coast and just came over land.'

But even after they had surrendered, 'several Japanese heavy bombers came over and started to drop bombs', Private John Prosser of the 2/40th wrote in his memoirs. 'I was blown out of the Bren carrier but not badly hurt. Several of our men were killed and quite a few Japanese, which was bloody good because they bombed their own troops.'

By the time Sparrow Force capitulated, surrounded by over 20 000 Japanese troops, it was discovered that only 76 of the 900 paratroopers were still alive. For the loss of 40 Sparrow Force lives.

———

Max Butler lay wounded in a truck. He had managed to pull another wounded of his platoon under some shelter, and Tom Bird, grabbing three other men to help, had moved straight into the line of fire, raced and pulled both of them back. They were lucky: the Japanese were bayoneting the wounded, as well as slitting throats, by then. And God knows what else.

The sun beat down, the wounded lay bleeding and in pain in the trucks; no-one had had water or rest or food for four days.

'Oh, it was terrible,' remembered Fred. 'I said to my mate Viv Jackson, "Well, I wished I'd copped it coming over the top." And he said, "Oh, don't be like that."

'We'd never thought of ever being taken prisoners. We'd thought of men being killed, or wounded, but never prisoner. It was so devastating. And that was one of the worst things of being a prisoner – the humiliation.'

Robbie Clare's good mate Jimmy Bock and his signaller partner, Joe Grant, were never seen again. Of the five boys who'd come from the tiny community of Wilmot, two were killed in the fighting – Jackie Knowles the first of them to go, killed on the first day. And Leslie John Richards, wounded on the first day, died the next in the Koepang Hospital. Len Mallinson, who was hoping to one day get a good job at the Railways or post office, would now never make it home to see his wife, Vie, and his two small children. And sixteen–year-old Thomas Robert Riley, who'd been with Max, would not see Blythe Heads again, his father searching fruitlessly for years for anyone to tell him of his son's last days. Many ordinary men died in those days, their deeds and actions unsung. But their own mates remembered. And remember still.

There were many men who, further inland, were given the order *every man for himself*. Three hundred and twenty-seven members of Sparrow Force escaped into the jungle but over a hundred surrendered in the following weeks: malaria, beri-beri, dysentery and the jungle conditions made it difficult to survive. Many joined with the 2/2 Independent Company Sparrow Force unit operating with their guerilla tactics in the jungle of Portuguese Timor. Several men are to this day listed still as missing, their fate not known.

'I thought it was a very poor command,' Don Woolley would say years later, his emotions close to the surface. For Brigadier Veale's order meant he was picked up by a Japanese submarine while attempting, with five others, to escape by boat, and he spent the next three and a half years separated from his battalion, one of only two Australians imprisoned on Celebes.

'I talk about it,' Lofty would say, decades later, speaking of those who were never to come home, ''cos *they can't* talk.'

<u>The Battle for Oesaoe [sic]</u>

Twas on February the 22nd
On that fatal Sunday night
We had struck more than we reckoned
was fair in any fight

A thousand Japs before us
Twenty-two thousand more behind
We had no time to think or cuss
Here's into it, never mind

The Japs were on the hilltop
And we were down below
But we had to take that hilltop
Or go where all good soldiers go

Just as the sun was setting
The word was passed around
to fix bayonets and at 'em
We'll take that bit of ground

And after the battle was over
And all the din had died
Of the 800 Japs who held the ridge
but seventy-five survived

Though victory was ours that night
We knew it were but a respite
For the Japs we could not hope to outdo
With the odds of one to about twenty-two

And we the next day had gone
We were the prisoners of the sons Nippon

And now at Oesapa-Besar
When we think of our dear land afar
We hope our effort was not in vain
And that Australia's gate is safe again

Composed by Private G Faulkner
Bn HQ 2/40 Bn 1942

The majority of Sparrow Force on Dutch Timor, captured by the Japanese, effectively disappeared from view.

PART III

17

The shadows

There is a purity which strikes you about Penguin. It is quiet, and the soul can rest here. On a fine day when the town is still and the tide is out, the sea sits glasslike and flat, the beach and rocks and sand softly pulsing with golden light, a vision of such tranquillity it both soothes and perplexes. For in that moment you can believe that all in the world is benign. Peace reigns – surely – and will do so evermore.

Sometimes on Sundays our father would wake us early; we would wave goodbye to our mother and he would take us to the rockeries at the eastern end of town. These were small stone pools which locals had constructed; rocks stacked high to create fencelike enclosures that trapped fish unfortunate enough to be too close to shore when the tide lapped out, those fish now left behind and easy pickings. We would wander through the maze of rock traps, breathe in the freshness and openness of the air, gaze – and poke, if our father couldn't see us – at the wonder of the sea life in each crystal-clear pool, the anemones, the crabs and the shells that moved.

We would take our catch home, all of us bundled together in the car, moving quickly up the steps of our back verandah. We were not allowed to run, for the abrasive concrete could scrape and tear if we fell, and the screams which might come would chill my father. Our mother waited for us, her eyes, her face, shining at our delight. She would take our catch and cook the fish in butter for breakfast, the salty aroma, the homely, warm splutter and sizzle as we waited, and our plates became beautiful with the silver shine of many garfish lined up, thin together, their long, unworldly swords hard to believe, each fish handsome and mysterious. All of it pure pleasure.

It is one of my abiding memories of my father. Him, at home, at the head of the table, light streaming in from behind him in the sunroom he had built himself, happy; his smile, his easy, patient ways; with us. Us together. And a plate of garfish, simple and unadorned, there before him.

———

There are stories which seem too sad to read, or even to hear. There are stories hidden and no longer mentioned. In

1942, when Singapore fell and the 8th Division AIF, along with all the Allied soldiers present there, were taken into captivity; when Sparrow Force capitulated with no other option – when despair entered so many hearts and would echo down the years – stories began to exist which would never know the light of day, the sadness and sorrow was so great. I am but one of many who is of that story. I am one of so very many.

And yet, like so many, that story was mine – and yet it was not. For when the men returned – or sadly didn't – the stories were hidden, often pushed down deep, the stories held close, many men wishing to protect others, their families, from all that their memories contained. And over time, for me, it came to feel as if I no longer had a story, or even a father who had once sat at a table, light streaming in from behind. It came to feel as if, instead, all there was for me was the emptiness that was left, that story belonging only to those who could speak of it, or who had close knowledge, or someone near. Not someone like me, from whom it had all disappeared.

And yet – and yet – I knew that story was still mine. And I so wanted to call my father back. I steeled myself, and resolved to go in search of it, to look into the places my father had never wanted me to go. For he was in there – they all were – there in the shadows; and if I wanted to find him, that was where I must look. I sought out men who had themselves been prisoners of the Japanese, and they understood – and their families understood – why I searched. For this was a story that belonged to all of us, together, each of us with a different strand. The men, the wonderful giving and courageous men, all helped me to find, to reclaim, my story again. The same story that belongs to so many.

Bill Coventry rang. To announce himself he launched into his rendition of 'Sally', a song from long ago that mentions – no question about that – my name. I know it from my childhood: *Pride of our alley/ When skies are blue, you're beguiling/ And when they're grey you're still smiling, smiling/ Sally . . .*

Everyone back then knew the song. It was from a time of peace, a film at first, *Sally Pride of our Alley*, starring Gracie Fields in 1931 and later known as a ballad alone, one which was loved and sung by many all through the Second World War, for it carried within the notes and words, memories, much needed and comforting, of home. And it spoke of someone who endured, who held on, through all those grey times. And the people who were fighting and dying; the people longing for news; the people grieving; the people faced with bleakness and uncertainty – well, they could do it too, so the song assured them. It was a song that picked people up, gave them the resolve to hold on. And a whole generation tried to have courage, tried to be no less than Gracie.

It was a song that has lived on long after the war as well. Like Bill Coventry.

'There are a couple of changes we need to make,' he said after his song fell away. And my heart sank almost to the point of despair. I had sent him a couple of chapters from this book, chapters in which he features. I intended the book to be about my experience of growing up in a family dominated by the Second World War, the experience of being the child of a prisoner of war of the Japanese. I wanted to write for all those who, like me, live in the confusion and sadness of the experience, still, these many decades later.

I wanted to somehow know the men who were there and those who came home, because many of us, the children, did not. My longing is one I have successfully suppressed for years and years. And it is a longing I try never to visit. For with the longing comes the grief, the sense of loss, the childhood gone; the grief I feel for my father; my incomprehension that men and women have ever been made to suffer what those prisoners had.

'It can all be changed, Bill. Everything can still be changed.'

I knew that my facts were correct, for I had stuck faithfully to what he told me: how he came home, when that was, what transport was used – ship or plane? And so on: answers easy to give. And he had told me over several visits what happened before and during the war, lent me his diary, photographs. I had done so much work. I was sure I was getting close enough to know, for he answered such questions as: 'What were you thinking of at the time, Bill? What was going through your head?'

I worry constantly that I probed too far, pushed men such as Bill back to the places they tried to, and needed to, forget.

'Bill, I want to understand,' I had said to him. 'I know bits: you got bashed, there was little food, you got sick and the suffering was grotesque. And many, many died. But Bill, I want to understand – beyond that.'

'I know,' Bill had answered, 'and that's why I'm trying to help. In some ways I wish that my Sally' – he took to calling me 'my Sally' after my second visit, which made me smile – 'hadn't come knocking on my door, because of my midnight troubles, you see. But I know it's important for people to . . .'

In his nineties now, and the Armistice announced well over sixty years ago, it is all still there for Bill, comes back so easily. And not just for Bill: for just about all those who are now left. 'I do not like the two o'clock 'til four,' he told me. 'Too many nights I'm awake. And I'll still be awake in the morning.'

'It isn't that you wake from a nightmare, then?' I asked. 'You are just thinking about it?'

'Oh, it all comes back – oh, nightmares. And then you start living it.'

'So what was wrong with what I wrote, Bill?' I said down the phone.

'You forgot the fear,' he said. 'If someone taps you on the shoulder: instant fear.'

———

When John Midgeley returned to Penguin in 1943 from his three years with the Air Force, having spent time as a cook both within Australia and New Guinea, he had learned a few things. He was now aware that Aussie diggers sure knew how to swear, especially after spending a night out in the pouring rain with an ineffective ground sheet over their heads, watching the pictures right through to the finish, over at the Yankee station, no matter how terrible the weather. Especially if they then had to clamber into the back of a truck which had filled up with water, and the thirty of them had to stand there for the five- or six-mile ride back to the squadron, getting wetter each bump and corner. He didn't understand why that was any different to any other time. You were always wet at Milne Bay; you'd put your ground sheet down on a clear piece of ground, and you'd just sink. In the morning you'd be buried.

He knew Air Force blokes didn't like having to peel onions in his kitchen when they got nicked by the sergeant for trying to scam their way before other men, to get the first bus into Ballarat on a Friday night. For three kitchens between them to feed 1200 men each day they were pretty big bags too, and when a fella has to peel two 150 pound bags before the sergeant will let him go, that's lots of onions, tears sure do stream, a fair bit of weeping goes on.

There were other things he knew too: that there were

many blokes from Australia, from around Penguin and Riana, who were missing. And he knew, from his time in New Guinea, of atrocities that the Japanese had committed.

 'That's bunkum,' his neighbours said of all the reports. And even after he had told them all he knew, of the Japanese cruelty to the native people of New Guinea, they still wouldn't believe it.

———

Families in Australia waited to hear, the strain immense. What had happened to the men? And were they still alive? They had slipped from view with the fall of Singapore. In a farmhouse in Wilmot, in the north-west of Tasmania, Jack and Nell Richards and their two young children sat in their bare sitting room, not much in there apart from their chairs and the wireless, although their room and house were no different from those of many other Tasmanian rural families. Or many who lived in the towns, for that matter. Nobody had much. They waited, hoping. It was as if no-one dared breathe.

It was Saturday night. 'Tokyo Rose' would soon be on – it was the programme where you had no choice but to listen to the Japanese propaganda peddled either side of it, just so you could hear those longed-for names. They would all gather, hoping: *Is he – could he be – alive?* Around Australia, 22 000 other families did the same. And thousands upon thousands of others. Only a few names were read at a time, from the cards the men themselves wrote to their loved ones, saying only what the Japs wanted them to say. People wept with joy. *He is! He is alive!*

Jack and Nell listened anxiously every Saturday night to hear, they hoped, of their son Leslie, the crack shot. Oh, he was good. But there was never any news – through 1942 and well into 1943. Until they needed to listen no longer. Sergeant Bell had managed to escape from Timor and, finally home, came straight up to see them. Jackie Knowles had gone first, he told them. And Leslie next, on the second day. The waiting for them was now over, but the grieving had just begun. They finally received official notification in 1945.

———

In Penguin Ruby sat, anxious and tense. Everybody was with her round the table on a Saturday night, including her sister-in-law Linda and her two boys, Barney and Trevor – Linda also a widow now, since her husband, Alf, had died tragically not long after Mort. Only thirty-two, Alf should never have gone in the boat in such weather when he was already ill. Everyone had said so when they had seen him off from down at the front beach.

Althea fiddled with the wireless, and argued with her brother Jack about just where the station was. *Oh, Althea and*

Jack! You know the station; leave it there. The wireless crackled and almost spat. And the two children argued and moved the dial back and forth, until it was obvious it had been another disappointing night. There had been no news; nobody they knew. Until people came, thrilled, and letters started arriving, one from a man in Victoria who wrote to every one of the families, just in case they hadn't heard. He knew what such news meant.

Did you hear? Max's card was read out! He's alive.

And he had used the few words he had been allocated to broadcast other men's names, to alert other families that their sons or husband were alive too. Words mattered on those cards, at least. He was a prisoner of war. Of the Japanese. *Relief.* If only they knew.

———

When I was a child my father chastised me once, the only time he ever did so, after I had argued with and made my mother cry. Turning to go out into the garden, I had passed my father on our back steps as he was coming inside.

'What did you do that for?' he had said, quietly.

My father, a gentle man who did not raise his voice or speak harshly, whose presence brought warmth and gladness, had been so upset by what I had done that he had spoken up from somewhere out of all the sorrows which we knew lay deep within him. Even as very small children, we tried never to cause him worry in any way. We knew from an early age that our father lived with shadows. We just didn't know exactly what they were.

18

POW

On Timor Les Poidevin, one of the medical officers (MO) with the 2/12th Field Ambulance as part of Sparrow Force, was grateful he had work to do. It helped keep his mind from revisiting the depression which had first swept over him on the day of the capitulation – that terrible day, 23 February 1942.

He could still see it, still feel all that he had been through: the barbed wire and guards; the machine guns which had been trained on all of them as they sat on the ground – as they had been ordered to do by the Japanese – outside the makeshift hospital at Champlong. On that day he had sat with his commanding officer, Major Roy Stevens, the other

MO, along with the staff and the wounded they had been told to bring out and place behind them – those lads who had been delivered to the hospital by ambulance on the 20th, the first day of fighting, the only day the vehicles had been able to get through: the day that grew too long in the waiting for the other wounded to arrive.

Seated on the ground, with the machine guns in both front corners waiting for the order which they knew was about to come, the two doctors had talked quietly of their families, Roy telling Les that today was his wife's birthday, and Les revealing it was his widowed mother's wedding anniversary as well as her brother's birthday. But the initial disquiet had subsided when the hours and the waiting had gone on, and finally it seemed the intention of the Japanese had altered: Les and the men were not to be gunned down that day. Then it was over, and they were locked back in their shed. Then nothing. Where were all the rest of the wounded men from the battle – the numbers there were sure to be?

It was the smell which first hit Les eight days later, when he and Roy and the medical staff were finally taken down to the main prisoner-of-war area at Usapa Besar, the usually picturesque spot amongst the coconut grass in front of the sandy beach. In the twenty-acre area, enclosed as it now was by barbed wire – the wire the Sparrow Force men themselves had erected to keep the Japanese out – the sick and the wounded lay littered everywhere, the air now hanging, after so many days, with the smell of pus, excreta and unwashed bodies. About 130 mangled men lay before him on the ground, with so few blankets between them as to be almost nonexistent, and so little water. And the Japanese had refused to allow stores to be transported. The few medical supplies the doctors Captain Brown, the MO of the 2/40th Battalion, and Captain Gillies, of the 2/1st Heavy Battery, had had with them when they had been captured had already been exhausted.

Les and Roy had worked quickly, doing what they could, making the difficult decisions. There were no antibiotics, such things still unknown then. And so very few antiseptics. Such appalling conditions, many dreadful wounds: gaping holes through men's legs; compound fractures with sometimes inches of bone missing; foul, pus-filled wounds; the filth, the sight of war and what it brings – all of it terrible. And yet, in amongst all that were men who refused to give in. Les had been filled with wonder at how these men didn't complain, and how each man seemed to think his neighbour was in a worse condition than himself and should be seen before him.

So much did they need – food, water, medicines, a roof to shield the wounded men from the burning sun, the tropical rain – and as prisoners, no liberty to obtain any of it. The over 20 000 Japanese on the island had commandeered all the beds and materials they could come by for themselves. Roy organised for some shelters to be built, at least. And within their compound the men from Sparrow Force who were fit enough chopped down coconut trees and split them, and – Tassie men from the land that most of them were – it wasn't long before a couple of huts had been built, and leaves from the coconut trees bound together for roofing, creating a covering effective enough to withstand the heaviest of those buckets of rain that hurled themselves down. Beds were made from the same materials and the worst of the wounded were then, finally, under cover, although not behind walls. The rest of the men and the officers slept in the open, and the malaria-spreading mosquitoes and pain-inducing scorpions feasted on them all.

It was July before a workable hospital was operational, albeit one with few medical supplies, with quinine in short supply and in such need for unconscious fever cases, and men suffering malignant malaria. And tropical ulcers.

Les worried at night, and worked continuously during the day. In the first few days when most of the men's wounds had become flyblown and filled with maggots, it had almost been a fright. Until he realised that the flies kept the wounds cleaner than he could in these conditions. But the stench!

There were deaths, but not from want of care or effort. Rather, they were from lack of medicine and equipment. And finally Les was relieved to be able to record: 'Michel, Butler, Kelleher, Jack, Halliday and dozens of others eventually survived their severe and fractured wounds . . .'

———

'His leg was broken. It ended up with a bend in it! Didn't you see it?' one of the men, Bill Atkison, says to me in amazement as if it were something a daughter would know. I didn't; my father didn't show it. What I did know – for my father did not keep the essential details of his life a secret – was that Max, the prisoner of war, had been shot. And in the hut where he lay convalescing a snake had slithered on him, and the most prudent course of action had been to freeze – or else. And I did know there were times in the jungle when he had so little food that he boiled grass in water, because he and the men were hungry. I knew also, for we had been told, that even one egg might mean someone could live. These are the things a child is told: clear and easy to understand.

But I grew up knowing much beyond the few words about the war that we heard. I knew of the quiet my father needed; no jolts upon his nerves. And no screams nor the sounds of sobbing. Especially sobbing. And I did know this: his photo was in a book – a book he never looked in. My mother told me years later that she hated the photo – his big smile – because he looked like a dazed man; not quite of this world. I can see now what she meant. For it was a photo which was taken too soon; too soon – but would it ever be far enough away?

———

On Timor Max and the men were not to know it yet, but there would be a time in their captivity when they would look back at their imprisonment on the island, and say of it – as Fred 'Lofty' Smith tells me – 'it had not been too bad'. For there was far, far worse that would come. Timor was but an introduction.

In the first few days after the men surrendered, the air was thick with a stench many would never forget: the smell of burning bodies as the Japanese burned their own numerous dead. Then the stench gave way to another – for life as a prisoner was at its most basic – the stench from overflowing latrines. The Japanese refused at first to allow the men tools to dig the deep trenches. And in the once idyllic palm grove where Max and A Company had originally made their camp and where, not so long ago, they had stood and watched the paratroopers float down, almost a third of the barbed-wire compound was fouled.

The thousand men had no choice but to sleep nearby; the cooking areas were close too. And dysentery and several deaths came. But every day the men worked and tried to control some of how they lived. They scrounged, and they planned, and they managed to dig the pits. And over time they built huts for them all so each man was off the ground. The problem was reduced with strict hygiene measures. But not the problem of the food. In the first few weeks the only food the Japanese supplied was several bags of 'broken dirty rice which was full of insects and grubs', said Reg Holloway.

Max and the men in his platoon, working together, added grass – or anything they could find – to water to make something called a soup.

The men were already becoming ill. Perhaps their condition might have been even worse if they hadn't been able to sneak out at night on the food-gathering expeditions they undertook, returning with coconuts, roots, cactus buds to make jam, anything they could come by, sometimes bananas and paw-paw. Many of the local people helped when they could.

It had been a surprise after the shock of the battle and the capitulation to find that the camp had been so loosely guarded. Some men were often out of camp several days in a row, gathering intelligence information to try to send back to Australia. Foch Dowling's hut had it all worked out with the hut next door. As soon as they'd been counted the man would just run around the back, slip in, and all were suddenly present. Or they'd just say the men were in the hospital. Bill Rainbow was out for four days at a time once. Bill Coventry thought him brave but foolish the way he ran a one-man war, burying rifles and ammunition under his bed, ready to lead a riot at any time.

The camp was casually guarded, but threats were never far away. There was the time the Japanese officer had all the men lined up in the middle of the town, had the machine guns trained on them and was searching, accusing them of stealing from the Japanese comforts fund. Bill Rainbow copped a bashing. Fred 'Lofty' Smith, who'd had to quickly jettison the small bag of sugar he had pilfered, says the Japanese officer put knuckledusters on to do it, and then the other Japanese officers had come down the line and slapped and belted all their faces. There were mutterings, agitation, men not going to accept such treatment. But then a couple of warning shots. And many seething men had to give in. Major Campbell had come to see what all the commotion was about, said his men would *not* do such a thing – and then his cap had fallen off and out had come a toothbrush and toothpaste. None of the men were giving in easily.

On Timor the prisoners had always pilfered what they could get whenever they were out of the camp. 'Hydraulics,' Bill Coventry says they were, including himself in the description, hydraulic lifters. They needed to be. By the time they left the island, transported in filthy, rat-infested overcrowded rustbuckets of unsanitary ships, vitamin deficiencies and the constant malaria, with the shivering debilitation, then the high temperatures, the inability to concentrate or walk without staggering, all were already taking their toll. And just about every man had a weeping scrotum from vitamin B deficiency. And the symptoms of beri-beri were there. Men had lost limbs from the gaping flesh-eating tropical ulcers that could start with a tiny scratch and in time expose the bone, a death from ulcers agonising and terrible. Fred Smith had seen one man with a hole in his back and a lung exposed.

'We were sick,' says Bill Coventry. 'By Jove we were sick. I was given soup to carry to feed my platoon, a three-quarter kerosene tin of some sort of liquid. And I've never ever forgotten it – *I couldn't lift it!* I was so weak. And as a lad I worked in a foundry and I could carry weights an average person couldn't. Oh, weak and thin straight out of Timor.'

They were indeed sick. And yet it was just the beginning.

In September 1942 Max was among the Sparrow Force prisoners of war when they were moved off the island, undertaking their uncomfortable, stinking, sweating, journey. For they were about to be disbursed across many camps and many countries, sent to wherever the Japanese decided; and for most of those on board, it was to the railway the Japanese wanted to build, to supply goods to the Japanese troops in and out of Burma – the Thai–Burma Railway.

Fortunately the Allied submarine which fired on their ship in the middle of the night was off target. But the Japanese hadn't been so inaccurate in the battle they had so recently fought for Java. The men, as they passed, counted seventy ships scuttled in Surabaya Bay. A worrying, tragic sight.

It was at their next camp, on Tanjok Priok on Java, where the ruthlessness, the discipline began to escalate. Korean guards kicked and punched the men the entire two and a half miles as they struggled under their packs, many of them so sick it was only willpower that got them from the railway station to the camp. The Korean guards 'were bigger and taller than the Japanese,' says Tom Uren. And 'their brutality was something out of this world. As a prisoner of war I was bashed by both Japanese and Korean guards with anything from an open hand to a closed fist, from wooden clogs to an iron bar about four inches thick and more than a metre long. They would just wallop into you.' Max, as a sergeant in charge of men, knew what such a bashing meant. And what it felt like. 'They lay into the sergeant first,' Bill Coventry tells me, 'and then get to the man they were after.'

Don Woolley, over on Celebes, had seen such treatment from the start. He had watched an English boy – who had been caught smuggling food into the camp – be laid across a table, and two Japanese soldiers had belted him with baseball bats until he was unconscious. They then poured cold water over him until he came round and bashed him once more, until he lapsed into unconsciousness again. Don says thousands died in this manner. 'I don't know how our camp in Macassar compared with others but I know that no camp could have had a harder, crueller malicious guard than we had in Yoshida. When he ordered a bashing session there was no end until the body was almost mutilated,' he says. Don, like most of his fellow Sparrow Force mates who he'd left behind when he escaped from Timor, was already sick too. He'd had malaria, dysentery, pellagra, beri-beri: and he had been starved. All standard treatment the Japanese handed out.

The men may have been afraid when that treatment came; Max too – for they never knew what could come next – but it did not cow them. What it did, it seems, was highlight their respect for fairness, decency, and equality among themselves. 'You didn't wear your rank in prison camp,' says Bill Coventry. All were simply men together. However, that was not what they encountered among their British comrades. And so, when what they considered unfair treatment showed itself in the compound next to theirs in Tanjong Priok, they could not stand by and let it slide. Someone had pilfered a marrow the British major – or rather, his batman – had been growing, that someone being the Australian boys.

'After we had finished working all day at the wharves, we came back, and the major and his sergeant-major had all these fellows lined up in their small compound, and they were made to march this way and turn around, march on and on,' says Bill Coventry. 'Oh they were giving orders! And were going to continue every night until he found out who stole the vegetable. The Aussie boys said, "this has got to stop". So we fellows broke the wire fence and we just boldly walked in between them. And when they said turn right and everything, they couldn't do a thing because we were standing in between them. We had a big bloke with us, we called him Tiny – he was a Queensland toughie. And when the bloke was screaming like mad, Tiny just walked up to him and stood with his face right against the major's. And he said, "I'm Private such-and-such in the Australian Army. We know what we're doing here!

What are you silly Pommy bastards gunna do about it?"

'They didn't go on parade again,' says Bill, with pride. You stand up for men. You step in. It's what you do. Even in a prisoner-of-war camp.

———

There are some placenames which thunder out images and complete scenes; names which bring back sadness, so much sadness. And memories of death and despair. Names such as Hintok, Konyu, Tonchan, Kinsyok, and so many more. Or simply Hellfire Pass. And even more simple than that: cholera camps; hammer and tap. And rice, watery pap, and not much of that. Beatings, too brutal and many to describe; blindness from the lack of vitamins; trench feet when the skin and flesh fell off the bottom of the feet when the rainy season hit – because it does with a vengeance in the jungle; boots and clothes having rotted long ago, malaria that hits again and again. Weeping open wounds, skin rashes, dysentery, weakness. Beri-beri and pellagra. Huge, stinking tropical ulcers. Doctors caring, copping beatings for the men, working miracles sometimes with nothing. And mates desperately looking after mates, cradling them, holding them as they died. All this lies within the sound of the name the Thai -Burma Railway. Max, with a group of men from the 2/40th Battalion, and along with other 'Sparrows' became part of Dunlop Force, a thousand-man force under the command of Lieutenant-Colonel Edward 'Weary' Dunlop, which had been the first group of Australians to be sent into Thailand.

It was January 1943. Rumours were flying among all the prisoners that they were to be sent away. Some were told straight out they were heading to Thailand. Some believed the stories: there would indeed be plenty of food, and little work. And even if the stories weren't true, there was hope. Sergeant Kenneth Harrison of the 4th Anti-tank Regiment heard a mate say, 'I've heard Thailand called the Rice Bowl of the East. We'll be okay.' Later Harrison was to write, 'none of us knew that the journey about to commence would take us back into the Dark Ages . . . complete with slavery and plague'.

Already, many of the men in Weary's force had few possessions – Max and the 2/40th group had little, as the Japanese had made a pile and set fire to their packs – and some were without boots. But there were others, especially those who had surrendered in Singapore, who had full kits. And at the railway station from which they were to depart, the orders to board the rail cars they could see before them, to take them to Thailand, shocked many of the men. It 'brought a chorus of incredulous laughter from the POWs for it seemed impossible that they could expect thirty-two men and their gear to cram into each truck. Once again we had underestimated our oriental friends who, with kicks and shouts, demonstrated that where there was a will, there is a way.' But it was just the start. It was all a nightmare, but especially bad at night, with men sick with dysentery, often embarrassed, trying to climb over people many times a night to hang out the doors, needing two mates to hold their arms so they didn't fall, a third to hold a man's wrists so he could hang his backside out the doors; and more and more of the men contracting it. Then there was the searing heat during the day; no ventilation; the freezing cold at night; the watery rice-stew supposed to be provided twice a day, but often only once. It was a four- to five-day journey with men racing out of the railcars at short stops to open their bowels then racing back in, guards bashing prisoners indiscriminately. And there was a lack of water.

Then, after a trip by truck, Max and the 2/40th men at the back of Weary's group, under Major De Crespigny, were marched down a mountainside, through the wild jungle country, with thick bamboo, vines, palms and trees, to Konyu camp. The rear party, having had little water for several days, arrived in the afternoon, so Weary Dunlop wrote, 'walking like men in a dream, 15 being practically right out of it, including De Crespigny, who was bathed in sweat, glazed of eye, and talking wildly'. And, in all probability, shaking with exhaustion.

And the work for them all was to begin. But first the pleasantries needed to be attended to, it seemed. When Robbie Clare of the 2/40th finally arrived at the railhead for the Burma end of the Railway, a Japanese officer paraded the whole four or five thousand POWs in front of him, and stood on a box to make a speech. 'You are the remnants of a rabble army,' Robbie would later recall the officer said. 'But we will not be hard on you. You have been given the honour of putting the railroad through, and it will go through over your dead bodies.'

As he stepped down, turned to walk away, a roar went up, the men in fits of laughter: he had two bullseye patches on the backside of his pants. The interpreter calmed him, somehow, with his answer.

And the work began.

By mid-1943 over 12 000 Australian prisoners of war were in camps scattered in Thailand and Burma. So many. But they were just part of the 61 000 Allied prisoners and 250 000 Asian labourers in the workforce. Max was just one. The Japanese wanted a bridge, and workers were expendable.

At the cutting, which became known as Hellfire Pass, where Max was, 'the men could not believe the Japanese engineer when he told them they were going to dig and dynamite their way through.' First the hammer-and-tap men had to hand drill into the rock, one man holding the drill, the other turning it after each blow, the other swinging a heavy eight-pound hammer. 'The changes in climate while they worked were incredible,' wrote Tom Uren. 'We would be perspiring as we worked on the cuttings, then the tropical rains would come down heavily, and before long we were freezing.' And they had to go into the jungle and drag out heavy logs by hand. All under the hated eye of the Japanese or Korean guards.

'It wasn't a matter of more than two or three months before people were keeling over with malaria, and probably the first dengue,' Lieutenant Fred Ransome (Smudger) Smith, who worked on the British end of the Line, tells me. 'By that time we'd all had malaria; we got all the symptoms of beri-beri, and the complications of that are enormous – eye trouble, stomach trouble, swellings. By about three months in, there were so many sick and dying – and then the cholera started, with the first cholera season. The deaths from that were unbelievable.'

'The Nips cashed in on our organisation,' he tells me. All my first work on the railway, they used us, for example, to look after my men and organise the bloody work for them. It was a very clever move.'

In the wet season the men struggled 'miles to work through the mud, sometimes knee deep, among thousands who were constantly bashed, lashed and stoned by the Nips,' says Barney Porter of the 2/40th.

'We were like zombies,' George Green of the 2/40th said of one of the jungle camps in the wet season. 'Blokes' eyes were sunk right back in their heads.' And back at the camp after a long day's work, the latrines overflowed, 'and the maggots were crawling out. We all had dysentery,' he said, 'and in the night you'd go to the latrines and walk without boots through the maggots, and you'd have to sit there while the maggots would crawl up your legs.'

When Fred 'Lofty' Smith came home after being out on the Line during the day, he would carry sick men from the huts so they could use the latrine. There was no avoiding the most elementary needs of existence. And there was no way of avoiding the grotesque cruelty of the guards. 'At the worst camp we were in,' he tells me, 'it was the 100 Kilo, one of the men had dysentery. A guard whose name was Mukkin was as mad as a hatter: bash you up for no reason whatsoever. Anyway, this bloke had dysentery and he was right at the end of the hut, and the latrines were outside. He didn't make it. He just got outside the door . . . it was an open door, no doors on it. He let go – 'cos with dysentery you just couldn't hold it. This Mukkin made him lick it up . . . The fellow died two days later. That guard was so cruel.

'They'd send the main group out to work, and then they'd put a blitz on the sick, line them all up – and if they had dysentery, they'd punch them in the stomach. If they had ulcers they'd whack them with a stick on the ulcer. That sort of thing.

'We were living on a knife's edge the whole time.'

But even when things were at their worst, says Lofty, 'we'd go to work, especially when it was the wet season, and things were pretty grim, and you'd be walking along, a guard would be walking on the side keeping you in line – and one would go past you and just to pass the time away you'd go "good morning you little yellow bastard," with a smile on your face. They'd say "Okay." "Okay." "Okay." Until you struck someone who could speak English – and then you'd get belted. It was worthwhile to take a belting just to have a go at them.'

And the boys from the bush, those boys whom Bill Coventry so admired, had their own means to boost morale – and sabotage as much as they could. Out on the Line, 'the timbermen and axemen from southwest Tasmania caught white ants in the forests' says Tom Uren, 'and kept them in matchboxes. No sooner had we put the logs in place than we would put the white ants into the crevices between them to create nests in the bridges and destroy the timber.'

There was a practicality about the Australians, so many with rural backgrounds like the Tassie boys. They were proud of it. And conscious of the advantage it gave them.

Alex White of the 2/19th, a young lad from rural New South Wales, could see how useful the fast-growing bamboo was to them all. It was a bugger to cut in the work he had to do, but it helped at least in the essential ways, perhaps in fact helped keep them alive. 'One patch we dug it was all bamboo,' he tells me. 'It was pretty solid. You got to get through that, and get it out and you cut it off. And it's all tangled up and down. It's sixty-foot high. And you'd be halfway through a stock of bamboo and it's still standing there . . . But that was the beauty of it, it didn't take long to make a bed.

'In one camp, where we got the cholera, we were in tents. They moved us in, and there was all rubbish and stumps and bits of nothing – and we had to clear it all, and put our tents up. Well, we slept on beds that night!

'We knew how to handle ourselves. And we were adaptable,' says Alex, 'We could make things out of nothing.

'Reg Newton [Captain Reg Newton, 2/19th Battalion] was in charge of us,' he explains, 'and you did it! Everyone in the tent did something. Some might go and scrounge a bit of tucker while we were doing something else. Because we were in tents we couldn't have high beds. We'd lay a few bamboo logs down, just lay 'em in slats. But we were off the ground.

'There was a hut full of Pommies across the creek, and they'd been here for months, and they were still sleeping on the ground. There was a Pommy major there – they had their batman still. And we passed them going to a camp late at night. The major asked, 'Who's going through?' His batman said, 'I dunno sir, but if they're sleeping on beds in the morning they're Australians. If they're on the dirt in the morning, they're Pommies.

'Reg Newton was very strict . . .When the cholera hit, anyone who was still in the camp' – that is, they were too sick to go out to work that day – 'they had to take the other side of the tents and throw it over to let the sun in; in the afternoon, the other way round. And we all had campfires so you leave the ashes and throw them in red hot. We had seventeen cholera patients in that camp. And our doctor saved ten of them. We only lost seven. The Pommies lost over one hundred in a night.'

'The British didn't have the roguery or something,' says Lofty Smith. 'We came from stock that was sort of pioneers. When things would be looking very black someone would come up with something, make a funny joke, make everyone laugh – or sing! And away they'd go!

'We'd all join in. The Poms and the Yanks would like to get with us, 'cos when things looked darker, the more we'd sing and carry on. Whereas they'd get down in the dumps. We'd get boosted up by carrying on.'

The quality of a man mattered more than ever in life in the camps, when men looked after each other. They noticed who helped and who didn't. Lex Milne, who had been sent to Sumatra to build a railway there, told me Sergeant Allan Kerkham, who was in charge of the Australians where he was. 'There were only about twenty-something of us at the finish,' Lex says. 'He would have our food ready when we came home. He'd have our food ready when we went out to work. He looked after us. Kerk was our chief. We never had any Australian officers on the Line after the first camp – because the Japanese sent all of them away. But at the first camp Captain Ransome started with us. He was a good bloke. He used to strip off to a G-string [a loincloth] and go out and get wood with the wood party as a private.

'At first I didn't think much of him – and that's when I

started to think a lot of him and he'd come round and talk to you. He did a good job.'

The Japanese brought forward the completion date of the Thai–Burma Railway and the conditions got worse very quickly. In February 1943 the 'speedo' period began, with the demands for increased work: 'We were working 'til after dark,' says Robbie Clare, 'and every man had to dig his two cubic metres of rock and soil before he could knock off. The diet was impossible on two pannikins of rice a day. You couldn't work on that. It was impossible. The starvation started getting worse. The men got very sick, and once you got sick, they cut your rations down. And the men who were fit had to share their rations with the sick ones.'

The men shared everything they had. 'If we were in a camp, say, with a thousand men,' Fred 'Lofty' Smith tells me, 'and say there'd be five hundred unable to work with ulcers and dysentery and all that sort of thing they'd only give us food for five hundred men. They wouldn't give it for the full camp. They'd supply us for just those who were working. So that amount all had to be split up for all, which was right! Those fellas couldn't be left.'

Alex White tells how the prisoners were always willing to take a risk. 'We went out of camp one night with another group – and Georgie had knocked off a tomahawk to try to sell, and we go out with them to flog this tomahawk. That was an experience and a half. They had the toilet pretty close to the bamboo fence and you had to sit there until you knew where the guard was. Then you'd go under the bamboo fence, back down here, then you'd lay there for a while in the dark – and suddenly there's a truck coming and the road's just there! But luckily it was timbered up a bit so the headlights went over the top of us. So we went out and the Thai didn't want to buy the axe. Because it was Japanese. If it had been an English tomahawk we'd have been right. We'd have got a few bucks for it. And we had it in a bag. In the finish he gave us two eggs for the tomahawk *and* the bag. Coming back we had to lay a good while, making sure there was no traffic, plus find out where the Jap was. Then we had to scurry under the fence and back into your hut and then you're lying in the hut trying not to be noticed, and wondering if he's been down and he's missed me in this bed – he could all of a sudden appear and I'm now in the bed so where have I been. It was a bit nerve-racking just laying there wondering and waiting. For a lousy two eggs!'

On the Thai–Burma Railway, Max and all the men were paid – if it arrived – ten cents a day. If they could find someone to buy from, perhaps someone who had come up the river in a barge, or sometimes the base camps had a 'canteen', they would try to supplement their starvation diet. And a portion 'went to buy stuff for the sick fellas,' says Lofty Smith. 'The really sick ones had to eat rice husks [to try to get them well]. It was horrible. Like chaff – and these little brown beetles. They were different from the rice ones. The rice ones had white bodies and brown heads. Our doctors wouldn't let you wash them 'cos you wash off [the goodness]. In the rice itself you had longer grubs – they had their nest in the rice – a silky nest and you'd just had to shut your eyes to eat it.'

After a while, on the Line, a different torture began, said Robbie Clare. 'Some little thing would happen and they'd line you up in two lines, facing each other, and you'd have to reach over and flip the man in front of you under the nose, and he'd flip you back, and it'd get that bad that he might flip a bit hard, so you'd flip harder and it wasn't long before we had bloody noses. And then the Japs'd have to stop the fight that started through frustration.'

Life dragged on, wrote Harold Cox of the 2/40th. 'Things were continually getting worse, all of us losing weight and getting weaker, amputation of legs becoming more frequent because of the ulcers. One of the boys, Bill Harper of Don Company who left Timor with me, lost his leg at the 55 Kilo camp. He had been shot in the mouth in the action on Timor and survived, and like many of we crook ones had been told he was going to a better hospital, but it was here in the jungle that we found ourselves. The doctors said it was the blowflies and the maggots that saved Bill's life. And of course there were plenty of those about. The doctors did a wonderful job, practically nothing to work with, no drugs or medication. Salt was used to cleanse out ulcers, and if that did not work, scrape them clean. So there was a lot of pain to bear.'

'The doctors were a wonderful inspiration to the men,' wrote Harold, 'and POWs are most grateful to them. Colonel Coates was a surgeon from Melbourne and he did many of the amputations in this hospital, using very crude instruments, a knife, a butcher's saw and forceps. And all done under such primitive conditions, but they saved the lives of many prisoners. And Dr Chalmers too would often be seen lugging bags of rice to relieve prisoners who were too weak and sick.'

And in the midst of all the suffering, the sickness, the men did what they could for each other, Fred Ransome (Smudger) Smith, says 'the Australian forces and the Australians as a personality have this curious – to us as Brits – matemanship; which is very intense, even to the state of staying behind and knowing you'd die of malaria or something. You wouldn't quit your mate. We had it built in as well, but we didn't have it quite as much in the British Army.'

And Lofty saw the same thing: 'Oh, Johnny Slater!' he says, 'he came from Ranelagh, across the Huon River in Tasmania. He was a sergeant and a bonzer fella. He had dysentery, I had malaria. And they were picking the work party to go out to work that day. The captain pulled Sergeant Slater out and said, "Sergeant Slater you can go out and take charge" – which meant you wouldn't have to go out, you'd be the man who would stand between the guard and repeat the orders to the men working in the thirty-man group.'

Sergeant Slater said, "No sir. If I do that, another sick

man's got to go out and take my place." He refused – and poor old Johnny died a couple of weeks later – that takes courage! Because he could have been standing there and he wouldn't have to do any work. But he refused.'

And he remembers an orderly, Jack. 'He was fairly elderly too, one of the older ones in one of our worst camps, in the 100 Kilo – he sold his watch [to help the men], which would have got him a lot of money, and he could have bought quite a lot – you know, eggs and bananas, and that in the canteen – but he didn't. He bought this iodoform – this gold dust – for the chaps for their ulcers. So the money he got for his watch he spent on them. I don't know whether he survived or not. But he could have died – while saving the others.'

'You got to know a man so well!' Bill Coventry tells me, 'that he was so close to you!

'When you sit on your bunk and so forth, a fellow man's head on your knee, and you're both as skinny as could possibly be, and the man's dying; if you're nursing a man in his last few moments of life there's no other secret or anything else. It's just sheer love.

'You'd give anything to save him – but you know you can't. That's the love I'm talking about. In stress times, continued *stress every day*, is where brotherly love comes out.

'You'd do anything, *anything* to try and save your mate.'

Major Bruce Hunt, a POW medical officer, said shortly after the war, 'I have on many occasions seen men tried up to and beyond the limits of reasonable human endurance.

I would say that [the Thai–Burma Railway] was the most searching test of fundamental character and guts that I have ever known. That so many men . . . came through this test with their heads high and their records unblemished was something of which we . . . may not be unreasonably proud.'

Max was a fortunate man. He had survived the Railway.

19

Hell on earth

The end of the war seemed tantalisingly close. There were so many planes, raids and bombing runs, which all the prisoners of war had witnessed and often run from, with too many sadly injured or dying as a result. In Nakom Paton, a large base camp hospital between Bangkok and Ban Pong in Thailand – or Siam, as the country was then known – Max and the other POWs watched the Allied bombers come in night after night, flying noisily and low over their camp. And then, in the distance, they could see the explosions and the smoke that arose as the planes dropped those thousand-pounders on Bangkok.

Optimism was rising among the men in the camps.

Maybe this would finally be the year! But they were wary of those thoughts, knew they should be pushed to the side – the hoping, the pining, the wishing to believe. For they knew of the men from their camp who had become too desperate for concrete news and snuck out at night to try to buy a newspaper, then hadn't returned. Instead they had been captured and tortured. It was best to just keep on. The men still managed, though, even after such a long and despair-inducing captivity, to keep up the banter, the talking of anything, the just being there for them all. When they were free from the Japanese or the Korean guards, the humorous asides and jokes would flow – 'Do you believe in the hereafter? Well, so do I. I'm here after a smoke. Have you got one?' Some would take delight in feigning disagreements to get a rise out of someone in another hut.

In Dunlop Force Colonel Edward 'Weary' Dunlop, their camp commander, had even insisted on an enforced cheerfulness when things were at their grimmest, no matter how the men felt. It helped. The men knew that. Over the three harrowing years there had been many techniques used on and by the men, to get them through.

Bill 'Crocodile' Kennedy, the Catholic padre of the Sparrow Force contingent – forty-five years old when enlisted – let rip time and again following an outbreak of cholera in the camp: 'I don't care if you go crook at me, or call me a bloody sky pilot, but you blokes are dropping your bundle! It's about time you pulled your bloody finger out and got stuck into it!' And many of the doctors along the way, all idolised by the men for their devotion, would also wade on using the same manner. Many times it was exactly what was needed. It was easier, though, if your natural disposition was on the optimistic side. Which Max's was. And under the grin was a steady determination.

Now it was partway through the year: April 1945. And Weary Dunlop was worried – he argued against 'sending off sick patched-up men prematurely', particularly the next lot which were to go. The Japanese had demanded that a thousand men be discharged and sent to work upcountry. Weary had experienced this many times since they had begun their lives as prisoners of war of the Japanese over three years before. He had nursed so many of these men back to life, to something that could approximate health.

Like countless of the courageous and dedicated doctors all through the prison camps, Weary had fought hard for the men. He had stood up to the Japanese guards and commandants, incurring many beatings; he had argued and cajoled and suffered himself, at one time enduring the agony of punishment for an offence which was not his own.

'If this goes on, you'll have to be punished,' the Japanese guard had said to him.

'God almighty, do you not think it punishment standing in this sun and being kicked and beaten by a pack of bandy-legged baboons?' Weary yelled. And then the retribution started. Rifle butts, chairs, boots, while he rolled in the dust trying to keep in a ball. They left him in the sun for the day. He lay motionless, beyond resistance, lying face down in the dust conscious of broken ribs and blood from scalp wounds. When they finally allowed him to leave and return Weary, wracked with pain but determined not to show it, said, 'And now, if you will excuse me, I shall amputate the Dutchman's arm who has been waiting all day.'

Weary was known everywhere as a tower of strength. He would race out through the mud and the slush when word came that one of the lads had been hurt on the Railway. He tended to the men constantly, moving among the sick, and time off duty for him was almost unknown. He organised food and medicines, the pooling of money, whatever he saw might help the men pull through.

There were many of the men in the camps who were convinced Weary never slept at all. He would be up before dawn to begin the argument with the Japanese – the bullying, the humiliations, the beatings, whichever it would be each day. For each day there was the question: how many men were there – men fit enough – to send out to work? Frank Foster considered that in Japanese eyes a man fit for work was one who 'could breathe, blink his eyes, walk a few yards without falling over, in fact any carcass which showed signs of life'.

Weary deployed many devious methods in his attempts to hold back seriously ill men from being sent out for the day. 'If they forced a few men on parade who were unfit to hobble two miles to work, he would give them a cue for them to fall over in the mud at a certain given time.' Before the Japanese 'could vent their rage, he would grab the man, put him on his shoulder, and rush him to the hospital as if it was an urgent case. And the Japanese, astounded, might just let it go.'

All of the men were ill. Fed only watery rice pap three times a day – that is, if they were lucky – few vegetables between many hundreds of men, even less protein, and sent on endless back-breaking and dangerous work out in the humid, disease-ridden jungle and the enervating heat, all of it meant that men were starving, suffering, their bodies breaking down. And then there was the brutality, the beatings. The sheer inhumanity. At one time while travelling by barge along the River Kwai Noi, Stanley Pavillard, an MO with D Force, saw from a distance what looked like a big cattle pen made of bamboo poles. But as he and his party drew nearer, he could see that it was men, about 500 of them, who were caged in there: living skeletons, each of them barely capable of any movement. Some of them dragged themselves painfully to the fence line in an attempt to speak. The Japanese had been delaying their evacuation in the hope that they would die, and had given the men practically no food at all. Captain Pavillard was able to see that it was a 'compound full of beri-beri, malaria, pellagra, dysentery, and great stinking ulcers'. He did not find out what happened to the men. When he returned several weeks later, the pen was empty.

And now, from the Nakom Paton base camp hospital, another party of men was to be sent away. The Japanese 'doctor' assured them that there was no need to be concerned, because the men were going south, where the climate was better and medical supplies were available. No need to take any at all, he told them, and certainly not quinine: there would be plenty there to meet all the men's needs. Men with malaria and beri-beri could go, as long as they were able to travel. The doctor then chose sick men who would 'benefit' from such an evacuation, and a number of fit men to assist them.

Weary, though, had heard such stories before. He knew what the men were in fact likely to face. He called Sergeant Max Butler, the NCO in charge of the Australian contingent, to his hut and spoke with him, giving advice on what to do and how to respond under the circumstances he would no doubt encounter – such circumstances now an everyday part of their lives – and he also gave him precious funds to spend on the sick. Perhaps Max would be able to buy some eggs from the local Thai people, perhaps some quinine.

Frank Foster, who was among the Australian party and had been selected as one of the 'fit', also said goodbye to Weary. 'We both sensed,' he wrote, 'that the future was ominous, but exchanged cheerful greetings.'

The thousand men – ill, already weak through malnutrition – departed in several large groups with the medical officers, bound for Mergui Road on the South Burma coast near the Siam–Burma border.

———

In the prisoner-of-war camps some men used strategies to help them last through the misery that never seemed to end. Des Jackson, of the 2/3rd Machine Gunners, had the six-month strategy: if he could just get through the next six months, then he could start all over again. And the way to do that, he had decided – if he could keep his despair at arm's length – was to go out, do the work, and somehow get back to camp. Harry Thorpe, the Fighting Digger Padre, would move around the camps and give talks on his strategy: 'Three more days.'

'Padre Thorpe turned up again,' wrote Private PJ Rea, of the Straits Settlements Volunteer Forces, in his diary, 'and gave us a cheering address. We all admire his cheerful manner and his addresses.'

Men sang songs to help them as they marched – if they still were able to summon enough breath, or if the Japanese or the Korean guards with them were in the mood for such foolishness – each lyric sung and felt in every ounce of its meaning by each man.

Alex White had a sheet of perspex which he carried from camp to camp, the remnant of a plane wreck he had found along the way. What was once a window was now his drawing pad, his lifeline to normality, and all he needed was charcoal. He sat when he could and drew his plans for the farm he would one day have – over, and over, and over. And each day he sat sketching, he was no longer in the jungle. He was back home, back in rural New South Wales. Most men had a strategy, hidden in their hearts. But you kept it to yourself. Just lived it. And hoped it worked.

It is not known if Max had a strategy to help him through. Perhaps he thought of his father, the man of resilience Mort had been; perhaps his mother and the family; the beach, the space and the wide open street. The freedom. Whatever strategy Max had been using, now would be the time to call on it again. For Mergui Road – which the party had been sent to cut into the mountain, joining it to Kirikhan Road – was to be an escape route for the Japanese troops retreating from Burma. With the war now turning against the Japanese, this road was one they were going to need. And soon. And it had to be finished before the monsoon rains set in. The party of men were not aware yet, but the job would be another 'speedo', just like the Thai–Burma Railway. Most of the men included in this party were already survivors from that. They had been through so much. And survived. So far.

—

There was nothing unusual about the discovery, so soon into the journey, that all assurances about food, medicine, hospital and convalescence from the Japanese had been nothing but lies. None of the POW doctors were taken in by such promises but there had been little, except protest, that any of them could do. And now they were without medicines. Captain Brouwer, a Dutch doctor, did manage to smuggle in a very small quantity of quinine as magnesium sulphate, which the guards had missed when they had searched everyone's kits. It was a pitiful amount, just enough for a few days; certainly not enough for the number of chronic malaria sufferers among the men. And also in the party was a large number of chronically ill men between the ages of forty and fifty-five.

There was nothing unusual about the train journey to Prachaup Khiri Khan with the dangerous open-sided trucks and thirty-five men packed on each; with so little food, and the men wet and freezing in the violent thunderstorms which hit them at night, then roasting in the scorching heat of the day. And by the time they arrived, to be forcibly marched up into the jungle when they'd had no sleep for two nights – nothing unusual about that. None of it was unusual with the Japanese. It's just that this time it was even worse than before – for the end of the war was biting hard upon the Japanese heels.

'Nippon very sorry. But many men must die,' had been the phrase used by a Japanese officer in 1943 in his speech to the POWs when announcing they were to build the Railway. Now there was the road, and no announcement seemed necessary. It had become procedure that many men would die. And, even more to the point, on 17 March in that year, 1945, a telegram had been sent to all commands from the Japanese War Minister specifying procedure, policy and, under the cover of ambiguity, spelling out the status of prisoners of war. The lives of prisoners did not matter. Only their labour did. The telegram meant that, indeed, many men would die.

> *Prisoners of war must be prevented by all means available from falling into enemy hands. They should either be relocated away from the front or collected at suitable points and times with an eye to enemy raids, shore bombardments etc. They should be kept alive to the last wherever their labour is needed. In desperate circumstances, where there is no time to move them, they may, as a last resort, be set free. Then emergency measures should be carried out against those with an antagonistic attitude and utmost precautions should be taken to ensure no harm is done to the public. In executing emergency measures, care should be had not to provoke enemy propaganda or retaliation. Prisoners should be fed at the end.*

Prisoners in the camps had heard rumours about such plans to exterminate them if or when the Allied troops landed, and prisoners in camps across all the countries now in the hands of the Japanese were trying to prepare in whatever small way they could.

Allan Moore in Changi had some rice ready in a packet.

He was going ... he didn't know where, but if the time came he at least had a chance – that is if he could find somebody on the outside to trust. Weary Dunlop had specially selected NCOs who were secretly stockpiling rocks, any sizeable and sharp objects which could be used. And all the POWs realised that the trenches that they had been forced to dig so close to the camps were most likely to be their own mass graves, if an invasion came.

Those on their way to Mergui Road – the men unaware of where they were heading and what they were to do – were to be used in the very manner spelled out in the War Minister's directive: 'They should be kept alive to the last wherever their labour is needed.' There was just one problem with that statement, for the Japanese were making no effort to keep them alive for long at all, and never had. Many a Japanese officer had been heard to tell a sick man, 'I hope you die'. It was a statement that would be heard again too soon.

———

Major Vincent Bennett RAMC had cut a mighty dashing figure in his Royal Army Medical Corps uniform in 1936, the year he enlisted in the British Regular Army. In his studio portrait it was easy to see his Irish charm and wit. There was a playful cheekiness, a lightness evident in his face. In the photograph taken nine years later, at the end of 1945, he appeared a man who had seen more than any man should. Major Bennett, who became a prisoner of war when Singapore fell, was the medical officer on the top camp on Mergui Road.

By the time Major Bennett was sent with the Mergui Road party, he had already dealt with a cholera epidemic at Tonchan South camp in 1943; he'd been beaten up by Japanese officers on several occasions for resisting their demands for more sick men to be included in working parties – and for his troubles lost a number of teeth – and he had seen much of what went on in jungle camps, as he had been sent to Thailand in 1942.

Now his party of 400 men, having had no sleep for two nights and arriving in the early morning, had been ordered to march after a short rest, seventeen kilometres up into the jungle. Major Bennett protested, but when the proffered alternative was to do thirty kilometres the following day instead, the men elected to march. The conditions in the thick, almost virgin jungle were grim from the outset. The sandy track they struck first was heavy going; the heat was intense, and their packs dragged at their shoulders. Iron cooking equipment had to be carried between men, who took it in turns. And the sick began straggling behind. There was no extra drinking water, apart from what they had started the journey with, and at the end of the first day's march their thirst was so great, and their throats so coated in dust, that they were unable to eat their food. At the end of the second day's march, after climbing higher and higher into the mountains, they slept without shelter in a dried-up riverbed. And the rains came down. But they had eaten: one pint of cooked rice each man, with a stew made from four marrows to feed the 400 men. On the third day's march through the jungle path – which had now become mud and slush from heavy rainstorms – many of the sick had to be carried over the mountain paths. Men were exhausted and starving and ill. And the work was yet to begin.

When the rail trucks delivered Major PD Dewe and his group of medical men to Prachaup Khiri Khan, the same assembly point from where Major Bennett's men had marched, he was already without any medical instruments, stethoscopes, syringes and any drugs. They had been taken from all medical officers a week before when 'K' and 'L' Forces had been transferred from Malaya POW Administration to Thailand Administration (Nippon). And even though Major Dewe, a doctor of the Indian Medical Service and the POW Officer in Charge of all the medical men on this job, had been given a small box of drugs to bring, the Japanese would not allow any of the medical officers to take any quinine with them – a curious directive in a jungle area, where mosquitoes descended like swarms of flies and malaria was endemic.

And the quinine directive was just for starters. Upon Major Dewe's arrival at Prachaup Khiri Khan the Japanese captain – with the POWs paraded before him as he was seated with great flourish in a chair that had been brought out from the house which was to be the headquarters – ordered Major Dewe to send the seventeen 'heavy sick' men in his party off to cook a meal for themselves and, while they were at it, prepare the morning and midday rations for the whole party which had gone ahead. The sick men were kept cooking until 4 a.m. the following day. And when the rations and those men were trucked out to join the party ahead, those sick men were then ordered out to march as well. Major Dewe protested violently, but a Japanese officer drew his sword and threatened him, and the order stood. On the forced march many of the men were so sick and weakened, Major Dewe was unable to persuade them to carry even the bare necessities for themselves, and a considerable amount of kit had to be hidden in the jungle. Major Dewe was at last given permission, after leaving the men six kilometres further on, to return to retrieve some of it: the pitiful eating utensils, dixies, spoons; perhaps a blanket if a man was fortunate; maybe the sacks some carried to sleep on. But it had been raided by the local people, and much was missing.

———

Each group of POWs who set out from Prachaup Khiri Khan followed the same route up into the jungle. In Max's group there were eighty-eight Australian and five British prisoners. The climb into the thick jungle became steeper and harder for them the further they walked, and as they went higher they passed Siamese workers coming back the other way, those men refusing to continue to work on the road any longer as disease was rife, and too many had died. They were going home, no matter that they had been paid ten shillings a day. It was better to live – that is, if they could get home.

Other parties of men were already hacking into the side of the steep mountain as Max and his group passed through, and a ledge, which was the road, was taking shape. After walking for four days and almost seventy kilometres, finally his group arrived – each man exhausted and close to starvation – at what was called a camp; in reality it was a few low huts: broken-down structures without full roofs, each of them bug and lice infested. A muddy stream ran through the camp, and the entire area was shaded by trees, which meant no sun could penetrate to dry packs or clothes. Sick men were already lying in the huts.

There was no shelter for Max and his men. As tired and as spent as they were, they hacked and split a few lengths of bamboo from the jungle to form low platforms so they would be out of the mud. And they slept in the open in the rain. 'It was a night of abject misery,' wrote Frank Foster.

With this camp as their base while they were here, they were to cut the final ten or twenty kilometres of road for the Japanese, linking it with the road being built by the gangs working from Mergui on the Burma side. Their work was about to begin.

———

'It was Hell on earth,' Alex White tells me when I meet him. 'It was Hell on earth,' Frank Foster wrote.

They were hauled from their wet bamboo beds at the first light of dawn and, loaded up with their picks and shovels and chunkels (a type of hoe), they moved out from the camp and struggled up the steep hill through the mud, carrying their morning rice. It was hard work just getting there. And the conditions on the road were the same. They were there to cut into the sides of the mountain, the same harrowing work they had undertaken for the Thai–Burma Railway.

They worked in large gangs, men close together, with picks and shovels swinging into the mountain rock. The work was dangerous and nerve-racking, especially at the speed expected of them. Frequently the rain pelted down, and the road was always slippery. Japanese guards paced up and down with their bamboo sticks, demanding greater and greater speed, the job so important that many guards worked with the men as well.

From the start men were suffering from dysentery, hunger oedema and malaria. Each day in this fortnight-long speedo period they started their labours at seven in the morning, working through into the night with huge bamboo fires to provide light. It was always after midnight when they were finally allowed back to camp seven kilometres away, and several times they did not make it back until two in the morning. Each day the only food provided was three meals of rice and a very thin stew or two ounces of dried fish, scrupulously weighed, not nearly enough in quantity or vitamins for such heavy and arduous work. Each day more men fell ill, but the number of workers still had to be presented to the Japanese and sent out, and sick men pushed themselves to go, not wishing to impose greater strain on the rest of their comrades.

At the camp the sick were too ill to help with thatching of the roofs, and the men working on the road were not given the time to do it either. In the persistent rain men sat huddled in groups, night and day.

When Max and his men came in from work each night they tried to dry out their bedding and their few items by big fires, which they lit. And each night, with no opportunity to build a shelter for themselves, the eighty-eight Australians and five British in his group slept on their platforms in the open, in the heavy rain.

The conditions during those fourteen days, so it has been said, were harder than any of the days on the Railway. But here there were only bashings; no-one was beaten to death. There was no need for it: the Japanese treated them in such a way the men began dying by themselves. But they lasted the Road. They did survive that.

Finally some of the 'heavy sick' men from the top camp of Mergui Road were allowed to be evacuated. This evacuation was, so Major Bennett recorded later, 'of the most brutal nature'. Four men had to be carried on makeshift stretchers fifteen kilometres, by twenty-five men who were themselves already worn out from overwork. And the 'walking sick' who were going with them had to carry one chunkel and one pickaxe plus their kit.

When Major Dewe was permitted to evacuate his group of 100 of the sick back to Nakom Paton, forty so-called strong men from other camps were selected by the Japanese to escort them on the way, and act as stretcher-bearers. The men, weakened already and overworked, carried those of the sick who were not able to walk.

Eight of the 'strong' men died between there and the hospital camp, three of them of blackwater fever. Major Dewe had a small amount of quinine, but it was an inadequate quantity for them all. The greatest suffering for the men on the four-day rail journey back to Nakom Paton, again in the open steel trucks, had been the many stops where they were left exposed and not permitted to seek shade in the blazing sun, and there was a shortage of drinking water.

Alex White had been among those brought down. Captain Cayley, the MO at the camp he'd just left, had been beaten about the face every day when he had presented himself to the Japanese at their mealtime, asking for any leftover food or scrapings so he could feed the sickest of his men. He had handfed Alex and an American POW, both of them suffering from blackwater fever. Alex had been unconscious for ten days and when he had finally come round the orderlies managed to hold him between them to try to make his legs move again.

When he was among those permitted to be evacuated, Alex had been carried on a bag stretcher down to where trucks could reach, the men slipping through the mud and somehow not dropping him – and not collapsing themselves. By the time he arrived back at Prachaup Khiri Khan he was recovered enough to go back and help an artillery man – who should have been on a stretcher himself – get back onto the road. The man sat down, asked for a drink, took a sip. And died.

'The Japs eventually sent a party with a stretcher to carry the body back to the camp,' Alex says. He did not know the man's name.

Up at Mergui Road, in the various camps situated several kilometres apart, it became harder and harder to field the numbers of workers that the Japanese demanded each day. Each morning the men were paraded and inspected; a required number, it was demanded, to be provided to work. If 270 out of 300 men were required, 270 there must be, even if those men could do not much more than crawl. At the top camp – the camp Max and his men were in for the speedo period – Major Bennett was forced to watch each day, and cop the brutal consequences when he protested, as the men, and the sick, were paraded each morning, no matter the weather or the conditions. Many of the sick were beaten to force them out to work. The doctors, who were enduring the same conditions, and with so few medical supplies allowed them, did the worrying for them all. The doctors were in their own private hell, with their enforced helplessness. No quinine for most of the time. No medicine, except for that which several MOs had smuggled in – or that which could somehow be wormed out of the Japanese. At an earlier time, before the road, in one of the jungle camps, one of the men had come across a doctor, Captain Frank Cahill, on his knees in the jungle, praying aloud for the men he had treated to be allowed to survive.

———

Mergui Road had finally joined, both sides now complete, the men having pushed themselves to do as they had been required. Max and his men – four of whom were now dangerously ill and the rest almost on their backs – were to start the journey back, so said the Japanese guard with them. They were to carry the sick – if they wanted them to make the journey too; the strongest among them could do it. And carry the blacksmith's tools, the anvil, the hammers, the picks, the crowbar – whatever they had been using – and their packs; plus all the camp equipment of the Japanese staff and guards. Also the cooking utensils which they would need to cook the rice – the rice which, the guard assured them, they would find somehow along the way.

They set off, skeleton-thin men, carrying those sicker than themselves on stretchers they had made from bamboo poles and rice bags. Men strained under the weights they carried: the blacksmith's anvil tied onto a bamboo pole and carried between two men; the stretcher-bearers in bare feet picking their way over the rocky ground, carrying the sick as well as their packs.

In Max's group no-one complained, Frank Foster reported. Instead those on the stretchers implored to be allowed to try to walk. They would catch up in a few days, they said. None of them wished to place a burden upon any other. Theirs, though, was an unsuccessful plea: no man would be left.

'We had long since moulded ourselves into a Digger fraternity,' Foster wrote. 'Every man was his neighbour's charge. Individualism was cast to the winds. It was a case of sticking together and we would get through in the same way we had got through the railway.'

They reached a camp after a day's march, each man anxious for the night's rest. But a fresh guard took over and they were forced straight through. The doctors and the orderlies 'cast dignity aside,' wrote Foster, 'and pleaded, implored and begged that the worst cases be left overnight. It was of little avail.'

A young English lad died first. He had been carrying the blacksmith's anvil. Frank Foster said he had strained his heart.

It was at the next camp – where conditions became even worse – that they discovered the Japanese had no intention of taking them off the mountain. They were here, on the road, for however long the Japanese decided: a job with no end. Or till they died. They were here for road maintenance, repair, bridge-building, whatever their captors demanded. And the road in the wet season was a never-ending quagmire.

It was the same all through: the men in camps all along Mergui Road had no prospect of getting out. 'Men who had withstood over three years' onslaught of brutality were dying at the rate of six every day,' wrote Frank Foster. 'In one camp there were only ten fit men out of three hundred and some of them worked their bodies to breaking point carting water, cooking, and in burying the dead.'

In one of the camps Donald Smith of the British Army (in a separate party to Max's) arrived at a camp where men lay motionless under their rags – which was all they had to cover themselves with – too ill to speak and too exhausted to struggle.

'Some groaned in their sleep,' he wrote, 'others gazed unseeingly into space, some plucked nervously with bony fingers at their straggling beards, others clasped and unclasped their hands as if in prayer. This was the breakdown of humanity, the final demoralising collapse of civilisation itself.'

Frank Foster in Max's group said, 'I found myself able

to hobble about in between bouts of malaria, like several others, and we devoted our time to grave-digging and giving our comrades a decent . . . burial.'

At the fourth camp that Max and Frank came to, Max had to leave forty-three of his men there, as they were too sick to continue. At that camp, Minowa, there were only fifteen fit men to look after all the rest. But it was the 20 Kilo camp, which Max and his men came to, which was too shocking for Frank Foster to relate.

'I arrived,' wrote Max in the affidavit that was presented at the War Crimes Trial into Mergui Road, 'at "Death Valley" 20 kilos in an easterly direction from Minowa, with 35 men. Also a party of 100 British arrived at the same time, camp strength 135. In two days there was not a fit man for work; there was no Doctor or Padre. Men started to die at the rate of two a day from typhus, fever, malaria, and beri-beri. The Japs then made this a base camp for work on the road. The Doctor and Padre arrived fourteen days after our arrival.'

'Suffice it to say,' says Foster, 'that hundreds of men were strewn on damp ground, writhing in pain in their vermin-infested rice bags. Men yelling in pain, sleep-walking, screaming for quinine.'

Max's affidavit continued: 'A Jap Sgt, known as "the Gorilla" (Sgt Hiroto) who was in charge of the work on the road was the cause of a lot of deaths. It was in his power to get us medical supplies. The MOs repeatedly asked for medical supplies, he would promise them in a week's time but they never came to light. He would also make the MO stand to attention and demand more men be sent out to work. At Death Valley, rations issued were very little and mostly rotten. The Jap Sgt who was in charge issued mouldy rice, which when picked over and washed was only half the amount issued at first. A Jap Private at Death Valley made life a little easier by his actions and kind treatment. He gave us quinine, not much, but it was all he could manage without arousing the Jap NCOs suspicions. Eggs, sugar, fruit, etc were all given to us after dark by him. He was the first to let us know on the 18 Aug. that the war had finished.'

———

When the news finally arrived that the war had ended, the heavy sick in Major Bennett's top camp were evacuated in bullock carts fifteen kilometres, 'drawn by men who had been sent from the nearest camp, over the world's worst road,' his report said.

'After 19th August (war ended),' he wrote, 'we received large stocks of quinine.'

For the entire four months Major Bennett's party of 400 had been on Mergui Road he had received, in June, one-half a kilogram of quinine, which on minimum doses had lasted ten days. In July, when over ninety per cent of the men had been suffering from malaria, he had received enough to last six days.

———

Some British men desperate to get off the mountain – and away from the certain death they would face if they stayed – set off however they could, enduring the blackouts, crawling, hoping to get away.

Donald Smith, who wrote *And All the Trumpets*, was part of the British contigent and the only one of his group of seven to survive Mergui Road.

———

Major Dewe brought himself to the point of exhaustion and was not able to rest until the last man was brought out of the jungle. He went over the road in a staff car, still finding men a week later. 'Final evacuation very erratic,' he reported. 'Light sick marched, heavy sick [were] crowded into trucks. Difficulty in controlling Jap drivers when driving stretcher cases on a very bad road. Trucks were used like buses by other Japanese who piled themselves and baggage on at various points after the trucks left our camps.'

Many men were still being found by American servicemen who, like Major Dewe, went into the jungle and searched. Major Bennett, in his camp, had written out his will.

Two hundred and sixty-four men died, and 200 were dying. Those 200 were recovered just in time.

—

Major John Stringer, himself a prisoner of war, compiled a report after the war.

'We had received information that approximately one thousand men from the hospital camp at Nakom Paton had some months previously been sent to Prachaub Kiri Kan [sic] to build a road to Mergui in Burma; that conditions in this area were extremely bad in regard to food, quarter, and sickness and that assistance was urgently required . . .

'(1) A large percentage [of men recovered from the road] were too weak to move

(2) Many resembled living skeletons (4 stone in many cases)

1. Mental condition of majority was such that no coherent information could be obtained. Some did not know their own names; and in a group a man's intimate friends had forgotten his name . . .'

———

Frank Foster wrote: 'Sgt Max Butler was a very popular NCO with his men . . . [H]e endeared himself to Australians, British and Dutch alike. Apart from seeing that no Digger was without anything that it was possible to obtain on the Mergui Road, he gave of his physical strength time and again to relieve the burden of his fellow-men. His name will live forever by those who knew his self-sacrifice in this colossal struggle of . . . men in the jungle.'

———

Tom Bird from Penguin thought he'd had a hard time himself in a POW camp high up in the Thai jungle. And he was now down at a base camp.

'When I saw Max,' he told his wife, Mardi, years later, 'I could have cried. I could have picked him up under my arm.'

———

Max wrote home to his family, said he had been in charge of work parties labouring on a road; and he'd seen Tom Bird. And in the pocket of his newly issued army shorts he placed the list he had compiled at the 12 Kilo camp – the list of deaths he had written on the back of someone else's letter, the only paper he could find.

———

Approximately 7500 Australians – more than a third of the Australian soldiers who became prisoners of the Japanese – died while imprisoned. Approximately 15 000 men made it home.

20

Homecoming

What a glorious day it is when war is finally over, even if it takes a while to sink in. In Melbourne on 15 August 1945, it took a few minutes for people hurrying in the street below to grasp the reason why people several storeys up were uncharacteristically leaning out of office windows and shouting 'Peace!' and 'It's finished!' By ten past nine in the morning, so the *Herald* reported, the news had spread, the city 'spontaneously erupting', then turning out into the streets.

And what a racket they made, this laughing, singing, shouting, pushing mob who thronged and cheered, while those still in their offices high up tore into shreds any paper in sight and tossed it out the window. Around the corner, in Swanston Street, revellers could be heard from a quarter of a mile away, belting out 'Australia will be there', 'Bless 'em all' and 'Pack up your troubles'. People grabbed people and danced; office girls formed 'crocodiles' and moved through the crowd. Returned soldiers and sailors came up with excuses for kisses and got their share. Bands played. A boy trying to get his bicycle through the excited, milling mob lifted it high above his head and was helped by a sea of upstretched hands — another 'crocodile' which instantly formed passing his bike across. It was a day when people were joined in spirit and exaltation.

The *Herald* reported that an old Chinese man stood across from Swanston Street, watching the scraps of paper raining down from above and asked, 'What for?' in answer to which a sailor slapped him on the back and told him the good news. The old man grinned. 'Japan too cheeky no more,' he said. 'No more trouble now anywhere.'

If only it was all so easy.

———

There was trouble brewing in the British and Dutch empires, for a start. Their veils of invincibility had been blown away, their reputations in tatters. The images they had presented, expounded upon, convincing themselves that it was indeed true — themselves as the heroes in the story, the benevolent overlords of might who would come sailing through because 'the empire belongs to them, as much as they belong to the empire' – had been shown to be puffed-up rhetoric, easy phrases which trip off a wordsmith's tongue.

The war had been more like a one-way street. The Australian forces had been used to shore up the British and Dutch empires; the Indian forces to the same end. And while Churchill's strategy had been to fight Hitler first, the rest of the Empire had been, well, sacrificed, along with many of the British. 'We saw a copy of Sir Lewis Heath's account of the Malayan Campaign,' Jim Rea had recorded in his diary on 2 January 1943. 'It was supposed to explain to the 18th Div. why they were landed in Singapore at the end but I don't think it satisfied them.'

And many Australians would not be easily satisfied with why they were landed either: Des Jackson's 2/3rd Machine Gunners, and Sparrow, Gull and Lark Forces to begin the list. The Empire was losing its grip on the power it once held. And now, in the Far East, many people wanted their countries back. Many had worked alongside the British and the Allies to defeat the Japanese, and now at war's end it was just a matter of continuing. In the prisoner-of-war camps the Javanese in the Dutch Army made no secret of what was coming: 'After this fight, we fight again,' they told Fred 'Lofty' Smith.

So, too, would the fight go on for the POWs who were now going home, but their fight would be of an altogether different kind. Now it would be the fight to create a life within a weakened and damaged body; to find a job, perhaps a career, which they could manage. And there would be the struggle to forget that which could never be forgotten.

And among the British ex-prisoners, the ordinary men had returned home with the disquieting knowledge that their burden in the camps had, often, been so unequally shared. There had been some exceptional officers, and then there had been those who were not. In a camp near Tarakan in Borneo the Australians and Fred Smith looked on, amused and impressed, at the large drawing which had suddenly appeared, pinned on the wall. It was an accomplished drawing by someone who knew what they were about. A ship was coming up the Thames and officers lined its decks. Churchill, waiting on the wharf to greet them, shouted up, 'But where are all the men?' The officers called back, 'They died that we might live.' The drawing was confiscated soon after. The culprit had been willing to risk the court martial which would have been readily given if he'd been caught.

There was much the men would face over the years ahead. But mostly they would have to face themselves. There are no clean finishes in war. Especially not this one.

———

It would take some time to collect the now ex-prisoners of war and repatriate them back to their homes. They were spread so far over many countries.

On Celebes an Australian Mitchell fighter bomber flew over the camp Don Woolley and Charlie Dodge were in, and dropped a note asking how many Australians were in the camp. Don and Charlie had first heard the war was over when a Dutch interpreter had taken the stand and addressed the men. There had been hugging and crying, and some men had prayed.

'Talk about excitement,' Don Woolley wrote. 'Never seen anything like it.' He and Charlie had remained locked in each other's arms for quite some time. Now they put two sheets of iron down in a yard to signal back to the bomber. Then another note fluttered down.

The men were waiting as instructed – they didn't need to be told again, Don said – at the airport the next morning. The plane landed, bomb racks opened; four men emerged with side machine guns ready for hostile Japanese. But there were none to be seen anywhere – cleared out for their own safety, Don presumed – and the bomber took off, a sudden rise almost straight up in the air, and with a swift manoeuvre and one wing to the ground, the other pointing skywards, turned, levelled out – and Don and Charlie peeled themselves off the ceiling, the very wits scared out of them on their first-ever flight.

Many of the men, including Don and Charlie, needed to spend time in hospital before they were allowed to join the others and begin the journey home. And all was not over simply because Japan had surrendered.

Harold Cox, who was now permanently blind as a result of malnutrition in the camps, was saddened by the men who kept dying after the war was over. 'They had suffered so much for so long,' he wrote, 'and now they would never make it home.' In remote areas the mopping-up took months. And many of the ex-POWs were already experiencing a foretaste of what they would encounter among those who had no idea what they had been through. The POWs had spent endless hours dreaming of life at home in their own countries, back with their families, with people who knew and accepted them. None of them had imagined what they would actually come home to face: the incomprehension, the brushing aside of their experiences; and from those who had heard some of the stories, there was often a refusal to believe it had been as bad as the reports stated.

In Siam the attitude was already evident at the base camp near Mergui Road. The paratroopers had been and gone, and the men finally all located and moved on. Now there was the need for official documentation and the finding of graves. This caused tension: Major John Mason Stringer refused to hand his report on the whole terrible road episode to men he encountered from the Contact and Inquiry Unit, so a representative from the Commonwealth War Graves Commission – a big, strapping, well-fed fellow – had been sent to fetch the report from the recalcitrant ex-POW. The War Graves representative wrote in his papers that he considered that many Australian POWs 'for reasons best known to themselves had a form of guilt complex' which caused them 'to carry a "chip on their shoulders" for all non-prisoners'. And, he explained, he did not like this chip when he met it. Nor did he like Major Stringer: '[a] lot of soldiers who had never seen a prison camp had faced some pretty tough times [too]. The prisoners had had no monopoly on hardship.' The gulf between those who had been there and those who had not was wide indeed.

Then there were those who were just beginning to find out what the reality had been. John Gandy had finally tucked some sea miles under his belt in the last six months of the war, after he finished his naval officer training course. He had been assigned to the *Gascoyne*, a ship which had been in the thick of several battles during the war, and had been lucky enough to have not seen a single casualty. The ship and crew, now released from naval duties and based in Balikpapan in Borneo under Army command, had been sent to Tarakan to pick up 700 POWs. Except when they arrived, they found none.

The men on the ship were shocked. Nobody talked. It was too hard to believe.

The ship and crew were still in Tarakan when they heard detailed reports: the POWs had been killed off. 'Marched to death. If they tried to escape the Japanese shot them; if they fell down the Japanese shot them.' This was Sandakan. And out of the 2434 prisoners only six POWs, all escapees, had managed to survive.

Later, when John Gandy and many ex-servicemen had returned home and heard of the Thai–Burma Railway, of the death rate and what the men had endured, they were incredulous. But John understood more than most. He had seen the hard and fierce Japanese front-line soldiers the *Gascoyne* had transported and delivered, those men who had now become prisoners themselves. And he wished to be as far away from them as he could be.

But those who had spent the war far from the camps would never really know. And nearly to a man, the returning ex-POWs did not – could not – speak of it in depth. Or at all.

————

The prisoners of war began to arrive home in Australia over the next few months. And strange feelings began to emerge – unexpected in many – almost a new despair.

'We were happy, very happy,' Fred 'Lofty' Smith tells me, 'but we were like zombies. Half with our own thoughts and half wondering what it was going to be like when we got back home . . . There wasn't much we could talk about . . . You're coming back, but you're leaving . . .' And his sentence trails away, but what he wants to say is clear: you're leaving your dead mates behind; separating from your living mates, who will go off to their homes; the closeness of their lives, the intensity of it all. 'You're leaving . . .'

On the homeward journeys most made by ship, the ships' captains took it slowly to allow the men time to readjust; some took three weeks to come down the Great Barrier Reef. The men wandered around on deck and were given tins of condensed milk and arrowroot biscuits to try to fatten them a little before they docked. Tom Bird, who had been thirteen and a half stone before his time as a POW, managed to get himself up to nine stone before the final leg back to Tasmania. Many men didn't wish their families to know, or see, their true condition and were grateful for the chance to do a bit of window-dressing on themselves – as much as could be achieved. Especially for the first greeting.

'The actual meeting of the repatriates with their next of kin is marked by emotions which have to be seen to be believed,' the Army's Adjutant-General Major-General CEM Lloyd, a desk officer, wrote in a memo. 'My own personal view is that these reunions should be had in the homes of the people . . . such a course would avoid the contagious emotionalism approaching hysteria . . . There is a feeling in the army, and I think in the country generally, that the flap concerning the repatriated prisoners is a bit exaggerated. The great bulk of them are fit and well, provided with large sums of money from their enforced period with no expenses, and now granted discharge from the Army. On the other hand, the soldier who has borne the whole deal comes from the continuing battle in New Guinea tired, diseased and NOT discharged and nobody but his next of kin are really very interested in him as an individual.'

It was here: the lack of understanding, the turning of attitudes, the World War I experience all over again. For now, at the end of 1945, long gone were the energy-filled days when the crowds watched men in khaki heading out, health radiating from them; able bodies primed to fight the foe; their spirits noble. Now, they were becoming nuisances. Already.

If the Adjutant-General concerned about the 'emotionalism approaching hysteria' had perhaps witnessed more ex-POWs' homecomings, he might have seen that not all family reunions were the joyous occasions he described.

Fred 'Lofty' Smith, arriving in Sydney on the *Highland Chieftain*, was astounded by the size of the crowds waiting on the wharf. One of his cobbers, who was already married with two little boys when he had gone off to war, was excited to be able to be with his family again, and was dying to see his young sons. When they disembarked he found his mother there waiting with his boys, not his wife. His mother broke the news: his wife had left him not long after he had been taken prisoner. He had not known, and had pined all those years.

'He broke down, really broke down,' Fred tells me. It was one of the saddest things he had ever witnessed. All the men crowded in on their mate, took hold of him, held him, and helped him. The memory of it saddens Fred still.

And 'joy' was not the word to describe Tom Bird's arrival home, either. He had come first on the *Highland Brigade* to Melbourne and now, on the final leg, here he was on the *Marana* sailing into Devonport, standing at the back, when he saw his sister-in-law on the wharf to meet him. He could not do it; could not go through it. He moved to where she could not see him, jumped over the side and 'took off' for a couple of days. He made his way home on his own, wanting to find his father for a private and personal meeting. No well-meaning greeting to be endured, no questions to avoid, no awkwardness which he could not face.

When your soul has been shredded and now lies close to the surface, too raw to so much as brush against, only the essentials matter. But, for Tom, a meeting with his father was not to be. His father, Alla Bird, the pest and health inspector in Penguin, a man known and liked all through the district – who had told all who would listen, as he did his rounds to the farms, that his son would one day come home, he would, for as he told everyone, Tom 'could go to work on just a slab of bread with butter and last all day. That's the type of man he is. No, he'll come home' – Alla had died not long before. And Tom had just discovered a whole new level of loneliness.

They had expected so much on the return home, the men, the boys. Oh, it would be wonderful, they had presumed, says Lofty Smith, happiness abounding, a Garden of Eden. But they stood, numb men nearly all – a different numbness these days – almost from the moment they set foot in Australia.

Groups of disbelieving men staring, uncomprehending, into this world to which they had returned. After years of fear, death, unspeakable cruelties; too many mates who had drowned on boats which had been torpedoed; starvation, and privations of which there could be no worse, none of what was now before them seemed real; nor the people with their chatter and their insignificant concerns, their living lightly in the world. Fred's brother told him how hard it had been because the taxes had been high.

The same loneliness which Tom Bird now knew was announcing itself to so many of the men – a further twist in the heart when war's end had promised new life. Many had no-one to come home to, Fred tells me: the wives and girlfriends had left them. And many couples and families were like strangers. This had never been part of the dreams of what freedom would bring, those dreams from back in the camps.

'We were to help with the returning prisoners of war,' Bette Wright told Patsy Adam Smith. 'They were to be reunited with their parents, but it seemed unreal to them. They didn't want to get off the buses when we got them to the meeting place. It was very traumatic.'

Fred Smith had been shedding mates all along his trip home. 'I'd been amongst the chaps all the time,' he says. 'And then they started to go to their homes.' Men left the boat in Brisbane, more in Sydney; he left his cobber with his mother and his boys in New South Wales; more in Melbourne.

And finally he hit Launceston. His parents, brother, sister and a friend were waiting, pleased to see him. After a kiss on the cheek from his mother, and the initial greetings and questions, and the relief to be home, there it was: he was no longer with his mates. And quite apart from the bleakness of the trip home to Queenstown in his brother's '36 Ford Coupe – with the flat tyres which happened on the way, and the dead grass they had to shove in the tyres as the only way to get home, then arriving home a day late and missing the neighbours' welcome party, which had been planned for the previous evening – the homecoming for Fred had been a parting of the ways. Where were all the men who knew what he knew? Oh, home was strange.

'Those men had all been around them. And as they died [in the camps], they got closer and closer together,' says Mardi Bird, Tom's wife. 'It's something like a baby that's always been wrapped up tight and suddenly it's out. And there's no comfort around it.'

Homecoming encompassed more than just a meeting on a wharf, though many people at home found that hard to believe. If you were home, and you were now safe, all would be well. The men could simply put it behind them and get on with their lives. Couldn't they?

21

A grateful man

When Max came back to Australia he smiled the smile of a grateful man, although there was a quietness to it. He was ready for life again, but he would have to ease on up to it, his body still weak. It had not been many months since he had been burying the men who had died at the 12 Kilo camp one on top of the other, the ground too rocky and hard for separate graves, and his strength and that of those digging with him almost spent. It had not been many months since they had watched Staff Sergeant Clive Tilbrook of the British Army be brutally bashed about the head at Death Valley for insisting that there were no more fit men at that camp to shift a load of ammunition for the retreating army. It was still all so close. And yet, now, at home, a man could believe it so far away.

The end of the war had been news beyond belief: they had long thought it near, yet it never came. And high up on the road, the job without end, the focus each day had been to stay alive and help as many men as they could to do the same. There had been no euphoria when the sympathetic Japanese guard, a Buddhist priest who had been pressed into the Japanese Army – banished there to the hellish backwater for his reluctance to fight, risking his life each time he helped them – told them it was over, especially when he couldn't tell them for some time if there had been a victor. Max and the few fit men had heard it with relief and excitement, but there had been 200 sick men in the camp, skeletally thin as they all were; the sick men diseased, and not fully in the world; in pain, many shivering then sweating in the swirl and dizziness of malaria rigors, most just holding on to life. They had to take care – a gentle telling – when they told those men the news. And even while Max had waited with several men at the train siding to be taken to a hospital camp and to safety, hoping to get there in time, another man had died. It had gone on and on. Sometimes you can't tell what a man carries inside and Max wouldn't talk of it. It was over. He was simply pleased to be alive.

Max arrived home from the war a few months after many of the others. He'd been held back, he said, to make a statement, but he didn't add it was for a war crimes trial.

He didn't say a lot at all; but, then again, although not shy, he never had been big on unnecessary words.

Ruby had travelled to Launceston to greet her son, collect him when the *Moreton Bay* docked. Her brother Jim, Max's uncle, had a car and he had gone through to Penguin, picked them up. Now they waited on the jetty. Althea was there, taller, her flightiness now reined in; a young woman proud and excited to see her brother again. She had last seen him when he had called into her school to say goodbye, just before he left. It had been so long since then. Max's brother Colin was with them as well, still in his Army uniform, for he had served in New Guinea.

It had been a big day, as all these homecomings were, and a local dignitary had circulated, chatting, shaking hands, doing his bit for the ex-POWs. Max had watched, amused, as the man approached and heartily pumped Colin's hand – and ignored Max the POW, who was once more in uniform and filled out a little from the condensed-milk-and-arrowroot-biscuits diet. He had improved so much that his previously wasted skin and bone was now merely an exceptionally thin kind of lean. In bulky khaki he could pass for any other soldier. And his appearance seemed to suggest he was healthier than his brother who, Max could see, had not come out of his New Guinea service well at all. All of them in this war had seen too much cruelty and the worst in men. And there were many along the coast who hadn't come home. Max and his family travelled back home to their small coastal town, entertaining themselves on the way with the story about the POW who couldn't be seen.

At home in Penguin Ruby made Max's favourite meal, which was ready to be served – the very dish he had requested when he had finally been able to send a letter home from Siam. He had been dreaming of her mince pie for the last three months, he said.

It was a wonderful moment for Ruby and Althea, and all the cousins and uncles and aunts who were there, when he walked in the door and down the hallway. His presence brought warmth, the house felt fuller somehow. He looked in all the rooms when he came in; the sitting room with his photo hanging high; the verandah with the sleepout where Uncle Tom had died; the big room, where he had last seen his father. And their pigeon loft out the back. Max would take that up again, the quietness, the memories of Mort, the birds flying free, swooping and wheeling then returning home. The club had always held their meetings every Friday night, around the kitchen table at Mort's house. And Hedley and his son, Bill, who'd just come home from the Air Force – Dick Oliver too, who was another World War I veteran – they'd all be there. Men who knew him. And who knew war. No need for it to be mentioned.

Ruby served his meal with some pride, pleased to give him something his heart desired. It was a scene played out in different settings, with different participants, in different families of POWs all around Australia; a scene which made people's hearts tighten almost in shock; a scene which disappointed so many cooks: the men, almost every one, could not eat the food they were given. Fred Smith couldn't even force his hands and the cutlery to his mouth. Lloyde Spencer could manage just a few spoonfuls of bread and milk. And Max, his body rebelling, couldn't eat the pie, couldn't force even one mouthful of the very dish he had craved. He pushed it aside and apologised. Some families were deeply hurt, not impressed at all. Ruby and her family, though, knew to let him be. There'd been too many men in this house who'd been to war for them not to know when something was going on. They would wait. He would eat when he could. Who knew what he had been through?

So many men had returned from years away. There had, of course, been disruptions in Tasmania, in the way people lived their lives. It had been like a time warp, Mardi Bird tells me: all the boys and men, as soon as war broke out, suddenly gone. Only those younger and older remained. There had been the enforced blackouts in the towns – especially the ports along the coast, Devonport and Burnie – and even going to the outhouse had meant your candle or torch had to be shielded. There'd been rationing and coupons for petrol and clothing. There'd been women working in jobs never before open to them. Joyce Jackson had become a mail-woman; after completing her job making Army uniforms, she then delivered letters to the door. It helped keep her mind occupied: her fiancé, Lloyde, was missing. But, regardless of the adjustments, it was difficult for the people who had remained at home to imagine or know what the men had been through. And there were those who didn't try.

In Queenstown Fred Smith felt a stranger – lost, only two other prisoners of war there and he knew neither. There'd been an official welcome home in which all the right words of support were spoken, and then nothing happened, many of the people in town simply wanting to get back to living in the same manner as before. No interruptions or intrusions. He couldn't wait to get away. But where to, or what to do, he didn't know. Sometimes he felt like giving up, giving this living game away. It was hard away from the boys.

'When I first came back, everything was strange,' Fred tells me when we meet. 'They still had the food rationing and the clothing rationing [going] on, and they would let us have a bit more meat from the butcher when they knew who we were. They let us have a bit of extra meat, but I was in a lost world. We expected everything to be like the Garden of Eden sort of thing. And there was the rationing . . . and everyone was down in the mouth.'

The aftermath of the war had left everyone home in Tasmania – in Australia – 'very downhearted', Fred says. 'And it was very strange. And a lot of us couldn't settle down – well, how could you – after being amongst men all that time. Hundreds of men – and all of a sudden, you're in a house! With four walls. We were living on a knife's edge the whole time, over there, and to come back and there's no fear! No danger. It was . . . totally . . . totally different. And it was hard to cope with.

'My mother couldn't understand why I couldn't stay in the house all day. I'd have to go and walk round the township. She'd get really upset about it because she expected me to stay home and just . . . and I couldn't do that – as I had to be go, go, go.

'And people would say, "Where did you serve?" "Oh I was a POW" – they sort of looked . . . but they didn't want to know the full story. And because ever since then we've been known as POWs and nothing said about the fighting we had. It didn't go for long. But it was pretty nasty.'

———

Along the coast, and in Penguin, the men were more fortunate: there were POWs by the score. Mates everywhere They saw each other, knew where they were, knew who wasn't doing 'too good', and who was managing. And they could get together down at the pub. Mates close by once more. The only problem was if you were one of the few who didn't drink. But regardless of how the men managed their lives, it was happening all over again. Men returning; lives altered; futures changed.

———

Max knew he was not well, and was advised to apply to the Repat for a pension. Which he would not do. He'd watched Mort, knew the struggle his father had faced to try to maintain a sense of who he was. Max remembered the subsistence living, with no possibility of rising beyond it. And he knew, regardless of how much of a good man Mort had been through it all, how his father's life had been impeded, how he'd had little chance of taking part in the changing world. And how much his father would have liked to have done so. They'd not even been able to afford a second-hand car like Hedley eventually had – the same one Hedley and his wife and the kids had been in that day in Ulverstone, when the back wheel had come off, and they had wondered whose it was as it went rolling past the car and knocked that man on his bike into the ditch. Max wanted a life for himself. Some money. A future. So, no, a pension was not for him. He would continue to work – if he could just find a job his body could now manage.

He returned to work at Fred Price's in Burnie, making cane furniture, but it was hard to settle. And he wasn't alone there: most of the POWs found it hard – the restrictions, the people, the strange settings.

Max wrote away and enrolled in sign-writing lessons which came in the mail, and he practised at the kitchen table: the script, the ornate lettering in many styles. Young Barney, still living with Ruby, watched. And he acted as Max's assistant, traipsing up the street, holding the ladder and helping with all the paint when Max got the job of repainting the sign above the River Don Trading Company in the main street. Max might just find a way to make a go of this.

———

It was hard for Max to make decent money out of his new sign-writing career in such a small town, and after only a few more small jobs when people tried to help him out, he had to call it quits. But he would try something else. He was well aware how he needed space, could not cope with confinement, wanted no-one to rein him in, especially after the years in the jungle. So when he received his back pay from the Army he bought himself a second-hand truck: a grey Maple Leaf Chev, a wooden trayback vehicle. He hoped there would be enough work in Penguin to accommodate another carter. There were already the established carriers: Harry Whittle did the bulk of the jobs and Oscar Mather still had his horse and cart. Max hoped, if it all worked out, to make a living from this.

He tried. He advertised at interval, or 'half-time' as it was known, at the local pictures which Spud Hall's dad ran on a Saturday evening in the Penguin Town Hall, there on the main street across from the beach. Max went about it as professionally as he could on a small budget, even had a 78 recording made, aluminium, and when the slide appeared –

featuring a photo of his truck – a voice would boom out each week telling the good people of the Penguin region that north, east, south or west, it made no difference to Max Butler. He'd travel anywhere.

Perhaps it might have been a success if he'd had the chance to continue it a while longer. But the fellow on the motorbike who ran into him on the road heading out from Penguin towards Ulverstone, while Max was backing out – just after he had shifted Linda and her children, Barney and Trevor, into a place down near Watcombe House; the same fellow who admitted to Max that he hadn't been looking and was in the wrong – that fellow then turned around and sued Max, and there was not much money left after that. He'd had to sell the truck. Someone had suggested he lie and claim he'd seen the chap far before it happened. 'No,' he said. 'There have been too many lies told already.' Max was as straight as a gun barrel, says Bill Deverell. Just like Mort. And another option in Max's life was gone. He did not mention the word 'disappointment'; you didn't back then. You didn't let any of it show.

So Max went back to wicker work – but this time as his own boss, setting up a workshop out the back of Crescent Street, in the old shed on the opposite side of the yard to the pigeon loft, which was now back in use. He was alive, he had freedom, and space; he had mates whom he met up with, and laughed and joked with down at the pub, and mates who called in, who came, sat and talked with him, when the jokes were gentler but still there. That life would do. It would have to. And anyway, you did what you could.

———

In time Max eased in to becoming the ex-POW you couldn't see. His body had returned to what could be described as lanky, and he was just another bloke around the town. It was the same with nearly all the men for after a while, once flesh covered their skinny frames it was hard to tell just who had been a prisoner of the Japanese and who had not. In Penguin men passed men in the street, uttered their good-natured g'days, went to the football, drank in the pubs, took part in activities in town, and those who did not know would be none the wiser.

Even those who bore bodily reminders were hard to pick: the men with the scars from rifle butts brought down hard; the ones with welts across their backs from the sticks and rods with which they had been beaten as they worked; those with disfiguring craters and large scarring from tropical ulcers under their clothes. Maurice Jones, though, was there for all to see, and he was a lucky man to have survived. He had been one of the miracles, his body put back together – almost – by Major Albert Coates, a surgeon in the camps, a man idolised by the men to whom he attended and operated on under the primitive jungle conditions. Daily they had seen Major Coates's courage as he had confronted the Japanese;

his skill and the care he gave; and his efforts to keep men alive, keep them going. All the doctors in the camps, POWs like the rest of them and enduring the same conditions, were regarded as heroes by the men. In Maurice's case his condition had been so bad that there had been little hope, yet he had managed to survive, coaxed and nursed back to life due to the devoted attention of an orderly. And, now home, he had a limp. And was now married. One of the many.

It was not the bodily scars which had the greatest impact on the marriages of so many of the ex-POWs. Instead it was the scars which no operation could remove: the dreams at night; the imprinted memories in the day; the visions which arose, triggered by a sight of some small thing – a smell which took them back, a sound perhaps – the times when what had been seared so brutally into their souls would rise up, unbidden, and take them over. For gentle Lloyde Spencer, it was the Maori Farewell which would cause him to jump sky high in shock at the sound, and rage down the street consumed with an uncontrollable urge to bash whoever was playing it. New brides, often unsuspecting of what could come, were now in marriages far different from the one next door.

———

It had been raining like the very dickens when Mardi met Tom Bird. She had closed the door to the electrician's office where she worked in Devonport, ready to head home, and turned to be confronted with just how wet a bike could become, the entire bike and seat streaming.

'You can't sit on that, love,' a voice spoke up from behind her.

'I'll have to,' she said, turning to the stranger who was standing, waiting there. For her.

'I'll wipe it down for you,' he said.

The following day he was outside the shop again. 'Don't you work?' she said.

Over the next few weeks, as he gradually revealed some of who he was and what he had been through, he came each afternoon to pick her up and take her home from work on the back of a motorbike he had bought, and she left her own bike back at the shop. And because her grandfather knew the Eastalls from Penguin, and they could vouch for Alla Bird's family – Tom Eastall saying he had grown up with them and knew Tom and all the brothers and sisters – it was sorted in no time. In 1946, less than twelve months after he had come home, eighteen-year-old Mardi married thirty-year-old Tom Bird quick smart.

Tom wanted it signed, sealed and delivered, almost there and then, and everything was to be perfect; it would surely follow that his life would be the same. He had imagined it for so long.

Mardi looked beautiful in a flowing satin dress, made for her by the dressmaker next door. Her veil draped onto the floor, a river of softness and elegance. Traditional cardboard horseshoes bound in ribbon hung from her wrist, and the several beautifully dressed bridesmaids and their partners completed the party. Tom, handsome and manly and fulfilled, beamed with happiness and pride. It was as perfect as he had wished.

But in no time at all the perfection in his life, and the hope which the prospect of such a life had given him, slowly unravelled and disappeared. He could not escape his years away: they were there, no matter how he tried to ignore them, every day. Mardi was stunned at what confronted her: his nightmares, his mood swings, his frustration with life; the sadnesses and pain he carried. It was all bewildering, especially when she knew he loved her. She walked on eggshells, she tells me now, so many years later. On many nights when Tom came home from work she couldn't look sideways, and could never tell why. And often he was quiet. So quiet. Tom, like so many, was struggling, drowning, in all his memories.

In Launceston Joyce Spencer was woken one night by her husband weeping in his sleep. 'I want to go home!' he said in his nightmare, over and over. 'I want to go home!'

'That's all they wanted when they were over there,' Joyce says. To go home. And even when he was safe in his place, the home he had longed for, Lloyde's nights were spent back in the camps.

In Penguin it was an almost nightly occurrence when, in a panic, Tom would fling Mardi to the floor then shove her under the bed to save her because the Japs were coming – they were! – over Gardiner's Hill, just at the back of where they lived.

Tom, like many of the returned men in town, bought a block of land with his deferred pay. There were many blocks available cheaply for the servicemen. And houses were slowly going up, even when timber was so hard to buy in those years just after the war. But Tom's house was never built. Mardi tried to suggest builders; tried to suggest he apply, like everybody else was doing, to the War Council for a loan. Why not him? But he didn't want to owe money, he said. Or whatever excuse it was this time. Mardi knew in her heart what troubled him, for his health had never been good since his return, and he'd been in and out of the Repat Hospital, tubes poked all over him.

He thought he wouldn't last; thought he had so little time left to live.

———

Bessie arrived in town after the war, an attractive young teacher who laughed readily and whose eyes beamed when she did so. She had not long returned to Tasmania from her own war service, with the RAAF, stationed in Sydney. It hadn't been an easy enlistment, for the Tasmanian Education Department had refused to release her, citing her teaching job as essential to the nation. But, determined, she had disobeyed and simply gone anyway, joining up instead in New South Wales. And at war's end she had delayed her return, wondering if and when she would be arrested by the military police, a thought which was not unfounded. For there were examples all knew about: Fred Smith had even been charged, and fined five pounds, for being AWOL in Launceston after returning from the prison camps in Thailand – because, so he was told, they were still in a state of war, long after the surrender had been declared and all his mates were home.

Bessie was in Penguin to teach at the local school. And boarding at Ruby's house.

It was at one of the weekly dances at the town hall, just across the train line and through the white gates over from Crescent Street – on one of the nights which were always packed, and the music and laughter could be heard well up the street – when Max and Bessie became an item. Bessie could dance well, and enjoyed it. She refused the last dance to a man who couldn't match her ability with the line, 'I've already promised Max', and there it was. They were soon engaged.

The two of them were lying on the grass together talking, over at Bessie's mother's house in Upper Burnie, when Max made his admission to her. He had nightmares, he said. She needed to know what would come.

They married at Devonport, for she was not from Penguin and did not want to be fussed over. She was not from

Tasmania, either: her mother – a woman of strength, just like the two daughters she had raised – had done the unthinkable back then and left her husband, bringing her girls across with her from Victoria. And Bessie, inheriting her mother's resolve, and her disdain of what she called 'show', married Max dressed in a suit and hat she had bought in Sydney, with only a few immediate family members as their guests.

Like Mort before him, Max had married a woman who, apart from knowing her own mind, possessed the strength to deal squarely with whatever her marriage would bring. Like Tom Bird, like Lloyde Spencer, he had been fortunate. They married women of loyalty, understanding and compassion.

For some wives, though, the marriages were too hard, what they faced too difficult. And some of those wives couldn't stay. But Bessie herself had been lucky. The way Mort had lived his life and faced his sorrows had taught Max steadiness. Bessie would never face anger or lashing out. Just grief. Terrible grief, when it rose. Under his smile and his laugh.

22

A small-town life

Bessie learned early that Max didn't like to be alone. Even when gardening on his own, all the way down the back of the big yard of the block of land they bought in Ironcliffe Road – a time when he wanted to be alone, for the quiet – he also needed to know that she was near. The knowledge that she was there, up in the house, calmed and reassured him. He dug his neat rows to the front of all the fruit trees, planted his vegetables and tended them. And had time on his own – of a kind. He needed that time; but he needed her there too, and she understood. She also understood that he needed her with him when he ate a meal, for he couldn't eat alone. She would sit with him while he ate; stay always while he needed her, for she knew from where his needs arose. She was devoted. And determined. And, if it should prove to be, she would have enough strength for the two of them. From the very beginning she sought to shield him from whatever harm or upset she could. She knew his fragility, and allowed him to live his life however he did. She loved him; and he her.

He continued to run his cane furniture business from down at his mother's house in Crescent Street, in the workshop in the shed out the back, on the opposite side to the pigeon loft. It was now providing sufficient income to support the family Max hoped to have one day – perhaps it would be soon. He and Tom Bird were making bets about who would be first to be a father. Max's reputation as a furniture maker of quality chairs and basinettes and prams was spreading along the coast, and with the orders increasing he now took on an assistant: young Barney, who, at fourteen, left school to come and work with him.

They worked side by side, with Max making the frames, and Barney – when Max had taught him – doing the weaving. As they worked they sometimes listened to the radio, sometimes talked. There were times Max would tell him of the camps: the good stories only; the successes; the times they put it over their captors; how they hid all manner of things under their loincloths, diaries, compasses, food. He told him of the kindnesses of the Thai and Chinese people who would press a bit of food, perhaps a lime or banana, in their hands when the prisoners were lined up, and then melt away, back into the jungle. He told him of Weary Dunlop, and how strong he had been, standing up to the Japanese for them.

Sometimes he would count in Japanese. Then, when he would send Barney across the railway tracks to buy some cigarettes from Elvin Ling's hairdressers and tobacconist shop in the main street, he would speak in Malay, tell Barney what to say, and Elvin – himself back from the camps in the jungle – would send a few cheeky comments back in Malay as well. The experiences were always there. Right there.

And there was the time when Max's black and white cocker spaniel, the much-loved Rex, had gobbled up a plastic membership badge which Barney had received from the 7BU kids club, and Barney was upset and crying. Max reached into the small box beside him, in which he kept nails and tacks and other small items, and he fished out whatever he had on hand to replace it: his 2/40th Battalion pin, which he always kept in there, right next to him.

'You take this one,' he said to Barney. For crying distressed him.

———

Max's workshop, so near to the main hub of the town, was in a good position for a man who now needed the close companionship of men. Ike Smith, an old 2/40th mate, would often visit when he had a break from his gang working on the railway lines. Hedley would call in regularly too, to sit and chat, his friendship with Mort living on in the son – and he was also checking on how Max was faring: an old soldier who knew, to a younger soldier just returned. Bill, who had been away in the Air Force, came and visited as well, spending many an hour there, for Max was enjoyable company. They would plan their next move: fishing, or rabbiting, or lobstering. One time they'd gone down lobstering near the big rock in the creek where the deep hole was, the place where they knew you could always find one or two, and there heading up the bank was a big – and happy – lobster, with a ten-inch trout firmly clamped in its claws. He was heading up to the deep hole too, to eat his catch.

'Well, I'll be damned!' said Max. And they watched in admiration. And let him walk on. And wished they had a camera.

Max did not stop working when all his mates dropped by to sit and talk: he had jobs to finish. And he was well used to conversation, asides, gags, funny lines continuing as you worked. In the camps that was how morale had been kept up. Here in Penguin, it was part of who they were; a recognisable Australian character trait which each of them possessed in spades. They looked for the joke in any story, sought always to find the funny side, especially with their mates. And there was much to talk of, and find amusing, in little interwoven Penguin, where everyone knew everyone.

And as Max and Hedley and Bill – Barney, too – were all in the Homing Society together, there were pigeon stories galore to remind the other of. There'd been that time when Charlie Close couldn't get the ring off the pigeon in time and, convinced his bird had set a new record, had tucked the whole bird under his arm and run flat out to where the central timekeeper was, on the foreshore across from the Town Hall, and he'd tripped and killed the bird. And it had been accepted anyway!

There was that fiasco when Mort and Hedley hadn't known whether to laugh or cry: the time when the entrant from Sulphur Creek – in a race for which the pigeons had been liberated from Wynyard – had won with the benefit of a tailwind, an obviously fudged handicap and the services of a professional bike rider to bring the ring to the timekeeper. When it was all worked out, it looked as if the bird had never left the loft, so fast did it appear to have been, and so sneaky had been the means to obtain the handicap. And they all enjoyed the story of Bill that one day when there was a big race on; when, running from his home towards the central time clock, his pigeon's leg ring in his hand – the time allocated to him one minute and 33 seconds, calculated by Max's brother Colin riding a bike down and timing himself – he suddenly found the bloody train across the line and had to go around, tear up along through the railway yard, and behind the Methodist Church, yelling, 'I'm comin' this way!' And then there were stories of the times back when Mort was still alive, when Althea had acted as his runner, and he would find himself consoling his plodding daughter with, 'Well, we were winning for a while there, dear.'

These days Max's time as a runner in the Homing Club were well and truly over: the bullet wound and fracture to his leg had seen to that, though his leg didn't trouble him too badly yet. He'd been advised to have it rebroken and reset on his return, but he'd decided against it. And it had held up pretty well in the football match organised for all the returned blokes who used to play before the war. In a town where so many had gone away, it had been a good turnout on the day. Henry Thomas, of the 2/14 Australian Infantry Battalion, had left his shop in his brother George's hands and fronted up as well.

However, it was in making up the numbers for the Penguin cricket team up at Riana that it had become obvious to Max that his more youthful sporting years were over. His old mate John Midgeley had bowled him three times, to the same spot where the wound had been on his leg. Each time Midge had appealed to old Mr Fielding, who was umpiring that day, but each time Max was ruled not out. And it was on the third ball that Max had crumpled, doubled over, to the ground, and all the blokes had raced and carried him off, for he couldn't walk. And he sat quietly, just watched, for the rest of the game, then went home with the rest. John Midgeley told Mr Fielding, 'Well, if you'd given him out on the first one, I wouldn't 'a bowled the other two!' Max gave cricket away after that; took up lawn bowls instead. The balls there didn't bounce as high off the green. And there weren't as many reminders.

———

Marriage brought Max happiness. It was a proud moment for him when he and Bessie had a son, Robert. He and Bessie, and baby Robert, and Bill and Mary Deverell with their son Butch, would go on picnics down to the beach near Grooms Corner. And they would call in at nights on the few neighbours who had already built up near where they lived, on the road which led up towards the small mountain. When a second son, Mark, came along, Max was thrilled. He loved his two boys following him around, and he and Bill would take them rabbiting on a Sunday morning, the two men and their little country boys, roaming and happy. Max always looked forward to his Sunday mornings.

———

By the time I came into the world as Max and Bessie's third child, two years after my brother Mark had been born, it had been a mere eight years since the Second World War had ended. It was 1953. I grew into a world which seemed as though there had never been a war or, if there had been one, that it had occurred decades before and was far removed from us all. It was possible to believe it had ceased to have an impact in people's lives. But in my house it had never gone away. We grew knowing about war from the day we were born. It lived in the curtains; under the carpet; in every room; in every glance from our parents, as innocently meant as those glances were. For we knew from the time our first cries were hushed, so as not to upset Dad, that our father was wounded in his soul somehow. We could feel it. And we could sense that we could accidentally wound him even further. We grew up trying so hard not to do that.

We knew that sometimes he had sadnesses that came to him. And that often he was not well – especially when we saw him after he'd had what my mother called his 'restless nights'. And yet we saw him smile, and heard his gentle jokes. And when my younger sister came along three years later, and we were growing children together, we would pile into my parents' bed on a Sunday morning and he would amuse us with the stories he made up about little dooks – little ducks. We loved him. And our childhood was full of longing for him to be whole. And happy. All the time.

———

It was around 1954, not long after my birth, when the strain from Max's cane business started becoming too much. Salespeople had taken to visiting him in his workshop; and there was talk of the need to expand, produce furniture for the major department stores in Victoria. With a larger family now, and Bessie precluded from teaching because she had married – a ruling hard to believe for women of a later generation – the financial pressures were rising: he would need bigger orders. There were already weeks at a time when Max would release Barney to work elsewhere – the orders too slow, or the cane hadn't arrived on the boat across Bass Strait, held up as it frequently was and stuck on a wharf somewhere. And there were warnings given, of how you then became a slave to the department stores' demands; of how your life was no longer your own, the hours long and the stresses great. And Max knew that he could not cope with that, for what he needed most was unburdened time after his years as a prisoner of war. And so he took a job – had to – to support the family, a job where the pay would come in and the hours were defined, and gave up the freedom his own small business had afforded him. He became a worker at the Pulp and Paper Mill in Burnie, left for work early, took a Gladstone bag with his lunch in it and came home exhausted. And often had to sit quietly to recover. But he was supporting his family. There are things you have to accept.

———

The town had recovered from the disruption of the war. Buildings were going up. A memorial library had been built on the foreshore, just over from the town hall, one of the few buildings in town with its back to the beach. Bessie was appointed the first librarian, a part-time position only, but it eased the worry with the bills. She would walk there, pushing her cane pram with her baby daughter – me – in it, down the sloping hill of Ironcliffe Road, turn right towards the town, walk over the railway line, until she was at the main street. She would park the pram and me just to the side of the library counter while she worked.

The large numbers of returned men in town had had their own plans for a building too. And they had all pitched in and built a Returned Servicemen's League Club for themselves at the eastern end of town, facing the sea. Men came home from work and would head straight down to the emerging club, see what needed doing next. And gradually, brick by brick, floorboard by floorboard, and wiring, and plumbing – all of it, all done by the men together – they then had a place. A haven. And they certainly made use of it. They needed it. They needed each other. And they came to life. We knew from an early age how our father was but one. And he too came to life when he was with the men.

Saturday night was the big one down at the RSL Club. Crowded and bustling, hilarity rising in waves, subsiding then bursting out again, the music blared into the night sky. And endless dancing, modern waltz, blues, foxtrot: the dance floor was filled with couples flowing and weaving through the others. Ex-POWs and servicemen, all with their wives, and social members of the club too. It was so popular that

Tom Mainwaring, an ex-POW, had to go down early at five o'clock and grab a table for his group to make sure they would get one: for his own wife, Edna; Max and Bessie; Max and Betty Dazeley; Earl Tregenna and his wife, Sue. And others who joined them. Tom Mainwaring wasn't to leave the table – that was his group's instruction – until someone else from the group came; he just had to sit and wait.

Max loved those nights. He and Bessie would dance. And he would get up and sing; so many of the men did: Basil Griffin, Max Dazeley, and Max and more. Max favoured the World War I songs, for they were the songs he knew when he went to war. The POWs first heard the new music and the World War II songs only when the war was over. Bessie didn't go down to the club, to the dances, as often as the others, for she didn't drink. When she did go she would instead sit with a block of chocolate in front of her – which Max would buy for her – to accompany her glass of water. But it didn't matter: the music and the company were what it was about.

The men were proud of the RSL Club they had built themselves, and it became a big part of many men's lives. It was the focus of the town for so many and the lifeline for some. You would always find a serviceman there, and the good cheer which people were ready to impart as soon as they walked in the door meant that the memories would be pushed to the side. For some, life became worth living – while they were there. There was companionship of the kind that could make a difference. And it was especially important on Anzac Day. The men, all well dressed and well combed, would gather there, meet after the Dawn Service – that time of a quiet so filled and heavy your heart almost breaks from the weight. It seems spirits float in the air at these services. It was just about the most important time of the year.

At the RSL Club the men would have a few while they told their stories to each other and remembered their mates who 'are still over there', and waited for the next service at 11 a.m., the service where just about the whole town, including the whole school, joined in the parade. The march came down the hill from where the cemetery was, past St Stephens Church, over the small bridge and along the main street. The beach and the sea and the huge sky were to one side; the railway line, Methodist Church and shops to the other. The march filled the entire street. Wreaths were laid at the War Memorial, which had been moved down from its old position on the hill to the foreshore opposite the town hall; and the bugle would begin, crystal clear and haunting, high above the town. The only sound. The only thing that mattered. The last post. And the whole town would be silent. And choking away the tears.

At home I always looked forward to the night once a week when my father would go for an hour or two to the club. We would wait to hear his car come down the driveway. And in he would come, pleased to see us, a box of Smarties each for the children, a block of chocolate for our mother.

And a *War Cry*, the Salvation Army magazine. No-one had to read it. But he bought it every week. One of his rituals. Our house felt fuller, complete, when he was home. And our mother would see to all his needs.

On some Saturday nights at home, my mother and father would have his mates and their wives over for a supper evening around the fire, and my sister and I would be in our beds listening as laughter and singing rang out from our sitting room, for we owned a pianola. And we would listen to Dad and all his party belting out the songs: 'Roll out the Barrel', 'The last time I saw Paris', 'When Irish eyes are smiling'. It was wonderful to hear.

And on a Sunday morning more would come, among them Earl Tregenna, Bill Whittle, Bill Ray, Arch Bryden, and Max Dazeley. More singing and a few beers. They would arrive while we were at Sunday school, and we would return to find them there. My mother would be cooking the roast while the men entertained each other; my brothers playing out in the yard or at friends' houses along our road. My father was happiest at those times: unabashed singing with the blokes brought him joy. So, too, did his family; his garden; an aviary with budgies he had by then; his activities in the town; and, in the summer, his Saturday bowls. He did not need or want anything more. He had his freedom, and a few simple pleasures. And he was alive. It felt as if he threw himself into those times, for he knew how precious they were. Life could be taken away: he knew that; he loved what he had.

Sometimes I knew my mother would have liked him with her more, for life could be lonely for the wife of an ex-POW who needed his mates near. Many times I knew her stressed with what she carried, with four children and often on her own. But she knew he couldn't take many hours of the ways of children, the squabbles, the shouting, the playing and the squeals, even of delight. For his nerves, after a day at work, were stretched tight. And the house would be tense, my mother on edge, in case we made too much noise – or any. She encouraged him and wanted him to take part in the simple things he did; for his sake she sacrificed much of herself in her early married life, to try to make him whole. And every morning she was concerned: how would he be today, his nerves and his health.

My father was promoted fairly rapidly at the Pulp and Paper Mill. He was now in charge of groups of men, working out in the open. Just like at the camps. I didn't know about the groups, or that he was in charge, but even as a child I would tell myself that this job would help keep him happy because there were men for him to be with. But often he would return home so tired, and we could see he was not well. My mother would sit him down and look after him. And we would quietly come, softly tell him our news for the day, worry that we had worried him, then leave him.

Sometimes my father would come home with small gifts for us that he had bought from men at work who had made them. One time he came with wooden jewellery boxes, one for my sister and one for myself. He had two, and we were to choose. My sister chose the one I wanted, the one with the hinge which allowed the top to lever back. I died a thousand deaths as I asked him if I could have one with a hinge too, if he could change it. He had given them to us with such love, wanted so much to please us. And I knew that. Yet I wanted another. And, child that I was, my desire overrode the truth that I did indeed know, even as I spoke: that any gift from him was enough to receive.

There were more financial pressures, for wages were not high in Tasmania. And my father would sometimes have some orders for cane furniture which he would gladly accept. He had built himself a workshop down the back near the vegetable patch, and I often used to wander through and just look around at this other world – see the cane soaking and the frames ready. I thought it sad his business was no longer viable, and the freedom he needed gone. All through my childhood I never forgot that my father had been a prisoner of war of the Japanese. I could never forget it. I knew at least some of what the men had suffered, for there was a book in the house with my father's photo in it, and drawings of men being punished. And suffering. My father did not look in it. And I could hardly open it, it made me feel so ill, but I would race past the pages to find the photo and read the caption:

Sgt Max Butler, a Tasmanian who demonstrated understanding leadership during days of adversity on the Mergui Road. And feel for him. And not know. Yet understand some of it, for it was there before me when my father was not well. And over the years, who he was and what he had been through had become part of who I was: I was of my father, of my family. We all were. We were of the grief.

I knew there was a shortage of money. Sometimes he would take vegetables to work to sell them, and keep a neat list of his sales; add them up. One time it was lettuces, and the list was lengthy: many 3ds in a long line. New clothes and shoes were rare, for my mother – who had lived through the Depression – was strict about such things, if we already had even just one. But every year one of my mother's friends, whom we called Auntie, would give my sister and me a new dress each to wear at the Anniversary celebration in the Methodist Church where we attended Sunday School. And we would show our father, who would nod approvingly. But I think it caused him pain; embarrassment.

One time I saw a pair of shoes in the window of the shoe shop in the main street: red with thin, black plaited straps across. I had never seen such shoes before, and such beauty I had never owned. I asked my mother if I could have them, and she explained that we couldn't afford them, and that I didn't need them. For there were other expenses which came first. The next day I pleaded, and had the same response. And the following day, when my father came home from work, he was carrying a shoebox. Smiling his kind, work-tired smile. Those shoes sit shining on a pedestal in my heart.

We had a normal Tasmanian small-town life. We would visit our grandmother and our Auntie Althea, and other of my father's relatives. And sometimes our father would take us on day trips, Mum in the front seat of the car with him, and him greeting every driver of every car coming the other way with a friendly salute – the roads were not crowded back then – in a lifting of his two forefingers from the steering wheel in a nonchalant, elegant Australian way. It was a *g'day mate* to them all, for he was a man of the times back then in Tasmania, of community and care. On those trips all four of us – my two brothers and my sister and myself – were squashed in the back. Hardly moving. For sudden noises from behind unnerved him. I'm not sure how he felt when my sister threw up down his back.

It was his response to noise and sudden movements – the knife wound it looked as if they caused him when they came – that made me sneak inside the day I fell while riding my bike on the road, after my mother had expressly forbidden me to ride there because of my inexperience. She had been right and I had fallen, the skin hanging from my shins, the blood and stripped flesh bright red and copious – at least to a child's eye.

I sat at the end of the bath, put the plug in and ran the water, intending to clean the evidence away. But when the water hit the exposed flesh, the shock and pain hit. I screamed. And screamed. And when my mother and father and brother raced to the bathroom and appeared at the door, I felt a knife wound to my own soul. For I saw my father's face: the fear exposed, the shock there, the suffering I no doubt gave him. And more nights when he would be back in the horror of the camps. My mother was not pleased with me. But whatever she said to me, it would never match the guilt and anguish that I felt.

———

Max and Betty Dazeley moved into Penguin the same year as the RSL Club was being built, Max in time to volunteer to help. The Dazeleys ran the garage in the main street, and sold cars, many cars, to the ex-POWs, and were a part of the town in no time once they had bought a house. Max D soon knew everyone around, joined in the town's activities and became one of my father's close friends — for they were similar, both of them men who were gentle, and both gentlemen in their demeanour.

Max D and Betty lived in a house out the back of their business, which was not far along the main street from where Bill Gandy's saddlery had been. Bill Gandy had had to leave the town he had been so much a part of several years before: age had caught up with him and he had moved to live with his daughter. In 1940 he had finally been given a pension to help him – one pound a week. But his sacrifice for his son had paid off: after his naval service John Gandy was now working in a bank. He would have a good life, just as his father had wished. My father ran into John in Burnie every now and then, and they would chat in the street. John never mentioned – for it would not have been right – how he'd been at the Burnie RSL one evening and heard how Max Butler had been so good with his men. And how he'd saved many lives.

John had been surprised by that. For although Max had been a friend, John had never thought him a leader. But John now knew that you can never really tell about a man. There were many stories – and so many more that people would never hear – about ordinary men, just like my father, who did what they did, and then returned to their ordinary lives. One man John played tennis against, Mark Crisp from Burnie, who had been a prisoner of war on the Thai–Burma Railway, had volunteered to help in the cholera area of a camp. Mark had risked his life every day he was there, nursing the men, helping them die; helping the far fewer number who would come through, being with them. Every day in the midst of so little hope, and so much suffering.

Courage comes in many forms. The courage of those cholera sufferers; and the courage, and love, of those who risked all for them. Humanity in the midst of inhumanity, from ordinary man to ordinary man: part of, and the heart of, the story which often goes unheard. What my father did, what Mark Crisp did, shows that you can never tell, you do not know, about a man – or woman – until everything is told.

23

Too late for goodbye

The world was changing in the 1960s, and I was aware of it. My father would bring a Melbourne newspaper home each evening in his Gladstone bag, and as I could read well – tutored as I had been by my school teacher mother (who had by then returned to teaching) – I would pore over it. It introduced me to a world different from that of my safe, pretty town: people missing, strikes and murders, all of it strange and somewhat grimy. But the Kennedys didn't feel like that. There was a lightness about JFK and Jackie. I loved to read about them – that is, as much as I could understand.

It was when my father brought home a television set, and carried it into the sitting room beaming with delight at his surprise for us, that I fell fully under the Kennedy spell. I would watch the news and see them, and somehow I sensed hope, although I didn't know what for. And JFK seemed a bit like my dad: decent and honest and warm. And I liked his smile.

I had just turned ten when President Kennedy was assassinated. I watched the television coverage of that day in Dallas, 22 November 1963; saw Jackie throw herself across the President to shield him, to take the next bullet should it come. I knew instinctively what she had done; her impulse; why she did it. I kept all the newspaper spreads – pages and pages of black-and-white photos. I could see the blood, and her distress. And her heroism. I wept over those pages; wept for what I knew. For she shielded him out of love. I knew that love. I knew the heroism of the men who shielded and tried to save others when they were prisoners of war; I knew it in the sacrifice of my mother at home; knew in my soul how my father would sacrifice himself to save us, if ever that day would arise. And I saw the faces of the men when they were together. I had grown knowing, and feeling, something far bigger than the confines of a family.

But Jackie had not saved him. The President, her husband, had died. My nights were disturbed – every single one – for the next twelve months, as I cried myself to sleep.

I did not realise for decades how intense my childhood had been. But I did know how strange it felt in other people's houses – the houses of families whose fathers had not been prisoners of the Japanese. In fact, I hardly knew what to say when I was in such houses. Their lives were so different, as if they didn't know what existed in the world: such utter brutality, over so many years, and the suffering which it caused. And they did not know that among them lived men – magnificent, ordinary men – who had helped men. And they did not know of magnificent, ordinary men who had tried so hard but not made it home. The air in my house was filled with it. There was an emptiness, for me, in other homes.

There were, though, other people in my town who understood that intensity, and who sensed what lay at the essence of it. They were the people so close to it, included in much of it, who could never fully take a part for themselves. They were the few with the grief that came; the guilt they felt at never having gone to the war.

Max Dazeley was eighteen – too young, in fact – when the war finally ended, but even though he had tried to join (his employer stymieing it) the guilt of not playing his part has never left him these decades later. 'I should have tried harder', he softly tells me, for other young men lied and put their age up, and were accepted.

At funerals – and they were regular – those who were not servicemen would have to sit further back, not up the front in the pews reserved for those who had served, even though at all other times those men mixed freely together. And there were specific functions and days around the town where participation was limited too; occasions such as Diggers' Day at the bowls club. My father had once called out to John Ingram, an older man who had emigrated to Australia and whose son was now the local chemist, 'You in the service, John, when you were in England?'

'Ooh,' old Mr Ingram replied, 'not really. But I did have a little bit of time in the home guard. You know – just weekends.'

'Oh, that's near enough!' said my father. 'You can come and play at our Diggers' Day!'

Max D, who loved his bowls like so many in the town and was there on the green on any other day, did not have a similar hazy link which could be used – otherwise I'm sure my father would have swung it – and could not attend. It was on those days, the ones when he had to consciously stay away – aware all through the hours as they passed, of what was taking place just round the corner, and that he was excluded – that the feelings arose again. But it was the Anzac Day parade, the slow, lengthy march which passed by every year, right out the front of his business on the main street, which brought all the suppressed regrets to the surface. He would stand inside the garage looking out as it moved along, and his guilt came, strong and too, too sad. Overwhelming. He could never bring himself to attend the day, all of it a torture. Max D was close enough, knew enough about the men together, to *see* them. His was a sad burden in a town like Penguin.

My father, though, was doing all he could to simply live lightly, to enjoy all he could. And he was fortunate to have come home to a place like this small coastal town. For there were many in areas and cities who lived lives separated from men who knew what they had been through. And many were struggling possibly far more than my father. One man from New South Wales whom Bill Coventry cared deeply for, and whom Bill had helped to survive in the camps, had come home, had four children, seemed to be coping – but then drowned himself in the bath. In Launceston Lloyde Spencer told the wife of a 2/40th man who kept taking off, kept running away for months at a time, 'He's only running away from himself. He'll be back.'

Lloyde himself would not accept a promotion at work because he feared he was no longer up to the task, worried that he would forget things; thought it a great kindness when the men with him reminded him about what needed to be done. In his family his wife, Joyce, always had the children bathed and in their pyjamas at five o'clock every night, so they could be put to bed and not disturb their father. And the children grew up being told that Dad wasn't very well, or he had tummy trouble. *And you need to be quiet.* Sometimes when things got too much for Lloyde he'd march up and down beside the house. Just march. It calmed him. And there were men from Launceston and further south whose doctors sent them for electric shock treatment to try to remove the memories.

The men from the coast instead had each other, although that didn't take it all away. But they looked out for the others. In Penguin, they worried for Merv Blight for a while. He was too quiet. And they were relieved when finally he married, and he seemed then 'to be all right'.

But men were dying, the numbers dwindling away – had been since the war – just like after the First World War, unnoticed. My father was unaware but Major Vincent Bennett, the doctor from the top camp at Mergui Road, died in 1962 aged only fifty-two, from causes attributed to his time as a POW. He had married, had four children and gone into private practice in Southern Rhodesia, looking after labour forces on farms and mines. Photos of him with his family show a far happier man than the one just returned from the war. He had found contentment. His son Patrick was just a child and away at boarding school when his father died. In the years after his father's death Patrick would look out the bus window and hope that perhaps he would see his father somewhere there, just there, in the crowd.

I don't know if my father worried for himself.

———

Max D and Betty were often at the receiving end of my father's determination to take each ounce of enjoyment he could find, for they were, like him, easygoing and tolerant.

There was the time that Max D, in a deep sleep, was lifted out of his bed, carried to his own lounge room – where a fire now suddenly blazed high – and a beer was ceremoniously placed in his hand, Earl Tregenna and my father having decided that he needed a late-night chat. There was also the time when again Max D was carried out from his bed, this time to find they had come with a goose, which they sat up in the chair next to him, and every time it quacked someone would casually reach over and close its beak, as if it should wait its turn to speak. No-one locked their doors back then in country towns. And Max D enjoyed the mischief making which occurred at the time when strong comments were emanating from the Council about the need to deal with the ragwort weed in the district. Not long after, ragwort suddenly appeared one morning in the newly planted garden in the front of the Memorial Library – courtesy of Max Butler and Earl Tregenna, both councillors at the time; they thought it a great joke. (But they could probably never match the impact of that time a few years back when Dick Oliver had decided to relive some of the larrikinism of his youth. Mounted on a horse, dressed in the khakis of his old 3rd Light Horse from World War I, complete with slouch hat and ostrich feathers, he had – after leading a special parade through town with Guy Harrington – decided to ride right through the Neptune Hotel.)

Since he had first moved to the town Max D had been aware of how my father grabbed at life. On the usual days at the bowls club, when Max D attended, he would hear my father down the end of the green reacting to every bowl as it was delivered: the delight in a good shot, the cry that went up with near misses, the happiness there in all the sounds. He would hear his laugh pealing out, and thought how much my father loved to be alive and back home in his safe small town.

And we knew that too. It's just that we saw the man inside as well. There was the time when my father's brother Colin, a soft, quiet man who was well liked at his job as barman at the Neptune Hotel but who had not coped with all he had seen of the war in New Guinea – and sometimes drank to forget – had fallen in the street. My father found him lying in the gutter. It was too much for Dad, the sorrow gone one step too far. He came home and sat in his chair in front of the fire in the kitchen. He put his head down and wept. My mother tried to console him. I believe my father wept for far more than his brother.

———

As the decade moved on, more changes were afoot. Decimal currency was coming; the old money of pounds, shillings and pence was to be replaced by dollars and cents in February 1966, and the metric measurement system was to replace the imperial. I had just turned twelve and couldn't wait to see the new money. I knew the world was shifting rapidly, could even see it in the advertisements in the Melbourne newspaper – the beautiful, stylised and elongated line drawings down the sides of each page to show the new fashions.

There had been changes at home for me, as well. With my mother back teaching – she had been working for a few years now, even though it wasn't until 1966 that married women were officially given the right to permanent employment – my parents were coping financially. Which meant that every now and then I would have some new clothes. My father particularly liked one of my dresses, a simple and short shift dress – one of the new styles of that decade – with its azure blue background and pair of large palm trees emblazoned on the front. It pleased me when he approved. But he approved of most things that we did. He had even defended my choice when I sang a Seekers song, 'A World of our Own', at the Methodist anniversary concert and presentation night, where we were all on display on the tiered platform up the front of the church. The organisers had expressed concern about the songs the young people were selecting to sing each year in this world of change: they weren't quite appropriate. There had been many *Sound of Music* songs sung that night too; I had sung one as well. Perhaps more variety could be considered, it was politely suggested, and not just the current fad. My father, who especially liked the Seekers, said I could sing what I liked. (Many years before, in the exact same spot, Jack Gandy had sung 'Twenty-seven Ginger-headed Sailors', complete with hornpipe and ropes.)

I had been thrilled that my father was there. He had seated himself close to the front and in the middle. To see him in this setting was strange, special, as he was not a churchgoer. But he was not going to miss it. He had already missed my no doubt stunning performance as a princess earlier in the year over at Ulverstone High, in the school production of *The King and I*, a musical which I loved – but set in Siam and containing the suggestion of torture, a flogging and a drowning, plus people who are slaves. My sister, who was eight and with not much more to her than skin and bones, had collapsed early in the performance from the heat and stuffiness. My father had carried her – his thin, unconscious daughter – down the aisle and out to the car, carefully placing her on the back seat, and looking after her. Then, with my mother, they drove home to Penguin. I do not know what the combination of all those occurrences brought forth for him. And I did not know about Siam. At the end of the night I left the dressing room with great expectations of the accolades to come and searched for my family. And stood in the blackness of the car park, staring and confused, my excitement long gone. There were no cars. A man tapped me on the shoulder and said at last he had found me, that my mother had asked him to take me home. My father had another 'restless night'. My mother had been anxious over it all. And my father had not seen me princess-like.

My mother came to watch me on her own on a different night.

———

Several people in town now had tape recorders. Ian Wallace, one of my father's friends, had been up at our house with his, interviewing us all for fun. My job was to play the same piece of music over and over on the piano for the background music. But I nearly lost my place when my father said his favourite sport was chasing the chooks around the backyard. It was the funniest thing I had ever heard. You think those things of the people you love.

It was school holidays. And my father was to soon go into the Repat Hospital, to have his knee seen to. Sometimes he wasn't well generally, but we were used to him spending a day or two in bed; then he would 'come good'. He'd garden quietly; perhaps come and get us to go down the back and see some ducklings or chickens; clean out the aviary which housed his budgies and the quails; stake the beans growing up the side of the two-roomed play house he had built for us and which I had commandeered for myself – it made a good library or post office for me to entertain my friends in the street. Sometimes he would pile us into the car – our quietness started once he was in the car too – so we could have our photo taken up on the top of the hill looking out to sea, the panoramic coastal view in the background. It was actually a spot in the cemetery, but the graves seemed a fair distance away. We thought nothing of it.

There were so many small-town things he found, and loved, to do. But a weariness was showing, even more than before. And I knew his hearing was going. Perhaps it was because Max Dazeley had his own small business – along with the memory of the freedom my father had once had – that the idea occurred to him to consider buying the local newsagency. It was an idea which had taken hold of him for several years now. And he would have liked to leave his job. But the financial insecurity, after the years they'd been through, worried my mother. My father accepted what she said, gave up the thought and continued taking his Gladstone bag – and recovering every night when he came home. He still didn't mention the word 'disappointment'.

The New Year's Eve celebration of 1966 at the Penguin RSL Club had been its normal bouncing, boisterous affair. My mother had attended with my father, and Max and Betty Dazeley and all the group had had a great night. Then they all continued down to the Dazeleys' house right there in the main street. My father was in fine form, chirpy and witty, and with the Dazeleys' new tape recorder in his hands he went around each person of the more than a dozen there and told them something about themselves, sometimes something funny, sometimes something real. They watched and listened and laughed. And were enthralled. *Oh Max, you're so funny.*

In the long Christmas school holidays I often walked down to the beach near the clumps of big rocks, just along from the Memorial Library, for a day of sunbaking and swimming in the sea. I would go by myself. This was the beach where my father would sometimes take us netting when he saw the conditions were right, those special still evenings when the sky and the town, the rocks and the beach, were all bathed in a magical soft glow; and in the twilight one of us would sweep, as noiselessly and as smoothly as possible, out into the sea in a crescent shape trailing a net, then walk into the shore, the net mostly full of fish. The stillness and the smooth sea, the lapping of the water, the sometimes streaked golden sky, and us in hushed tones moving and working together, spoke to me of purity, heaven sent, even at that age. So when I went to the beach by myself I would clamber over the rocks and walk around to the rockeries if the tide was out, just to have a look. And a think. In January Mrs Zoe McCarthy from across the road came to ask my mother if I would like to accompany her family and her daughters, Jan and Catherine, on a picnic to Brickmakers Beach, further along the coast to the west, I was inclined but not particularly anxious to go. For I had a beach I could go to by myself. And my father was in bed. Not well. It felt strange leaving him there to go away.

My mother and Mrs McCarthy were chatting out the front near the road and called me to them. When I said I wanted to go inside, to say goodbye to Dad, my mother said he would understand, and to hurry along, to not keep them waiting, for he would still be there when I returned.

It was just after lunch when Tom Bird walked into the bowls club. Mardi was pleased he had gone. He was always better if he had something to keep his mind occupied, and especially if there were enough of the men there, and they had an afternoon on the green.

'What are you doing here?' they said as soon as he walked in.

'Why wouldn't I be?' he said.

'You died this morning!'

'No bloody way! I didn't.'

'Well if you didn't, who did?'

'I don't know, but I'll soon find out,' he said.

Up at the doctor's surgery Betty Dazeley was sitting in the waiting room when another person arrived for their allotted appointment.

'The doctor's late,' they were told, 'because Max Butler died this morning.'

Betty didn't believe them. People got things wrong in small towns, she knew.

'No! He couldn't have done,' she called out – he had looked so well a week ago. 'Not Max Butler! It can't be!'

But it was.

'Yes. Bessie's husband,' came the reply.

Betty couldn't bring herself to lay him out as they asked her to.

———

I spent some time that day at Brickmakers Beach walking by myself, even though the McCarthys were all my friends and kind to me; but I was ready, wanting to go home and the sky was now too grey for me.

We drove home, and as we came up Ironcliffe Road Mrs Dick, Mrs McCarthy's mother who lived along the road too, flagged us down. She had been waiting. Looking out her window for some hours. I thought it unusual, and that someone must have died, and was glad it was nothing to do with me. The adults spoke, and Mrs McCarthy opened the door and took a seat in the back next to me. My mind was suddenly blank. Whatever was about to happen, well – it couldn't be.

———

The blinds were drawn, every one, when we pulled up outside my comfortable weatherboard house which my father and his friends had built; the house now full of people who were strangers to me. My mother was waiting, and took me by the hand to where we could be alone, away from them all. My heart pounded. None of it made sense. It felt like I was on a road, one I couldn't get off; I had to just keep on going. And up the passage near the cupboard where my father kept the ginger beer he made – and which frequently exploded, causing us to race to check how many bottles had gone this time – she told me, 'Dad died this morning.'

I grabbed at her, and she held me, holding back the crying she would not allow herself to do, not in front of people – these people who, as helpful as they may have been, had taken over our house. But our dad had never really felt as if he had been ours alone.

She was waiting, it seemed, for what would come.

'But you didn't let me say goodbye!' were the words I could not help.

She was ready: 'I know,' she said.

There was only sadness for us there. She blamed herself. I know she did. And I blamed her too, anger in amongst my grief, until I grew and learned to understand. And felt remorse.

So many layers of longing, regrets, grief and incomprehension. It was how we had lived our lives, all the way through.

———

My dad was forty-seven. Many former prisoners of war along the coast died at forty-seven. Others worried as the age drew near. 'If I can just make it past forty-seven,' they told their wives.

———

The RSL moved into action, as they had certainly had enough practice by now, and the funeral was the very next day, just as Mort's had been.

I wasn't allowed to attend the funeral, a standard practice in my town, an attempt to protect the children. But my mother arranged for me to walk to the church with Mrs McCarthy and her daughters, and watch from outside. I chose a dress fit for my father's funeral: my azure blue shift dress with the large palm trees emblazoned on the front. I was determined. For my father would have approved.

We walked down the sloping hill where my mother used to wheel me in the pram to the library, along the road behind the railway station in front of the creek. And we stopped and stood, and looked up the hill towards the cemetery, but we did not go over the bridge. For we could see: a coffin being carried out, shiny and red–brown. And men, many, outside St Stephens Church.

I watched, and wanted this to be only a dream from which I would awake. But what I wanted most was to see the man inside that coffin.

He was buried in the cemetery on the top of the hill looking out to sea, in the very spot where he used to seat us, those days he would pile us into the car, drive us to the cemetery and with the panoramic view in the background take our photo, his four children, us together.

———

My father's death set us adrift. Our focus taken, in an instant. He had gone, and so had the men, the singing, the Sunday cheer, the fishing. The dancing for my mother. The worrying we did for my father. Now there was just the grief. And emptiness, loneliness, when the house had been so full. His workshop stayed as it was, everything in its place, for years.

My mother continued teaching, and took up many interests, filled her life: travel, bushwalking, badminton, volunteer work. But too many times she would just sit and stare. And decades later, on one of the few occasions when we would mention his name – for the grief our mother carried felt so raw and deep we couldn't bear to bring it to the surface, it clawed my soul to see her, our controlled and strong mother, cry – she told me, quietly, almost a confession, that she regretted not allowing my father to buy the newsagency. Perhaps she blamed herself, thought he may have lived longer. She had tried so hard. Heartbreaking. We saw all that.

For no matter what she had done, how she sought to shield him, as happened to Jackie Kennedy, her husband had died.

24

Unsung ordinary men

'There is no glory in being a POW,' Ron Cassidy tells me.

It is a statement which contains the huge well of disappointment that the prisoners of war of the Japanese felt – and that those who remain still feel – about the treatment they have received over the years, their sacrifice not included as part of the Australian war effort, their sacrifice often not acknowledged at all. The story of the war is about soldiers, heroes, not prisoners who are a sideline to the main event.

When the prisoners of war came home at the end of the war, they were an embarrassment. No-one knew what to do with them.

'No-one wanted to know us,' Bill says about coming home to Victoria.

'We soon found out,' says Fred Smith in Tasmania.

And the problems began: the doctors who didn't understand or know; the search the men often had to undertake, for years, to find one who did; the problems to settle down to the humdrum, the mundane; the body breaking down; the memories. And the search they faced to find meaning, a will to live, in the life they lived back here. For they had to do it firstly in the face of many people not understanding so horrific an ordeal; and perhaps far harder to face was a country's denial of their worth.

'Ah, so you raised the white flag,' said a fellow worker to Fred Smith.

'We had been on a hospital ship,' Harry Medlin told Hank Nelson, 'and we were made to feel a little bit guilty that we had not conducted ourselves properly by capitulating; that we should have fought on and been knocked off – for what purpose eludes me. On the ship there was a broadcast to ex-Japanese prisoners of war telling them that they should not feel guilty, that their country was proud of them, and [all] this [sort of] crap.

'We had no guilt. We were the ones let down, even betrayed.'

Harry Medlin had been on Timor. There was reason to feel betrayed. And so, too, for the soldiers in Malaya and Singapore. For the fall of Singapore had been placed on the backs of the Australian soldiers, Britain doing a fine line in passing the buck. And in Australia surrender is not the Australian way, so the legend goes. The ex-POWs came home to a country that didn't want to know.

Historians Christopher Bayly and Tim Harper hold the view that '[t]he global publicity of the fighting record of ANZACs was a matter for resentment by British officers, and may explain in part the scapegoating of the Australian troops and their commanders after the fall of Singapore'. And in Britain in 1993, papers dealing with the defence of Malaya and Singapore were finally released – twenty years beyond the normal release date for official files. What they contained was too sensitive. 'The newly published government papers confirm,' said an article in *The Independent*, 'that British efforts to scapegoat Australian forces and the Governor of the Straits Settlements for the most humiliating debacle in the history of the Empire could well have been motivated by a wish to deflect attention from Whitehall's far greater dereliction of duty.'

———

In 2010 I travelled to Adelaide to attend a memorial service for the nurses who were massacred at Bangka Beach, machine gunned by the Japanese as they waded into the sea, as they had been ordered. Only Vivian Bullwinkel survived. Harry Medlin, whose brother had died while a POW in the camps and who also had been a friend of Ms Bullwinkel, was giving the address that day. I attended a lunch he organised at which an ex-POW made a short speech. He reminded those there that what one of their departed comrades had most desired was the vindication of the 8th Division. Ex-POWs were more than just prisoners. But mostly it was only their families who knew that. It's the men and the families who feel it still.

———

In 2009, sixty-seven years after the 81 officers and 1505 men of Sparrow Force faced more than 20 000 well-trained, well-equipped Japanese soldiers on Timor, Fred 'Lofty' Smith – who had been a young reinforcement thrown without much training into the shock of the battle – returned to Timor. His nephew, David Hepworth, took him there: along with friends David Cunnington, Robert de la Rie and Kevin Parker, they had spent over $8000 of their own money to restore the memorial at Usau Ridge, where the bayonet charge had taken place.

Fred saw the shops, which hadn't changed much, perhaps updated a little; had a look at the seawall where they had to unload Japanese stores from the barges when they were prisoners; was horrified at the sight of the once-pristine Usapa Besar beach, now used as a dumping ground for rubbish by visiting fishermen; saw the Champlong hospital, which appeared not to be in use; had a look at the limestone caves where the Japanese had machine guns set up; and went looking for relatives of a Timorese man.

Germais, the head man of his village, had organised his people to hide and help twenty-three American airmen to escape – a perilous six weeks in which four of the men died as they waited for the submarine sent for them to be able to safely stay on the surface for long enough. Germais was then tortured by the Japanese. At the end of the war the Australian government had presented an RAAF citation to him for his brave deeds during the war, and promised him forty pounds – which he never received. Using an interpreter and a taxi driver, Fred and the younger men found Germais's two sons. They were given the money. And there was great excitement.

But it was at the memorial service – one they organised themselves in front of the memorial which they had paid to have restored – when Fred became a soldier once more. A group of local Timorese stood in the pouring rain and watched as the young Australian men each took a role. David Hepworth read the campaign history of Sparrow Force; David Cunnington recited the ode to the fallen and departed comrades; Robert de la Rie read a poem written by an ex-POW. Fred, wearing a slouch hat the boys had given him, felt compelled – he just walked forward in the rain, up the steps. And saluted.

'I thought of all my mates, the fellas,' he tells me. 'It was very emotional.'

The young men all cried at the sight. And for Fred something lifted right then, he says; something rose from his shoulders.

'It was the proudest moment for me,' he says. To recognise 'the fellas who were left there.'

———

No-one has forgotten, even all these years later. In 2002 the younger brother of a prisoner of war who didn't come home remembered, as he did every year, that it would soon be his brother's birthday. Len Andrews's brother George died on Sumatra three months before the war ended. And now it was a milestone year: George would have been eighty. Len has never forgotten George, in all the years. He placed calls, he sought information, he wondered how to place flowers on his brother's grave. And the Australian Military Attaché did it for him, placed the flowers with ceremony, and sent photos to him. Len was deeply moved, and grateful. A brother never ceases to be a brother.

———

When my mother passed away many decades after my father – and after we had scattered her ashes just over the hill from where my father had been born – it took us many months before we could bring ourselves to go through her possessions. It was hard to believe that after living in such a connected fashion – our family life always in the shadow of what the Japanese treatment of our father had delivered upon him, upon us – that she was no more. For she had tried so hard for all of us.

It was my sister who opened the writing desk, when we discovered the letter with the list of deaths on the back, the letter which so shocked us. She was eight when she saw my father die, saw him collapse and my mother try to catch him, hold him at the side of the bed.

'Oh, you silly thing,' my mother had said to him, to try to make light of him knocking over the side table. And then she realised. 'Run!' she said to my sister. 'Go and get Mr Mainwaring.' And my sister ran, not knowing that it was already too late.

It took some time before we discovered just what that letter was. My father, as the sergeant – for no other officers had been sent, a deliberate policy by the Japanese to prevent official witnesses to their treatment of the prisoners – had been in charge of the Australian contingent on Mergui Road, and it had been his duty to record and report the Australian deaths. The letter, written to James Wemyss by his wife, Janet, was the only paper my father could find at the 12 Kilo camp at Mergui Road. James Wemyss died on the 8th of August, 1945, ten days before they knew that the war had ended. Janet would never know how her husband had carried that letter with him all the terrible years, no doubt hoping, yearning, to see his new son, trying to make it to the end. Who knows how many times he read it? I don't know which is sadder to read: the letter or the list of so many deaths.

———

Time moves on, as it always will do. Penguin is still a town of beauty with the shops facing out to sea, overhung with a huge sky. And it remains a place where a sense of peace reigns. But there have been changes as the years have passed. The RSL Club, which was so much part of the town when I was growing up, has been sold. No longer does the sound of old-time band music echo from that building up the street, nor waves of laughter push out into the air, rising and falling, accompanied by the clinking of glasses. Nor are there cars aplenty parked nearby in front of the sea, which is often silver speckled in the moonlight. The Saturday nights at the club when you couldn't get a table unless you sat and waited – these are no more. The RSL Club now meets in a new, larger complex up on the road towards the small mountain. And there are few from my father's generation left in the town now. Many who live there – and along the coast – no longer know the stories of the towns, the men, the courage, the sacrifice they made, the struggle of the families. For it is a story that is fading away: that story of courage and sacrifice and endurance beyond belief, of those ordinary Australians from their ordinary backgrounds – farm labourers, cabinet-makers, concrete workers, factory hands, chaff cutters, miners, fishermen, train drivers, quarrymen, drovers, sawmill hands, textile workers, orchard workers, butchers' assistants, teachers, electricians, bread carters, bootmakers, builders, drapers, plumbers, shop assistants, policemen; that story which continues, even now, to play itself out. I have come to believe that for many of these unsung ordinary men who were not heroes, the word 'hero' will never be enough.

List of POWs

Australian survivors of Mergui Road recovered from Prachaup Khiri Khan Area at the end of the war:

NX/7780	Pte Ambrose	2/20 Bn *
TX/4272	Cpl K Anders	2/4 CCS
VX/33338	Gnr S W Batson	4 A/T Regt
NX/6932	Pte R Bland	2/19 Bn
NX/36994	Pte C D Boden	2/19 Bn
TX/5384	Pte L Bonney	2/40 Bn
TX/4047	Pte A Brown	2/40 Bn
A/27728	LAC D W Bruce	RAAF
WX/7542	Pte G L Burdon	2/4 MG Bn
TX/3462	Sgt M L Butler	2/40 Bn
QX/23311	Pte R. Callanan	2/19 Bn
VX/19689	Pte P Cay	105 Tpt Coy
VX/57401	Pte H Collins	2/2 Pioneers
NX/49862	Cpl G E W Collins	2/19 Bn

WX/10048	Pte E J Cosson	2/4 MG Bn
NX/60046	Sgt A G Croston	2/15 Fd Regt
NX/42974	Pte H J Cutler	2/19 Bn
TX/3402	Pte W J Dawe	2/40 Bn
TX/2638	Pte M S De Jersey	2/40 Bn
NX/59762	Pte F H Doherty	2/20 Bn
402287	Sgt G R Donald	RAAF
NX/51080	Sgt K Douglas	2/19 Bn
QX/18086	Gnr J W Dowling	2/10 Fd Regt
VX/45002	Pte T D Dowling	4 A/T Regt
NX26351	Sgt WG Dykes	AASC
VX/18093	Cpl W Eastwell	105 MT Coy
VX/39152	Cpl F F Foster	2/2 Pioneer Bn
QX/14661	Gnr R F Fitzgerald	2/10 Fd Regt
NX/44014	Pte T E Francis	ORD
QX/12966	Pte H Franklin	2/3 MT Coy
38174	Sig. Fraser	2/1 FS★
NX/32576	Pte J K Glasby	2/20 Bn
WX/13836	Pte Golding	2/3 MG Bn★
NX/32398	Pte Gordon	8 Div HQ★
NX//66965	Pte D A Gosling	2/19 Bn
VX/37975	Pte D M Griffith	2/3 MG Bn
QX/13593	Gnr G M Hamilton	2/10 Fd Regt
WX/6778	Pte J B Hills	2/4 MG Bn
VX/29303	Sgt D W Howie	2/4 MT Coy
TX/2566	Pte L R Humes	2/40 Bn
NX/53759	Pte K C Turrall	2/19 Bn
SX/13231	Bdr J H Langford	2/1 RAA
SX/5837	Dvr J C Jacka	2/2 MT Coy
WX/14746	Pte R G Krygger	2/2 Pioneer Bn
NX/72732	Pte T J Cumiskey	2/20 Bn
TX/3080	Pte T Lewis	2/3 MG Bn
NX/31623	Pte M Lynch	2/20 Bn
NX/28616	Cpl G McDonald	2/18 Bn★
QX/20798	Sgt RJD McKay	2/3 MT Coy
NX/71956	Dvr J A W McRae	2/3 MT Coy
NX35285	Pte R McMaster	2/19 Bn
VX/5301	Sgt G Marshall	2/8 Bn

VX/23651	Pte Matthews	2/2 Pioneers
WX/8441	Pte J B Mellor	2/4 MG Bn
NX/34158	Sgt W T Monro	8th Div HQ
NX/31796	Pte R C Morrish	2/20 Bn
VX/46397	Gnr T W Muir	4th A/T Regt
VX65446	Pte M P Moss	2/10 Ord
QX/18436	Gnr Parrott	2/10 Fd Regt★
SX/9257	Pte R C Pope	Pay Unit
WX/36780	Gnr C Porter	2/1 Hy Bty★
NX/48914	Dvr A D Price	2/3 MT Coy
TX/5114	Pte C M Rainbow	2/40 Bn
WX/7621	Pte W W Reeves	2/4 MG Bn
QX/9439	Gnr G R Roberts	2/10 Fd Regt
SX/5565	Pte J A Root	2/3 MG Bn
NX/10963	Gnr W V Sainsbury	2/15 Fd Regt
NX/31594	Dvr S C Sampson	AASC
NX/14446	Pte W J Saunderson	2/19 Bn
VX/42510	Pte O K Scoullar	105 MT Coy
SX/30694	Pte Shillingford	AASC★
NX/54281	Pte S H T Smart	2/20 Bn
SX/5936	Pte G G Smith	2/3 MG Bn★
VX54631	Pte T R Smith	2/29 Bn★
TX/4184	Pte J A Sowter	AASC
NX/46081	Gnr D A Stanborough	2/15 Fd Regt
QX/7813	Bdr J M Stewart	2/10 Fd Regt
WX/10794	Sgt P A Sturtridge	2/4 MG Bn
QX/9812	Gnr S M Summers	2/10 Fd Regt
WX/9134	Pte J Sumner	2/4 MG Bn
SX/3236	Pte R J Sutton	2/3 MG Bn
NX/58322	Pte L T Taylor	2/20 Bn
NX/45208	Sgt D Taaffe	2/20 Bn
WX/7248	Pte F D Thaxter	2/4 MG Bn
NX/71868	Pte W J Thompson	2/20 Bn
NX/19923	Gnr C S Townsend	2/15 Fd Regt
VX20698	Pte A S Vandervord	2/2 Pioneers
VX/61707	Gnr C Watts	4th A/T Regt
QX20454	Gnr D E Wheeler	2/15 Fd Regt
NX/35474	Pte C H Wilkinson	2/19 Bn

1149	A B Williams	R.A.N ★
QX/8352	Gnr J Winterbottom	2/10 Fd Regt
NX/59260	Dvr C W H Woodley	8th Div HQ

Reconciliation of figures of personnel sent to and recovered from Prachaup Khiri Khan in the days after the war ended:

	Living	Dead	Total
English	368	178	546
Australian	93	40	133
Dutch	252	46	298
American	7	0	7
	720	264	984
Prisoners originally sent from Nakom Paton			1000
MOs and orderlies sent from Tamuang			11

136 Prisoners and 1 MO plus 8 orderlies had returned to Nakom Paton.

NX/44989 Alex White had been among the men evacuated with the MO Major Dewe. Pte White was one of the 'heavy sick' with black water fever. He survived. The names of the other Australians among that group are not known.

This list is taken from the affidavit of Major John Mason Stringer, War Crimes Trial of Japanese officers/NCOs involved in the Mergui Road Episode: National Archives Kew England.

★ denotes information that appears to be incorrect, and that cannot be verified. The condition of the men at the end of the episode would have meant some were either too ill to give their own information, or even to remember their own details.

Selected bibliography

Books and Australian War Memorial

Adam-Smith, Patsy, *Australian Women at War*, Penguin, Ringwood, 1996

Adam-Smith, Patsy, *Prisoners of War, From Gallipoli to Korea*, Penguin Books, Ringwood, 1997

Adam-Smith, Patsy, *The Anzacs*, Hamish Hamilton, London, 1978

Bayly, Christopher, and Harper, Tim, *Forgotten Armies, The Fall of British Asia, 1941–1945*, Allen Lane, London, 2004

Bean, C.E.W, *The Official History of Australia in the War of 1914–18 Volume V1, The A.I.F in France*, University of Queensland Press, St Lucia, 1980

Bean, C.E.W, Diary AWM38 3DRL606/58/1

Braddon, Russell, *The Naked Island*, Penguin Books, Ringwood, 1993

Cannon, Michael, *The Human Face of the Great Depression*, Today's Australia Publishing Company, Mornington, Victoria, 1997

Carlyon, Les, *Gallipoli*, Pan Macmillan, Sydney, 2001

Carlyon, Les, *The Great War*, Pan Macmillan. Sydney, 2006

Corfield, Robin S, *Don't Forget Me Cobber, The Battle of Fromelles*, Melbourne University Publishing, Carlton, 2009

Daws, Gavan, *Prisoners of the Japanese, POWs of World War II in the Pacific*, Scribe, Melbourne, 2008

Dunlop, E. E, *The War Diaries of Weary Dunlop, Java and the Burma-Thailand Railway 1942–1945*, Penguin, Castle Hill, 1990

Ebury, Sue, *Weary, The Life of Sir Edward Dunlop*, Penguin Books, Ringwood, 1995

Feldt, Eric, *The Coast Watchers*, Lloyd O'Neil, Hawthorn, 1946

Flanagan, Arch and Martin, *The Line, a man's experience; a son's quest to understand*, One Day Hill, 2005

Forbes, Cameron, *Hellfire, The Story of Australia, Japan and the Prisoners of War*, Macmillan, Sydney, 2005

Foster, Frank, *Comrades in Bondage*, Skiffington, London, 1946

Freudenberg, Graham, *Churchill and Australia*, Pan Macmillan, Sydney, 2008

Gammage, Bill, *The Broken Years, Australian Soldiers in the Great War*, Penguin, Melbourne,1982

Graves, Robert, *Goodbye to All That*, Penguin Books, London. 2004

Hearder, Rosalind, *Keep the Men Alive, Australian POW Doctors in Japanese Captivity*, Allen & Unwin, Crows Nest, 2005

Henning, Peter, *Doomed Battalion, Mateship and Leadership in War and Captivity, The Australian 2/40 Battalion 1940–45*, Allen and Unwin, Sydney, 1995

Horne, Gerald, *Race War, White Supremacy and the Japanese Attack on the British Empire*, New York University Press, New York, 2004

Jackson, Desmond, *What Price Surrender? A Story of the Will to Survive*, Allen and Unwin, St Leonards, 1989

Jeffry, Ray, *Scout Association of Australia, Tasmania Branch*, c 1990

Lake, Marilyn, *A Divided Society, Tasmania During World War I*, Melbourne University Press, Melbourne, 1975

Leemon, Jack (Lt) Holder, *The Body Snatchers, Australian War Memorial*, AWM MSS 8011

Lloyd, Clem, and Rees, Jacqui, *The Last Shilling, A History of Repatriation in Australia*, Melbourne University Press, Melbourne, 1994

McKernan, Micheal, *The War Never Ends, The Pain of Separation and Return*, University of Queensland Press, St Lucia, 2001

McMullin, Roland, *Pompey Elliott*, Penguin, Hawthorn, 2002

Moremon, John, *Australians on the Burma–Thailand Railway, 1942–3*, Dept of Veterans' Affairs, Canberra, 2003

Nelson, Hank, *POW, Prisoners of War, Australians under Nippon*, Australian Broadcasting Corporation, Sydney, 2001

Nish, Ian and Kibata, Yoichi (General Eds), *The History of Anglo-Japanese Relations, 1600–2000, Vol. 2, The Political-Diplomatic Dimension, 1931–2000*, Macmillan, 2000

Pavillard, Stanley S, *Bamboo Doctor*, Macmillan, London, 1960

Peek, Ian Denys, *One Fourteenth of an Elephant, A Memoir of Life and Death on the Burma-Thailand Railway*, Macmillan, Sydney, 2003

Peng Chin, *My Side of History*, Media Masters, Singapore, 2003

Perry, Roland, *Monash, The Outsider Who Won a War*, Random House, Sydney, 2004

Poidevin, Leslie, *Samurais and Circumcisions*, Published by the Author, 1985

Power, F.W.G, *Kurrah! An Australian POW in Changi, Thailand and Japan, 1942–1945*, R.J. & S.P. Austin, Macrae, Brunswick, 1991

Rivett, R, *Behind Bamboo*, Penguin, Ringwood, 1991

Silver, Lynette R, *Sandakan, A Conspiracy of Silence*, Sally Milner Publishing, Bowral, 2000

Smith, Donald, *And All the Trumpets*, Panther, London, 1960

Stewart, John, *The River Kwai, Two Journeys, 1943, 1979*, Bloomsbury, London, 1988

Thompson, Peter, *Pacific Fury, How Australia and her Allies defeated the Japanese*, William Heinemann, Sydney, 2009

Thompson, Peter, *The Battle for Singapore, The True Story of the Greatest Catastrophe of World War II*, Portrait, London, 2005

Travers, Richard, *Diggers in France, Australian Soldiers of the
Western Front*, ABC Books, Sydney, 2008
Uren, Tom, *Straight Left*, Random House, Sydney, 1994
Wright, Pattie, *The Men of the Line, Stories of the Thai-Burma
Railway Survivors*, Melbourne University Publishing, Carlton,
2008
Wyett, John, *Staff Wallah, At the fall of Singapore*, Allen and
Unwin, St Leonards, 1996

Other Sources
Newspapers
The Advocate
The Examiner
The Sydney Morning Herald
The Tassie Digger
The Weekly Courier

Articles and papers
Larsson, Marina, 'A Disenfranchised Grief: Post-war Death
and Memorialisation in Australia after the First World War',
Australian Historical Studies, 40:1, 70–95, March 2009
Larsson, Marina, 'Restoring the Spirit: The Rehabilitation of
Disabled Soldiers in Australia after the Great War', *Health and
History*, 6/2 45–59, 2004

Interviews conducted by the Author 2009–2010
Baker, Pat, wife of the late Mervyn 'Tiny' Baker, 2/40th Btn,
Tasmania
Bennett, Patrick, son of the late Major Vincent Bennett,
RAMC
Bertram, Allan, 2/19th Battalion and his wife Lorna, Victoria
Billett, Phill, wife of the late Basil Billett, 2/40th Btn,
Tasmania
Bird, Mardi, wife of the late Tom Bird, 2/40th Btn and her
daughter Cheryl
Brett, Fred, 2/40th Btn and his wife Janet, Tasmania
Bunton, Beryl, sister of the late Thomas Robert Riley, 2/40th
Butler, Althea, Tasmania
Cassidy, Ron, 2/40 Btn, Tasmania
Coventry, Bill, 2/40 Btn and his wife Dorothy, Victoria

Dare, Doreen, wife of the late Ernie Dare, 2/3rd Machine
    Gunners, also his son Greg

Dazeley, Max and Betty, Tasmania,

Deverell, Bill, 60 Operational Base Unit, RAAF, and his wife
    Mary, Tasmania

Dowling, Foch, 2/40th, Tasmania

Dunham, Barney, Tasmania

Finch, Ray and Betty, Tasmania

Gandy, John, RAN, and his wife Betty, Tasmania

Hay, Peter, son of the late Reg Hay, 2/40th Btn

Lawson, George, 2/40th Btn, Tasmania

Lutterall, Steve, son of the late Joe Lutterall, 2/40th Btn

Medlin, Harry, 2/1 Fortress Engineers, South Australia

Moore, Alan, 2/9 Field Ambulance, and his wife Betty, Victoria

Midgeley, John, 1 Embarcation Depot RAAF

Milne, Lex, 22 Dental Unit, Victoria

O'Brien, Vic and Betty, Tasmania

Shields, Graeme, son of Darrel, 2/40th who escaped Timor, and
    rejoined 2/12th Btn, and Graham's wife Gloria, Tasmania

Stone, Rod, son of the late Ernie Stone, 2/40th and his wife
    Betty, Tasmania

Smith, Fred (Lofty), 2/40th Btn and his wife Daphne, Tasmania

Spencer, Lloyde, 2/40th Btn and his wife Joyce, Tasmania, and
    their daughter Glenys

Ransome Smith, Fred (Smudger), 5th/ Suffolks, British Army,
    Victoria, and his wife Mary

Uren, Tom, 2/1 Heavy Battery

White, Alex, 2/19th Btn NSW and his wife Rose, New South
    Wales

Woolley, Don, 2/40th, and his wife Betty, Tasmania

Correspondence

Dewe, Mike, son of the late Major D.P. Dewe IMS

Moss, Simon, nephew of Craftsman Charles Gordon Moss, 18th
    Division Ordnance Workshops, who died on Mergui Road,
    4th July 1945

Transcripts

War Crimes Trial of Japanese officers/NCCs involved in the
    Mergui Road Episode. WO235/981: Folder, consisting of

reports and affidavits; character witnesses for accused; and
Defence and Prosecution cases.

*Unpublished Reports, Private Diaries and Personal Written
Histories*
Clare, Robert Francis, 2/40th Btn, Personally recorded history,
and transcripts
Coventry, Bill, Private Diary
Cox, Harold, 2/40th Btn, Personal Written History
Dolbey, Ken, 2/40th Btn, History compiled by Ken's son, Jeff
Dunham, Louise, 'Two Brother Soldier Settlers on the North
West Coast of Tasmania after the Great War: A Case Study'
(Masters Thesis)
Hollaway, Reg, 2/40th Written History
Mallinson, Len, 2/40th Btn, Letters provided by his son John
Medlin, Harry, Personal Written History
Prosser, John, 2/40th, Written History
Rainbow, Bill, Private Diary
Rea, James (Jim), Personal Diary, now in the Imperial War
Museum, London
Winstanley, Lt. Col Peter (Ret'd) OAM RFD JP, Articles about
Prisoners of War of the Japanese. Including the Burma–
Thailand Railway, 1941–45
Woolley, Don, Personal Written History

Internet Sources
Australian War Memorial, Canberra, www.awm.gov.au
The Australian Dictionary of Biography, online edition,
www.abd.online.ed.au
www.britain-at-war.org.uk
Children of Far East Prisoners of War, COFEPOW, UK,
www.cofepow.org.uk
Far East Prisoner of War Community, fepow-community.org.uk
www.greatwar.co.uk/ypres-salient/museum-talbot-house-
history.htm
The Independent, http://www.independent.co.uk/news/uk/
incompetence-that-led-to-fall-of-singapore-1477824.html
www.toch.org.com
Winstanley, Lt Col Peter (Ret'd) OAM RFD JP,
www.pows-of-Japan.net

Endnotes

All chapters compiled from information received during personal interviews conducted by the author; from papers and information held within the Butler family; from reading the selected bibliography; from the transcript of the War Crimes Trial into Mergui Road; and with the addition of the following:

Chapter 2

Page 14 – 'Kick the kerosene tin': story related by Bill Deverell, Max Butler was there as well. Kerosene tin – in all probability – used when no whistle at hand. There are many books which detail the battles and the slaughter on the Somme. Several to consult include Travers, *Diggers in France*, Carlyon, *The Great War*. And of course Bean, *The Official History of Australia in the War of 1914–1918*, and his diaries which are available online through the Australian War Memorial.

Page 15 – Population and death figures: *Tasmania's War Record, 1914–1918,* edited by L. Broinowski with an introduction by Sir J. Gellibrand, published for the Government of Tasmania by J. Walch, Hobart. Pages 210 and 214.

Chapter 3

Page 25 – 'True role of the infantry ...': quoted in Travers, page 2.

Page 26 – For Gen. Haig, see books above on the Somme and World War I. For conscription in New Zealand, see Lake, *A Divided Society*, page 123. For recruitment in Tasmania, see Lake, chapters six and seven. For deserter hiding in wardrobe, see Lake, page 108. For economic recruitment, see Lake, page 33 and throughout.

Page 27 – For refusal to employ single men, see Lake, page 33. For

General John Monash, see Travers and Roland Perry *Monash*. For a description of 8 August, see Bean, *The Official History*, page 605.

Page 28 – 'Staff work, timing . . .': private diary of the Chestnut Troop, quoted in Bean, ibid, page 605. 'Sight of the various services streaming up . . .': Bean, ibid, page 605. 'It was a *trés bon* stunt . . .': an unnamed digger quoted in Bean, ibid, page 606. For a description of Gen Haig meeting with three divisional commanders, see Carlyon, page 664. 'You do not know what the Australians . . .': Carlyon, page 664. 'Tears down . . . cheeks': Carlyon, page 663. 'Sacrifices for the whole': Carlyon, page 663.

Page 29 – 'Grinding out': Bean: Bean, *The Official History,* page 874. 'few yards useless advance . . .' Cafes operating, pass through Picardy: Adam-Smith, *The Anzacs*, page 188. 'They appeared . . .': Sergeant E. J. Rule quoted in Adam-Smith, page 192.

Page 30 – 'Jabbering . . .': Rule in Travers, page 82. 'It is awful to see crippled men . . .': Adam-Smith, page 194. 'If you are killed you are left there . . .': Lance Corporal Arthur Foxcroft quoted in Adam-Smith, pages 192–3.

Pages 31 and 32 – 'Six pushes': Travers, page 89. 'Wearing down . . .': Bean, *The Official History,* page 874. 'I stayed to have tea' and 'Littler wore a beard': Bean Diary, 2 and 5 September, 1916. (AWM 3DRL606/58/1)

Page 35 – 'The Australians suffered more than 29 000 casualties . . .': Travers, page 96.

Page 36 – Letters to Morton Butler, and those containing information regarding his brothers are from his military file obtained through the Australian War Memorial.

Chapter 6

Page 43 – See Lloyd and Rees, *The Last Shilling, A History of Repatriation in Australia.*

Page 44 – 'That in view of so many returned to Penguin . . .': quoted in Lake, page 145. For detailed information about strikes, unemployment, attitudes to returned soldiers, 'shirkers' and employers, white feathers and conscription, see Lake. Attitudes to returned soldiers also in Adam-Smith, *The Anzacs.*

Chapter 7

Page 63 – 'Nuisance': Adam-Smith, *The Anzacs*, pages 345–356.

Page 72 – Letters from Charles and Herbert Butler's file, Australian War Memorial.

Chapter 8

Page 76 – Allocation of funds: *The Advocate*, 1931.

Pages 76 and 77 – Cannon, *The Human Face of the Great Depression.* Allan Bertram interview. Frank Power: Cannon, page 133. Gen. Harry Chauvel: Cannon, ibid, pages 266–7.

Page 80 – Burnt out digger: see Larsson, 'Restoring the Spirit', *Health and History*, pages 45–59.

Chapter 9

Page 86 – Toc H: see www.toch.org.au and www.greatwar.co.uk/ypres-salient/museum-talbot-house-history.htm

Page 89 – Francis Marriott: information from interviews; also Jeffry, *Scout Association of Australia, Tasmanian Branch*; also *The Australian Dictionary of Biography,* online edition.

Pages 91 and 92 – 'False glamour . . .': Tassie digger, quoted in Dunham, *Two Brother Soldier Settlers* (unpublished thesis), page 129. Money paid to soldiers and wives: discussed at length in Lloyd and

Rees. Jokes regarding job training: Lloyd and Rees.

Pages 92 and 93 – 'Sapper Healy dies . . .' and Hugo Throswell commits suicide: quoted in Larsson, 'A Disenfranchised Grief', *Australian Historical Studies*, pages 79–95.

Chapter 10
Page 95 – Jeffry, *History of Scouting in Tasmania*.

Page 97 – Confirmation Mort Butler first scout leader in Penguin from interviews with John Gandy.

Page 102 – Information regarding interview, and Dunham, L.

Chapter 12
Page 126 – 12/50th men enlist individually, Youl: in Henning, *The Doomed Battalion*.

Chapter 13
The definitive book on the 2/40th Battalion is Peter Henning's *The Doomed Battalion*. Chapters concerning the Battalion have been compiled using Henning; interviews; and personal papers written by men from Sparrow Force.

Chapter 14
Page 158 – 'At Battalion Parade on 7th Dec, the troops were told . . .' Henning, pages 38–9.

Page 159 – Sparrow Force figures sailing that day: Henning, page 39.

Chapter 15
This chapter has been written, informed by the following: Freudenberg, *Churchill and Australia*; Horne, *Race War, White Supremacy and the Japanese Attack on the British Empire*; Bayly and Harper, *Forgotten Armies, The Fall of British Asia, 1941–1945*; Nish and Kibata, *The History of Anglo-Japanese Relations, 1600–2000, Volume II, The Political-Diplomatic Dimension, 1931–2000*.

Pages 161 and 162 – 'the Empire belongs to them . . .': quoted in Freudenberg, pages 19 and 20.

Page 162 – Leader of the 'Asiatic peoples': Bayly and Harper, page 1.

Page 163 – Exclusions from clubs and society: Bayly and Harper. 'Poor whites': ibid, page 65.

Page 164 – Bad stock: Churchill in Freudenberg, page 1. Indian Troops rebel, Bayly and Harper, page 66.

Page 165 – Penang taunt and evacuation: Bayly and Harper, page 120. Fifth Column Activity, ibid, pages 5–8; also interview with Fred Ransome Smith; also Pavillard, *Bamboo Doctor*, pages 4–5: In Penang, Pavillard saw for himself how coconut trees had been felled and whitewashed and left pointing like arrows towards ammunition and petrol dumps. '*Read this Alone and the War can be Won . . .*' quoted in Bayly and Harper, page 82.

Chapter 16
Page 177 – Lt Col Roach on Ambon, could not hold vital localities more than a day or two: in Henning, page 57. 'Put up the best defence possible . . .': quoted in Henning, page 57. 'As far as I can judge position at Ambon not critical . . .': quoted in Forbes, page 190. General Lavarck in Java. in Gen. Wavell decision held instead: Henning, page 73.

Page 178 – 'It's not the first time a few thousand men have . . .': quoted in Forbes, page 190. Massacre Ambon, Gull force: Forbes, page 191. Official war memo regarding Rabaul, 'They must be hostages to fortune . . .': quoted in Forbes, page 202.

Page 191 – '327 members of Sparrow Force escaped into the jungle': figures from Henning, page 110.

Chapter 18
Information on Timor 'wounded' story taken from the personal papers of Leslie Poidevin, provided by Rosemary Poidevin and Lt Col Peter Winstanley. Also in Leslie Poidevin,

Samurais and Circumcision published in 1985. Also from the detailed information on 2/40th Battalion in Timor in Henning.

Page 210 – 'Michael, Butler, Kelleher, Jack ... survived their severe and serious wounds ...': in personal papers of Leslie Poidevin.

Page 215 – Korean guards 'were bigger and taller ...': Uren, *Straight Left*, page 26.

Page 219 – 'Rumours were flying ..

.' *Australians of the Burma–Thailand Railway*, pages 14–15. 'I've heard Thailand called the Rice Bowl of the East. We'll be okay ...': quoted in *Australians of the Burma–Thailand Railway,* page 20. 'None of us knew that the journey about to commence would take us back into the Dark Ages': quoted in ibid, page 20. 'Brought a chorus of incredulous laughter from the POWs ...': quoted in ibid, page 22. Journey by rail and trucks: ibid, page 23.

Page 220 – 'Walking like men in a dream ...': quoted in Ebury, *The Life of Sir Edward Dunlop*, page 385.

Page 221 – POW figures: Nelson, *POW*, page 41. 'The men could not believe the Japanese engineer when he told them ...': quoted in ibid, page 41.

Page 222 – 'Miles to work through the mud ...': quoted in Henning, page 211. 'We were like zombies ...': quoted in ibid, page 210.

Chapter 19

Mergui Road story compiled from information in War Crimes Trial file, affidavits and reports contained therein; Foster, *Comrades in Bondage*; Smith, *And All the Trumpets*; information from COFEPOW; and interview with Alex White, survivor. Additional information from Pavillard, *Bamboo Doctor,* as well as information on Doctor Bennett from a story written by Lt Col Peter Winstanley. Also interview with Dr Bennett's son

Patrick Bennett, in Sydney.

Page 234 – 'Capture and torture ...' cited in Foster. 'I don't care if you go crook at me, or ...': quoted in Henning, page 209.

Page 235 – 'Sending off sick patched up men ...': quoted in Ebury, page 501. 'If this goes on you'll have to be punished ...': quoted in Ebury, page 496.

Page 236 – Weary stories in Foster.

Page 237 – 'Could see it was a compound full of beri-beri, malaria ...': in Pavillard, page146.

Page 239 – Des Jackson strategy in Forbes, page 310.

Page 242 – 'Prisoners of war must be prevented from ...': quoted in Forbes, page 434.

Page 243 – NCOs stockpiling rocks, and weapons: Ebury, page 504.

Chapter 20

Page 267 – From Leemon, *The Body Snatchers.* 'If they tried to escape they shot them, if they fell down they shot them ...': quoted from interviews with John Gandy.

Page 269 – 'The actual meeting of the repatriates with their next of kin ...' quoted in Forbes, page 491. Attitude that they could put it all behind them: this attitude was referred to in many of the interviews.

Chapter 21

Page 275 – Staff Sgt Clive Tilbrook in Foster.

Page 276 – 'Job without end ...' from Smith, *And All the Trumpets*, page 147.

Chapter 24

Page 332 – 'We had been on a hospital ship ...': Harry Medlin quoted in Nelson, page 207.

Page 333 – Australia forces scapegoated: Bayly and Harper, page 315. *The Independent* http://www.independent.co.uk/news/uk/incompetence-that-led-to-fall-of-singapore-1477824.html

Index

railway sleeper squaring, 115–116
Rainbow, Bill, 153, 155, 156, 180, 213
Ransome, Captain, 226
Ransome Smith, Lieutenant Fred ('Smudger'), 166, 169, 170, 173, 222, 230
rationing, 279, 280
Ray, Bill, 305
Rea, Jim, 263
Rea, Private PJ, 239
recruiting quotas, 26
recruits, 124–125, 133–135, 140, 184–185
Red Cross, 35–39
'Repat' (Repatriation Department), 79–80
Rhodes, Bertram ('Shorty'), 141
Richards, Jack and Nell, 202–203
Richards, Leslie John, 141, 190, 202
Richardson (Motor and Cycle shop), 51
Riley, Thomas Robert, 143, 190
River Don Trading Company, 53–54, 75, 76, 283
River Kwai Noi (bamboo cages), 237–239
Roach, Lieutenant Colonel, 177
Roff, Captain, 178, 182
Roosevelt, President, 167
Rowell, Major-General Sydney, 177, 178
Royal Army Medical Corps, 243–244
RSL (Returned Soldiers' League), 127, 128, 302–305
RSSILA, 44, 91–92
RSSILA (Returned Soldiers and Sailors Imperial League of Australia), 44, 91–92
Rule, Sergeant, 29–30
Russia, 158

S

St Dunstan's Hostel for Blinded Soldiers and Sailors (London), 90
St Helens (Tas), 145
'Sally' (song), 198–199
Scouting for Boys (manual), 95–96
Second World War, 124, 147–148, 256, 261–262, *see also* 2nd Australian Imperial Force
Seekers (group), 321
79th Anti-Aircraft Unit, 188
Siam. *see* Thailand
Singapore, 163–164, 169, 170–174, 197, 201, 217, 261, 332–333
Slater, Sergeant Johnny, 330
Smith, Chocko, 187
Smith, Donald, 254–255, 257
Smith, Ike, 295–296
Smith, Private Fred ('Lofty')
  drawing of Churchill, 264
  fined for going AWOL, 290
  inability to eat, 277
  in POW camps, 212, 213–214
  ex-POWs, 268, 270–272, 280–281, 332
  returns to Timor, 334–336
  Thai–Burma Railway, 220–221, 223, 224–225, 226, 228
  in Timor, 179, 181–182, 184–189, 190, 191
Smith, Sergeant, 187
smoking, 150, 234
Snelling, Captain Rewi R.L., 171–172
social exclusion, 163–164
soldiers
  attitudes towards ex-POWs, 266–268, 280, 331–332
  as 'hostages of fortune', 178
  NCOs (Non-Commissioned Officers), 136
  pay deductions, 71
  public attitudes to returned soldiers, 91–93, 96
  role of infantry, 25
  soldier-settlement holdings, 101–102
  Soldiers' Children's Education Scheme, 82
  'soldier's heart', 80, 121–122
Somme, Battle of, 14
soup kitchens, 76
Sparrow Force in Timor
  Battle of Usau Ridge, 182–183, 185–188, 191–192
  campaign history, 335
  capitulation of, 188–189, 197, 207
  disbursed as prisoners of war, 215
  'every man for himself' order, 190–191
  forces of, 159, 191, 207, 209
  Japanese invasion, 174–176, 178–188
  Padre, 234–235
  on Thai–Burma Railway, 218–219
  wounded, 189–190
Spencer, Gordon, 134
Spencer, Joyce, 279, 288, 317
Spencer, Lloyde, 134, 136, 183, 279, 286, 288, 317
Stevens, Major Roy, 207–209
strikes, 46
Stringer, Major John Mason, 258, 266–267
Sumatra, 226–227, 336
Sunda Straits, 168–169
Surabaya Bay, 215

T

Tarraleah (Tas), 138

Acknowledgements

When I set out to write this book, I did not know where it would take me. Over time, the book seemed – somehow – to set its own course, and much of what I had planned still sits, waiting its turn, perhaps for inclusion in a further book. I am grateful to so many for sharing all their information and stories, and wish that more had been able to find its way into this book. In truth, it is all in there, the understanding all the stories gave, the broad view it permitted me. And I am deeply grateful to all who helped me. I extend a heartfelt thank you especially to the many ex-prisoners of war and their families, each of them more than generous, always caring, and who welcomed me as if I were family.

To Fred Ransome (Smudger) Smith and his wife Mary; Fred who so shocked me when I fronted at his door with my copy of *Comrades in Bondage* in my hand: for Fred announced – with a big smile at the coincidence – that he had designed the cover and drawn the inside illustrations, all those years ago, for Frank Foster the author. He explained the rationale; the idyllic island scene, and the keyhole there, intending to suggest that something other than paradise was contained behind it all. To his wife Mary who lovingly and patiently explained that they all still live in a prisoner-of-war camp. 'We laugh about it,' she says, 'but that is how it is.'

To the other Fred Smith - (Lofty) - and his wife Daphne, both of whom gave so much of their time to me; to Harry Medlin, and his daughter Anna, and all the much appreciated messages of support; to Alex White and Rose, who welcomed me so readily into their home; to Alan Moore and Betty, who didn't think they could help, but indeed did; Ron Cassidy, with his humour.

And the openness of them all: Fred Brett and his wife Janet; Lloyde Spencer, his wife Joyce and daughter Glennis; Lex Milne, and Jeff and Marion; Allan Bertram; George Lawson and his daughter Julie-Ann; Foch Dowling and his family; Maureen White who went to so much trouble for me; Tom Uren; Don Woolley; and to Dorothy – Dottie – and her husband, dear Bill Coventry who passed away the day after I received a letter from him, in which he had sent me some tips on how to manage the too many things in my life. I was touched when I received it, in fact, shed a few tears, it felt so father-like. All the men gave so much to me; far beyond the words they said.

To Lorna Bertram who spoke for so many wives and families when she spoke to me of her husband, Allan. 'Oh, I felt so sorry for him,' she said. 'You've got no idea. I still feel sorry for him. You wouldn't read about what goes on. Unless you've lived with a bloke. I used to feel terrible about my girlfriends and other people who knew that he had been a prisoner of war. They would ask me questions. And I was so embarrassed because I couldn't answer them. I never talked about the war to him at all. I just let him have his own way and I knew he'd have to get it out. But I felt so sorry for him because I knew him before!' Her husband Allan has only been talking about the war in the last couple of years. I am grateful to them both for opening up to me.

I am grateful too, to the people originally from my home town who were so generous with their time and their stories. To Barney Dunham; to Althea Butler who is my father's sister and my Aunt; to Bill and Mary Deverell; to Mardi Bird and her daughter Cheryl; to John Midgeley; Muriel Wright; Max and Betty Dazeley. And especially John Gandy and his wife Betty.

And thank you as well to the many people who shared their information about their fathers, brothers, uncles and grandfathers with me. We are all part of, all share some aspect of this story.

Thank you to Rod Stone, and his partner Jacqui. Ron for taking it upon himself to become my unofficial Tasmanian secretary for quite some time, in a very generous and open Tasmanian gesture; and who told me so much of his beloved father Ernie and mother Betty, the boss's daughter whom his father married, and her father's furniture factory in Launceston which employed a number of the POWs on their return. And how hard life became for his Dad; how his mother struggled through it all, and kept going. And all the funny lines his father came out with when he and his Dad were alone; and how his Mum died so sadly the day before I was to meet her, when she had her papers all ready, wanting to tell her story.

Thank you to Vic O'Brien and his wife Betty, and Vic's brother Bruce who gave me his childhood memories of their adored Uncle Max De Jersey, who survived the Railway and Mergui Road, then came home and found his girlfriend had married someone else. And Bruce told me of his uncle's sadness; the emotional pain; the difficulties he like so many faced back home.

To all the people who forwarded information thank you: to Lyn Johnson; Glad Garwood; Charles and Anke Cameron; Sally Jones; Thelma Baldock; Craig Woodhall and his wife Nellie; Lindy Hingston who felt for her father, Lt Cpl Lindsay Hedditch of the 2/40th, who was unwell when he returned, and had difficulty facing people behind the counter where he worked. And who wouldn't allow celery in the house because it smelled of the Japanese guards, so he said.

To Tony Blight, whose father Neil Blight of the 2/40th escaped Timor after evading the Japanese by spending what he estimated was twelve hours sucking air through a cane reed, and lying underneath a creek. Neil remained in Timor for a further six months with other Sparrow Force members, son Tony says, their mission to get valuable X-ray, hospital and medical equipment into 'safe' caves in the mountains and not let them fall into Japanese hands.

To Fred Brett who said he coped with being a POW pretty well, but his wife Janet spoke up from the corner, 'Remember those times when…?' 'Oh yes,' said Fred, 'I forgot about those.' He sometimes thinks about when he came home, the time he arrived back at the farm, and all his little brothers and sisters raced up over the paddock so excited to meet him. And he didn't respond the same way. It's a regret he still carries. 'I didn't meet them in the right way. I often think about that,' he says. But he also remembers when the war finished and he was sent to Okinawa on an aircraft carrier, (UK leased) and they were like school kids he says – each one having rides on a jeep around the decks, all lined up. He'd never seen anything like it.

To Mrs Marjorie Quinn who told me how she, like many, had to get to know her husband again; to Mrs Flo Bell, and her husband Jack who battled, Barry Smith, about his father Gordon; Lindy Hoodless, about her father Ronald Hoodless: Chris Matthews for his father J.E. Matthews, who suffered from nightmares; Russell Broomhall for his friend Ted Sweetman of the 2/40th who still goes for a walk on the beach at Burnie most mornings; Heath Fellows, for his grandfather; Graeme Simpson for his father Alfred Leonard Simpson; Maggie Amos for Sgt Les Wootton.

To Deryl Dowling and Barbara, and Peter Duckert for Foch Dowling; to Len Andrews; to Mrs Pat Baker; to Margaret Elliston for her husband Max; to Cindy Jones, whose grandfather Hector Davidson of the 2/29th died on the Thai–Burma Railway; Shirley Stafford; Kerry Porter; John Hill; Raelee Adams for her father Maurice McFadyen; Alan Rowe, about his father Mick Rowe, an ex POW, who had been in the 4th Anti-Tank Unit, and who after the war was another of the POWs in town, and owned the grocers 'Rowe and Elliott' in Penguin on the way to the beach; Mary McLachlan for Sgt George Milsom; Mrs Vonnie Bennett for her father Terry Lee Ambrose.

To Mr Cyril Butcher for information about his brother Robert Henry Butcher, of the 2/40th who had been a Bren Gun Carrier; Daryl Bramich, for his father Russell (Joe) Arthur Bramich. And Tas Browning for his Uncles, William R Browning, who was Killed in Action, and Thomas John, who drowned with so many when the POW ships on the way to Japan were torpedoed by Allied ships. Two sons gone. So much sadness spread throughout a family.

To Graeme Shields for his father's sad story: of shock at what confronted him, first to survive, and escape from Timor; then to go on and fight in New Guinea where he and his platoon were subjected to torture and mindless cruelty by the Japanese. Graeme told me with great sadness (for both his mother and his family) what happened in the family: the nightly rages, and the family fleeing to sleep outside. His father came home, disturbed, a different man from the one who had gone away. And his mother remained loyal, and lived for the family occasions, Christmas, the birthdays. Now on Graeme's wall, portrait shots of those who would be Darrel's grandchildren, and great grandchildren are neatly arranged, all of them appearing happy, secure. Darrel may not have achieved that for himself in his own life, but he fought for, and helped give his grandchildren the life they now lead. He helped give them that.

Many thanks to John Mallinson for kindly permitting publication of his father's letters; John was seven when he finally heard his father would not be coming home. The mail came, and they all cried, in the yard.

Thank you as well to Roxley and Eileen Day for Harold Cox's story, Eileen's 'kind' uncle who came home blind; to Jeff Dolbey for his father Ken Dolbey's history; Ken was another who came home, lived a quiet life, had a loving stable family, and yet still had nightmares in his late 70s and 80s. And he was never able to take up again his interest in rifle shooting, his time as a POW had affected his sight.

To George Richards, for the story on how it felt at home in the sitting room, his father and mother there, anxious to hear his brother's name, to know he was still alive. And how it affected the whole community, five boys in the 2/40th set out together. None returned. Two were killed in Timor, and three drowned together on the POW ships heading to Japan. Seven from the entire district didn't return. George still gets emotional on Anzac Day.

To Lyn Gleeson for her delightful, yet ultimately sad letters. *To my Darling Mother,* her brother had written, and signed *with a pile of love from your only baby boy, Wilton. XXXX Write soon. Love Wilton.* Pte Wilton Bricknell drowned on one of the ships carrying POWs in June 1944.

To Mr Kerry Seens, for the POW card that his uncle was permitted to send home from Japan. With only 15 words by the time he'd written his own details as he was required to do:

Service NX 32637 Rank Private
Name G Yard
Unit 2/10 Field Ambulance
Country Malaya

The word count was taken. He put the card in his pocket in disgust, went outside the building, and came across a Japanese soldier tearing them all up anyway.

To Betty and Des Hinds, and to the Clare family for Robert Francis Clare's evocative and moving story. *A wonderful dad.* To Vivian Rainbow for Bill Rainbow's diary. To Mrs Beryl Bunton and her family, for the story on Thomas Robert Riley, whose mother refused to believe he was dead. 'Tommy'll walk through that door one day. He's not dead.'

Steve Lutterall, whose father Joe was captured in Timor and spent the war in the camps in Thailand after finishing on the Railway. Joe was in a bad way when he came home, in and out of hospital. He married one of the Army nurses. He was sick, but his pride would not let him apply for the pension, for he was determined like many men, to provide for his family. On the medical forms there was never enough room to list what was wrong with him. Eventually he was accepted as a TPI. He worried. Everything had to be fully completed, the house paid for, nothing left undone, in case he didn't survive. He was so happy to have a family, his son Steve tells me, and spent a lot of time with his grandchildren too. But he also needed to be by himself a lot, and would go down to the workshop for that time. 'Our saddest thing,' Steve tells me 'is that he didn't see my boys, and my brother's daughter grow up to see what they became.'

To Greg Dare for his great kindness, and to his mother Doreen Dare, whose husband Ernie was in the 2/3rd Machine Gunners; To Len Andrews, for the photos and the moving story of his brother; to Jack Farrell of the 2nd/2nd.

To Ethel Wells. And also Mrs Ellery Carr and the sense of loss and sadness she still carries about her brother Pte H B Sushames who returned, his back covered in scars and welts, to the personal sadness he was to find waiting for him in his marriage. He would put his head down, when reports came to him, and say, 'Don't tell me Mum, don't tell me.'

To Mrs Ellery Carr for the list of the boys who went off to war together: Jim Hayes, Fred Hayes, Bill Emmerton, Mr Lockett, Harry Wandett, Neil Sturzaker.

To Francis Rhodes and her loving story of her husband David, who'd had cerebral malaria in the camps, and yet, like so many on his return from being a POW (wanting to get back to a normal life), told the doctors at the interview before his discharge that he was perfectly fit, which Francis wrote, 'was far from the truth'. For years he couldn't sleep on nights when the moon was full, for it had always been a full moon when the US bombers would come and bomb the bridge at Kanchanaburi. (Several of the men I interviewed had nightmares about the Allied raids, and the bombs coming down.) And decision making and communicating was hard for him, the stress from the war still all there. And how she had coped, and helped him.

To John Prosser's family; so too Reg Hollaway's.

To Janet Uhr, and the Fepow Community; to Mrs Rosemary Poidevin.

To Peter Henning – apart from taking the time to search among his records for me – for writing the *Doomed Battalion*, the bible for the 2/40th families. To have something to fill in the gaps and explain all those silent years, means much to so many, to me as well.

To Patrick Bennett, son of Major Vincent Bennett, for so

kindly permitting me to see his father's papers, and providing access to Jim Rea's diary.

To Mike Dewe, son of Major DP Dewe, without whose help a crucial part of this book would not have appeared. We worked together – many messages by email – to try and locate the full transcript of the Mergui Road War Crimes Trial, and finally we succeeded. The index of the transcript Mike created is an organisational triumph.

And to Simon Moss in England, of the Fepow web community who already knew where the War Crimes Transcript was, so I then discovered! Simon's uncle, Charles Gordon Moss of the British Army, died on Mergui Road, 4 July 1945. And Simon, like so many around the world still longs, and seeks, to find somebody who knew his uncle back then in the camps. Charles's sister, now in her late eighties, still grieves, still wants to know why: why the men, and her brother suffered so, and how could such suffering ever have been visited upon another?

To the daughter of a still living Tasmanian ex-POW who with love and concern removed one of the photos from the album her father shows to people, for every time he came to that photo, it made him cry. She wishes to spare him that.

To Peter Hay, whose father Reg won the Military Medal for his courage and leadership in the bayonet charge on Usau Ridge, who earned the respect and gratitude of his men in the POW camps and who returned from his time as a POW to lead his quiet life in Wynyard, run his grocery store, never to talk about the war – but each year circled just one date on the calendar. Peter never knew what that date meant. Neither did his mother. Sometimes Alf Williams, a fellow 2/40th member, would come over from across the road, and he and Reg would sit down the back and talk, quietly, over a beer, huddle in close.

To the 2/40th Battalion remaining members; for permission to publish *The Battle for Osoe* by Private G Faulkner; and for welcoming me at their lunch meeting.

To Jason Butler for helping me with research. To Liz Butler for tolerating my too many phone calls. And many thanks to Vanessa Radnidge from Hachette and Sophie Hamley of Cameron's Management for pushing me, with so much understanding and support, over the line.

Also, I owe a big debt of gratitude to Lt Col Peter Winstanley for his constant support, his willingness to help, and his friendship.

I apologise if I have inadvertently omitted any of those who so kindly assisted me on the way.

To all, thank you.

Sally Dingo was born in Tasmania in 1953. After completing a Bachelor of Arts degree in politics and history at the University of Tasmania, she left the Apple Isle to see if life really was different on the 'mainland'. After a variety of jobs, including waitressing at the Last Laugh Theatre Restaurant in Melbourne, youth worker and proofreader's assistant at *The Age*, she stumbled into the world of television, working first in promotions, then in sales, before transferring to TCN 9 in Sydney and on to radio at 2Day FM. However, an urge to write saw her back at study, obtaining a Diploma of Journalism at Sydney's Macleay College, after which she worked for an insurance company and did freelance work. All of which was put on hold with the arrival of children. She is the author of the bestselling book *Dingo: The Story of Our Mob*. Sally lives in Melbourne with her husband, Ernie, and their two children, Wilara and Jurra.